CAPITALISM

Edited by

**Ellen Frankel Paul, Fred D. Miller Jr,
Jeffrey Paul and John Ahrens**

BASIL BLACKWELL
for the
Social Philosophy and Policy Center
Bowling Green State University

Typeset in 10 on 12 pt Ehrhardt
by Columns of Reading
Printed in Great Britain by Whitstable Litho, Kent.

Contents

INTRODUCTION

The central ideological conflict of this century – and one which permeates much of contemporary thought on cultural and political issues – is the clash between capitalism and socialism. For capitalism and socialism seem clearly to be more than just *economic* systems. They are also the overall frameworks within which are constructed two radically different ways of organizing our collective affairs. Thus, each gives rise to a host of ethical and conceptual issues which go well beyond the technical concerns of economics.

The essays in this volume address some of these issues in connection with one of these systems – capitalism. The first six essays are concerned primarily with the moral status of capitalism. One way of approaching this issue is to ask whether or not competitive markets allocate goods according to a principle of desert. That is to say, do people deserve what they get in competitive markets? John Christman argues, in "Entrepreneurs, Profits, and Deserving Market Shares," that they do not. The concept of desert has as one of its components a requirement that there be a proportionality between the deserving action and what is said to be deserved. But market shares are determined by factors that are independent of the value of the action in question (i.e., market conditions), and hence this proportionality requirement is not satisfied.

Desert is also a central concept of one of the most common arguments on behalf of socialism, and thus against capitalism, viz., that the consequences of "bad luck" are so harmful to those whom they befall that government must undertake coercive methods of "redress." In "Luck," Richard A. Epstein argues that this is not a cogent position. Centralized attempts to redistribute wealth so as to "equalize luck" present such problems of design, implementation, and administration that they are almost certainly unworkable, and certainly less reasonable than voluntary approaches to this problem. Hence, Epstein concludes, this common and superficially plausible defense of socialism fails.

A central component of a Lockean defense of capitalism is the notion of self-ownership: the notion that we own, prior to any social agreements, our bodies and the powers and abilities that inhere in them. This notion is used to ground an argument that capitalism is the only economic scheme that can accommodate the presocial rights – rights of self-ownership – that individuals have. In "Capitalist Persons," Andrew Levine investigates the notion of self-ownership and finds that it depends on an unviable view of persons. And this, he concludes, leaves capitalism with only a defense in terms of the incentives necessary to maximize production.

Andrew Kernohan also investigates the connection between capitalism and self-ownership. In "Capitalism and Self-Ownership," he argues that the claim that capitalism preserves self-ownership is a "false and stultifying myth." Kernohan's argument turns on the connection between ownership of a power and the right to exercise that power. Because, he argues, capitalism may result in situations in which the means necessary to exercise one's powers are unavailable because they are monopolized by others, one cannot really be said to own one's powers at all.

A common objection to capitalist economic institutions has been that they render some or all of the members of society unfree or, at least, substantially less free than they would be under some other set of institutions. G.A. Cohen, in particular, has urged this objection in a series of papers. In "Against Cohen on Proletarian Unfreedom," John Gray argues that Cohen is entirely unsuccessful in establishing this objection. And Gray advances a set of arguments designed to show that workers are likely to be less free under socialist economic institutions than under capitalist ones.

One of the more provocative of recent critiques of capitalism is that advanced in *Habits of the Heart*, by Robert N. Bellah, Richard Madsen, William M. Sullivan, Ann Swindler, and Steven M. Tipton. The central argument of this work is that the individualism which lies at the heart of liberal capitalist democracy may be destroying our ability to preserve the political community that supports freedom. In "Capitalism, Citizenship, and Community," Stephen Macedo concedes that the proponents of liberal capitalism must take this concern with "community" seriously. However, he also argues that individualism need not and, in fact, has not seriously undermined community. The core of Macedo's argument is a reinterpretation of Tocqueville's still cogent analysis of American democracy.

The next three essays are all concerned, in one way or another, with the concept of "efficiency." Traditional defenses of capitalism have frequently given primacy to a criterion of efficiency, and only secondary importance to other evaluative criteria. In "Capitalism and the Democratic Economy," Gary A. Dymski and John E. Elliot reject this defense on two grounds. First, efficiency is itself a socially determined measure, and hence cannot be applied independent of other social variables. And second, there is good reason to think that efficiency can itself be enhanced by enhancements in equality, autonomy, and other normative desiderata.

The socialist calculation debate, at least as it was perceived by Mises,

Hayek, and other leading participants, was primarily a debate over the technical issue of whether or not central planners would be able to make the calculations needed to run a socialist economy with any appreciable degree of efficiency or, indeed, to run it at all. But Israel Kirzner argues, in "Some Ethical Implications for Capitalism of the Socialist Calculation Debate," that this debate also has implications for the normative assessment of capitalism. The core of his argument is an analysis of the discovery processes that characterize entrepreneurial activities in a market. This analysis exposes the similarities between discovery and creation and, hence, provides a foundation for the claim that the distribution of wealth that occurs in a market is just.

In "The Dynamic of Capitalist Growth," Antony Flew notes that Marx and Engels themselves credited capitalist social arrangements with an incomparable degree of effectiveness in producing wealth (i.e., efficiency). Yet they have little or nothing to say in answer to what is obviously a crucial question: Why is this so and how may this virtue of capitalism be preserved under alternative arrangements? Flew argues that Marx and Engels simply failed to understand the incentives and disincentives that Adam Smith characterized as the "Invisible Hand" and, hence, were unable to provide a satisfactory answer to either part of this question.

Finally, one may raise the question of whether or not it is even possible to compare capitalism and socialism in order to make a rational choice between these two competing systems. In "Capitalism and Socialism: How Can They Be Compared?" Peter Rutland seeks to establish both a methodological point and a substantive point about comparisons of capitalism and socialism. The methodological point is that such comparisons are, arguments to the contrary notwithstanding, possible, and that they are best carried out in empirical rather than abstract terms, i.e., by comparing the performance of existing socialist systems with that of existing capitalist systems. Against objections that such empirical comparisons are not possible, Rutland provides one and argues for the plausibility of its major components. The substantive point is that capitalism fares better in such a comparison, although this is tempered by the difficulties inherent in collecting and interpreting the relevant data.

There can be little doubt that the clash between capitalism and socialism will continue to loom large in the intellectual life of both the industrialized and the developing world. These essays, along with those in a forthcoming companion volume on socialism, delineate some of the concepts that are central to this debate.

CONTRIBUTORS

John Christman received his Ph.D. from the University of Illinois at Chicago in 1985. He is an Assistant Professor in Philosophy at Virginia Polytechnic Institute, and was a Visiting Assistant Professor at the University of California at San Diego in 1987–88. He is the editor of a forthcoming volume, *The Inner Citadel: Essays on Individual Autonomy*. He has published articles in ethics and political philosophy in such journals as *Philosophy and Public Affairs*, *Ethics*, and *The Southern Journal of Philosophy*.

Richard A. Epstein is James Parker Hall Professor of Law at the University of Chicago Law School and has published widely in the fields of legal philosophy and economic law. He is the editor of the *Journal of Legal Studies*. His book *Takings: Private Property and the Power of Eminent Domain* was published by Harvard University Press in 1985.

Andrew Levine is Professor of Philosophy at the University of Wisconsin–Madison. He is the author of *The Politics of Autonomy* (University of Massachusetts Press, 1976), *Liberal Democracy: A Critique of Its Theory* (Columbia University Press, 1981), *Arguing for Socialism* (Routledge and Kegan Paul, 1984; 2nd edition Verso, 1988), and *The End of the State* (Verso, 1987).

Andrew Kernohan farms beef cattle in Parrsboro, Nova Scotia. He received a Ph.D. from the University of Toronto in 1984, and is now an Adjunct Assistant Professor of Philosophy at Dalhousie University. During the slower months of the farming year he has been able to enjoy the hospitality of the University of Toronto Department of Philosophy, thanks to a grant from the Social Science and Humanities Research Council of Canada. He has published papers in nuclear physics, political theory, and philosophy of psychology.

John Gray was born in 1948 and educated at Exeter College, Oxford, where he read Philosophy, Politics, and Economics, and received his doctoral degree. In 1973 he was appointed to a Lectureship in Political Theory at the University of Essex, and in 1976 he was elected a Fellow of Jesus College, Oxford. His books include *Mill on Liberty: A Defense*, *Hayek on Liberty*, *Conceptions of Liberty in Political Philosophy* (edited with

i

Z.A. Pelszynski), *Liberalism*, and *Liberalisms: Essays in Political Philosophy*. He is currently at work on a three-volume critique of Marxism.

Stephen Macedo is an Assistant Professor in the Department of Government at Harvard University, where he studies and teaches political theory and American constitutionalism. His publications include a monograph, *The New Right v. The Constitution*, and a book, *Liberal Virtues: A Liberal Theory of Citizenship, Virtue, and Community*, the latter of which will soon be published by Oxford University Press.

Gary A. Dymski received his Ph.D. in Economics from the University of Massachusetts at Amherst in 1987, and is currently an Assistant Professor of Economics at the University of Southern California. In 1985–86 he was the Leo Model Research Fellow in Economic Studies at the Brookings Institution. His recent papers include "A Keynesian Theory of Bank Behavior" (forthcoming in the *Journal of Post Keynesian Economics*), "Banking and Financial Fragility," "Illiquidity, Uncertainty, and Bank Innovation," "Coercive Signals, Bank Lending, and the Latin American Debt Crisis" (with Manuel Pastor), and "Some Analytics of Narrow Banking" (with Robert E. Litan).

John E. Elliott received his Ph.D. in Economics from Harvard in 1956, and is currently Professor of Economics and Director of Political Economy and Public Policy at the University of Southern California. His major interests are the history of economic and political theory, comparative political economy, and Marxian political economy. His articles on these subjects have appeared in such journals as *Economic Inquiry*, *Quarterly Journal of Economics*, *Journal of Economic Organization and Behavior*, *Review of Social Economy*, and *International Review of Ethics and Economics*. He is the author of *Comparative Economic Systems*, 2nd edition (Wadsworth, 1985). He currently serves as Vice President of the History of Economics Society and President-Elect of the Association for Social Economics.

Israel M. Kirzner was born in London, England, in 1930. He subsequently lived in Cape Town, South Africa, attending the University of Cape Town. Moving to the U.S. in 1948, he received his B.A. from Brooklyn College in 1954, his M.B.A. from New York University in 1955, and his Ph.D. (under Professor Mises) from the same institution in 1957. Since 1957, he has taught at New York University, where he is Professor of Economics. Professor Kirzner is the author of six books, including *Competition and Entrepreneurship* (University of Chicago Press, 1973). At New York University, Professor Kirzner heads the doctoral program in Austrian Economics.

CONTRIBUTORS

Antony Flew is Emeritus Professor of Philosophy at the University of Reading and a Distinguished Research Fellow of the Social Philosophy and Policy Center. He is the author of *Hume's Philosophy of Belief, Evolutionary Ethics, The Politics of Proscrustes, Thinking about Social Thinking, Darwinian Evolution, David Hume: Philosopher of Moral Science, The Logic of Mortality* (with Godfrey Vesey), *Agency and Necessity, Power to the Parents*, and other books. He is also the editor of the Penguin Classic, Malthus's *Essay on the Principle of Population*. Professor Flew is a founding member of the Council of the Freedom Association, the Education Group of the Centre for Policy Studies, and the Academic Advisory Board of the Adam Smith Institute.

Peter Rutland is currently an Assistant Professor of Government at Wesleyan University, and has taught previously at the University of Texas at Austin and the Universities of York and London in England. In 1984–85 he was a research fellow at Harvard University's Russian Research Center. He has spent over two years living in Eastern Europe and the USSR, including study as a visiting scholar at three Sovieteconomics institutes. His publications include *The Myth of the Plan: Lessons of Soviet Planning Experience* (1985), and articles on topics ranging from Soviet industrial management to nationality policy. He has just completed a book manuscript on party supervision of the economy in the USSR.

ENTREPRENEURS, PROFITS, AND DESERVING MARKET SHARES*

BY JOHN CHRISTMAN

INTRODUCTION

The question I wish to take up in this paper is whether competitive markets, as mechanisms that initiate the distribution of scarce goods, allocate those goods in accordance with what participants in those markets deserve. I want to argue that in general people do not in fact deserve what they get from market interactions, when "what they get" is determined by the competitive forces coming to bear on the market (the laws of supply and demand). This more general claim is meant to apply to all participants in the market (workers and their wages as well as capitalists and their profits). However, my strategy here is to focus on the particular case of the role of entrepreneurs, as I will define them, and whether they deserve the profits they reap in a competitive capitalist market. In particular, I will argue that the claim that entrepreneurs deserve their profits, when spelled out precisely, is indeed not plausible. Generalizing from this claim, I want to suggest how moral desert is inappropriate as a justification of market shares whenever competition determines the magnitude of those shares.

I should stress, though, the particularity of my central claim: it is that "(strictly speaking) entrepreneurs do not (strictly speaking) deserve their (strictly speaking) profits."[1] This is not to say that, for *other* reasons (for example, reasons of entitlement or utility), people should not receive the rewards doled out by a market. My claim is only that desert has nothing directly to do with it.

I am deviating significantly here from the usual strategy for denying the relevance of desert claims to principles of distributive justice.[2] These

---

* A shorter version of this paper was read at the Pacific Division Meetings of the American Philosophical Association in Portland, Oregon, March 1988. I would like to thank Professor Jeffrey Paul for his comments on that version. I am also grateful to Thomas Christiano, Alan Nelson, and Allen Buchanan for their helpful comments on earlier drafts of this paper.

[1] My arguments here apply to all profits, positive or negative. So my full thesis should read: "entrepreneurs deserve neither their profits *nor* their losses"; more generally, the market simply does not distribute resources (including profits) according to what people deserve.

[2] Cf. John Rawls, *A Theory of Justice* (Cambridge: Harvard University Press, 1971), pp. 15, 310–15; and Joel Feinberg, "Justice and Personal Desert" in *Doing and Deserving* (Princeton: Princeton University Press, 1970), pp. 55–94. For a sympathetic account of "desert defenses"

strategies either include a challenge of the moral value of the benefit provided by entrepreneurs and capitalists (the provision of goods to consumers), upon which claims of desert are based;[3] or, like Rawls, it is argued that the winning of profits in the end emanates from the possession of talents and dispositions which are not themselves deserved.[4] My argument, however, will not depend on either of these sets of claims. In fact I will assume that selling goods via market mechanisms can provide some benefit to willing purchasers,[5] and whatever talents entrepreneurs utilize are themselves deserved. Despite these assumptions, I will claim nevertheless that entrepreneurial profits are not deserved.

I will begin, in Section II, by defining the relevant terms. I will clarify the notion of "an entrepreneur" as I am using that term, followed by a description of how profits arise in markets. I then will explicate the structure of desert claims. In Section III, I will consider an argument that entrepreneurs in fact do deserve their profits, and I will raise several objections to it. In Section IV, after briefly considering Rawls's argument that desert should not be a basis for distributive principles, I will set out my own argument that entrepreneurs in particular do not deserve the profits that accrue from the production and sale of goods in a market. I will close by showing how this particular argument can be generalized to all participants in a competitive market.

I. ENTREPRENEURS AND PROFITS

The term "entrepreneur" has been used variously to refer to anyone from a robber baron to a small shop owner to a money lender. There seem to emerge, however, two components to these usages that also fit with some of the standard economic definitions.[6] These are that the entrepreneur is the primary organizer of production and that she is the person or persons who holds primary title to the capital assets of the firm. Both of these notions can be summarized by calling the entrepreneur, simply, the person

---

of markets, cf. John Hospers, *Human Conduct: An Introduction to the Problems of Ethics* (New York: Harcourt Brace, 1961), pp. 433–46.

[3] Allen Buchanan, in *Ethics, Efficiency and the Market* (Totowa: Rowman and Allenheld, 1985), pp. 51–53, makes this point.

[4] Rawls, *A Theory*, and Feinberg, "Justice," pp. 88–94, follow this strategy.

[5] This centers around the claim that preferences revealed by market behavior are true reflections of an agent's welfare. This view has been widely criticized; cf., for example, Amartya Sen, "Rational Fools: A Critique of the Behavioral Foundations of Economic Theory," *Philosophy and Public Affairs*, vol. 6 (1977), pp. 317–44. Also see below, section IV.

[6] Cf. Paul Samuelson, *Economics* (New York: McGraw Hill, 1967), ch. 31; Frank Knight, *Risk, Uncertainty and Profit* (New York: Kelly and Millman, 1957), ch. 9;. and Hal Varian, *Microeconomic Analysis* (New York: Norton Press, 1984), p. 6. For a revision of the "standard account," cf. Israel Kirzner, *Competition and Entrepreneurship* (Chicago: Chicago University Press, 1973), ch. 2.

who owns, or comes to own, the productive factors of a firm.

This obviously collapses the familiar notions of an entrepreneur, considered the creator of a new business who seeks investors to back the venture, and the capitalist, considered the investor of her own capital in anticipation of positive returns. Combining these roles in this way helps to clarify the question of whether profits are deserved by imagining a single person who both organizes production and collects the profits of the firm. This broad characterization lends the most plausibility to the claim I am denying, for I am thereby considering a wider range of activities and characteristics which could serve as the basis for a claim of moral desert.

An entrepreneur who owns the capital assets of the firm will have final say over how those assets are utilized. The entrepreneur is the *primary* organizer of production in that she holds ultimate organizational control even if she chooses to delegate managerial functions to representatives – i.e., she could hire consultants and managers. But in such a case, the entrepreneur still has the primary organizational control insofar as whomever she hires, she can also *fire*, if not tell what to do. So in this sense, the entrepreneur is the primary organizer of production. In short, the entrepreneur is the person who perceives a certain malallocation of resources, information, or technology, and exploits this situation by starting a firm.[7] Even if all the start-up capital was borrowed, even if managers and consultants were hired to carry out the organizational tasks, it is the entrepreneur who begins the process and thus is the focus of my inquiry.

Turning now to "profits." This notion has also been variously rendered in the literature, with meanings ranging from merely "interest on investment capital," to (the morally question-begging) "reward for innovations and risk taking."[8] Generally speaking, however, profit is the difference between the market price for a good and the total cost of its production. Hence, in imperfect markets, the price of production (where that includes wages, rents, interest on borrowed capital,[9] etc.) may differ from the price of the good produced yielded by the market. Pure profit is this difference, whether it is positive or negative (though here I simplify and only speak of positive profits).[10]

It is important to remember what production costs (the aggregate price of all input factors) include: the wage bill, interest payments, resource costs, and depreciation costs. An input factor is any component of production that makes

---

[7] I simplify here by only talking of starting a firm. An entrepreneur can redirect production in an already existing firm in a variety of ways. The arguments I make should apply in those cases as well, though.

[8] *Cf.* Samuelson, *Economics*, pp. 592ff. *Cf.* also Knight, *Risk*, ch. 2.

[9] This includes interest on capital that the entrepreneur "borrows" from herself.

[10] *Cf.* Knight, *Risk*, p. 280, where he speaks of the "residual income" of entrepreneurs.

a marginal contribution to the monetary revenue of the firm. So an entrepreneur's contribution here is not, strictly speaking, an input factor, since payment for whatever services she renders is not part of the wage bill (by definition).[11] Her "income" is whatever is left after the complete bill is paid for all inputs after a cycle of production and sale, i.e., profits.

Now under conditions of perfect competition – ideal markets – an equilibrium will be reached at which profits for all firms will be zero. This results from constantly emerging competitors entering any market sector where firms are enjoying positive profit, thus driving prices down until they do not exceed the costs of production. But in real world markets, positive profits emerge when there is not completely free and costless shifting of resources. This malallocation of resources (where that includes information, technology, or even credit) allows for the market price of a commodity to stabilize above the marginal costs of the production of that commodity. An entrepreneur exploits the opportunity to produce such a good at a cost lower than the price the market will yield and to do so before others do.

So profits only arise when there is a sufficient lack of competition from other potential producers of the good. What *determines* the margin of profit is the presence of effective barriers to the entrance into the market of other producers. This could be caused in any number of ways: monopolies of various kinds (on resources or technology), high transaction costs, lack of credit for start-up capital, lack of information about consumer demand, etc. None of these factors are things an entrepreneur brings about herself (we are supposing), but they are nevertheless crucial in the determination of the size of the profit returned to the firm (and thus to the entrepreneur).

This is not to deny the importance of consumer demand for the economic success of a firm. But an essential determinant of that success – what determines the margin of profit – is the relative competitive threat posed by other producers. So entrepreneurial profits are the result of *both* consumer demand and the presence or absence of competing firms. This point, as we shall see, is crucial to my argument.

We come now to the concept of moral desert. This notion has been given a much recognized structural analysis by Joel Feinberg along the following lines: "S deserves X in virtue of F, where S is a person, X some mode of treatment, and F some fact about S, [and] the values of F (the desert bases) are determined in part by the nature of the various X's in question."[12] So a person deserves some benefit or loss (simplifying the possibilities) when there is some fact about her that is generally accepted as

---

[11] If she contributes to the management of the firm, her salary for those services will be computed in the wage bill, but this will not be part of her contribution *qua* entrepreneur. Recall that I am using the term "entrepreneur" in its strict sense.

[12] Feinberg, "Justice," p. 61.

providing a reason grounding such a claim. And the response in question is both appropriate for, and proportional to, the relevant characteristics of the desert bases.

In addition, the concept of desert is an essentially nonconsequentialist notion. The justification of a particular claim to deserve something cannot, by the logic of the term, make reference to the results or consequences of the person's getting the reward or punishment in question. This is not to say that consequences are barred from consideration at the level of evaluating the bases of the desert claim. We do say, for example, that the criminal *caused* harm and therefore deserves punishment. But it is inappropriate to justify the reward or punishment *itself* with regards to *its* consequences. We will see in Section IV the relevance of this fact. Also, for the purposes of this paper, I will view desert claims as *prima facie* moral claims, which provide a defeasible moral reason that the deserving person(s) should receive the thing or mode of treatment deserved. This is not to say that denying the appropriateness of a desert claim rules out various alternative justifications for the receipt of some treatment, but the desert claim can be separated out of the justification and tested for its independent plausibility.

The conditions of propriety and proportionality necessitate further attention, as they will be crucial in the arguments to follow. For a person to deserve, for example, a favorable mode of treatment like praise, there must be some fact about her that provides a basis for that praise. If she performed some difficult and noble act, for example, then we would say the praise is deserved. But what must also be true for it to hold that she deserves the particular bit of praise offered, is both that praise is an appropriate response to the behavior in question and that the amount of praise given is proportional to the goodness or nobility of the acts. If the condition of proportionality[13] is violated – when the response is too much or too little – we say that the person in question does not deserve *that*.[14]

Another way to put the proportionality condition is this: it must be the case that the magnitude of the benefit or harm deserved is *determined by* the moral evaluation of the factors upon which the desert claim is based. Proportionality does not mean merely an accidental correlation of one with the other, but a relation between the two where the person receives a certain mode of treatment *because* of the characteristics calling for that treatment. That is, S deserves X in virtue of F only when the nature of

---

[13] From this point on I drop consideration of propriety, since my argument rests on the proportionality condition alone.

[14] This is distinct from saying that a person is (simply) undeserving. She may, for example, deserve praise, but not the particular praise offered, when it violates this condition.

X – its magnitude and quality – is determined in strict accordance with the value or disvalue of F.

With these conditions in mind, then, upon what basis might it be claimed that entrepreneurs deserve their profits? What is it that entrepreneurs do, in the course of their roles as primary organizers of production and owners of productive factors, that might ground the claim that they deserve the economic surplus after the production and sale of their goods? In Section IV, I will consider two answers to these questions: one is that the entrepreneur takes the relevant risks with the initial capital investments and so deserves the resulting profit; the second, which is my main point of concern, is that the effort and skill that entrepreneurs display in spotting the relevant demand for a product, and then meeting that demand, results in the provision of a benefit to the consumers of the product, and for this she deserves the resulting profit. Before considering these issues, though, I would like to spell out, and respond to, an attempt to defend the claim that entrepreneurial profits are deserved.

II.   A Defense of Entrepreneurial Desert Claims

In "Profits and Desert,"[15] N. Scott Arnold defends the claim that the fact entrepreneurs do deserve their profits. Arnold's strategy for supporting this position is along these lines. He accepts, in general, the Feinberg-type analysis of "desert" I discussed, but he spells out an additional kind of desert claim which he calls "institutional." What he has in mind is a desert claim which may be valid based solely on its relation to an institutional setting of some sort. An example is a baseball game, where the best team deserves to win because it is part of the "essential goals" of the institution of baseball that higher quality teams should win. So to understand the meaning of these sorts of desert claims, one has to know the goals of the institution. Desert claims are distinguished from entitlements in that the latter are generated directly by the "achievement rules" of the institution, while the former are based on the essential goals of the institution.

Entrepreneurs, for Arnold, are those persons whose creativity and alertness to malallocations of the market enable them to pursue new production strategies to meet the demand created by that malallocation.

---

[15] N. Scott Arnold, "Why Profits Are Deserved," *Ethics*, vol. 97, no. 2 (January 1987), pp. 387–402. *Cf.* also Edward Nell's criticism of Arnold in the same issue (pp. 403–410). Professor Nell makes some similar points to the ones made here, though his discussion is more technical and does not deal with the concept of desert more generally. He spells out how conditions having nothing to do with entrepreneurial activity can determine the rate of profit and thus dislodge any claim of desert. While some of my arguments here rest on a similar kind of claim, the conclusions I want to draw extend beyond his criticisms. *Cf.* also Arnold's reply to Nell (pp. 411–13); nothing of what he says there addresses the criticisms of his view I adduce below.

Markets, on his view, are an institution which have a central directive of distributing scarce goods to consumers. The essential goal of a market, then, is to allocate resources as efficiently as possible. Entrepreneurs engage in activity which contributes directly to this goal by redirecting production and distribution in response to perceived malallocations.

Arnold lists three ways in which profits are the "appropriate reward" for the contributions made by entrepreneurs. First, when entrepreneurs are allowed to keep the profits that the market returns to them, this provides an incentive to continue to pursue the kinds of production that are the most responsive to existing need. As he puts it, "if he [the entrepreneur] is allowed to keep the profits, the cost of not correcting a perceived malallocation of resources is quite high."[16]

Second, allowing entrepreneurs to keep profits keeps valuable financial resources in the hands of those whose success indicates a talent for effective investment. Those who have gained profits must be doing something right, so keeping those profits allows them to keep doing it. Finally, "the winning of profits by some serves as an effective signal to competitors to follow suit by making appropriate changes"[17] in their production strategies to respond to the newfound demand. Again, keeping profits functions as an incentive, this time to others who would enter that particular successful market sector.

The argument, then, can be summarized this way. Desert claims made in an institutional setting derive their validity from the essential goals of that institution. The essential goal of a market is the effective distribution of scarce resources. For the reasons just listed, entrepreneurial activity contributes to this goal (when profits are kept), so the profits are "fitting" rewards for the activities in question. Hence, the profits are deserved.

My criticism of this argument will be along several lines. First, is it the case that institutional frameworks are necessary for the determination of the validity of desert claims? Take Arnold's baseball example. Is it only because there is a principle *internal* to the game of baseball (that the best team deserves to win) that the desert claim (by the best team) gets its *moral* force? I think it is obvious that the principle (if it is a principle) that underlies our intuition that the best baseball team deserves to win is *not* based on anything internal to the rules or spirit of baseball. The entire phenomenon of games, or of competition generally, carries with it the idea that the best team, or the team or player that effectively exerts the most honest effort, deserves to win. And since the entire phenomenon of competition cannot be considered an institution, the intuitions that ground

[16] Arnold, "Why Profits Are Deserved," p. 397.
[17] *ibid.*

these claims are not tied to any particular institution at all.

This leads to a more important objection. If there are indeed goals internal to institutions that can be the basis of a desert claim, the *moral* status of the claim will depend solely on the moral status of the acts sanctioned by those goals. Evil institutions with evil goals should not be the basis for the desert of positive rewards. Arnold reminds us that desert claims have only *prima facie* force. My point here is that this force is *moral* only if the moral evaluation of the acts upon which the desert claim is based correspond to the moral worth of the thing deserved, (e.g., if they are good, then the things deserved must be good), *independent* of the institutional goals which those acts may promote.

Arnold is sensitive to this objection. He mentions it by way of imagining the Mafia, which may contain certain "institutional" rules and goals which would provide a basis for desert on his analysis, even though such an institution's goals are themselves immoral. His response is to remind us that the claims of desert here are indeed only *prima facie*, and thus would be overridden in this kind of case by the other moral considerations that make the actions of the Mafia immoral. But this response won't do. Imagine, for example, that the Mafia's institutional achievement rules demand that a person kill another person in order to avenge a minor insult made against the godfather. Imagine also that the effective carrying out of this action successfully contributes to the institutional goals of the syndicate. It will not do to say that the henchman who does this job well deserves a reward, in the *morally relevant sense*, but that this desert claim has only *prima facie* force. It has no moral force *at all*. It is immoral to kill someone to avenge an insult, so doing so does not deserve praise or reward. To say that there is an "institution-relative" sense in which the person deserves this merely is to use the word "desert" in a nonmoral manner. It strikes me as straightforwardly false that a hitman of the sort described *morally* deserves praise, and a view that entails this is thereby defective.

Now Arnold could demand that the goals of the institution in fact be morally beneficial ones, thus ruling out examples of this sort. This would in fact avoid these obvious counterexamples, but it would then remove the claims being made from the class of desert claims. This leads to a second major objection to Arnold's account, namely that his defense is actually a *consequentialist* defense of a claim of desert. This, as we have said, is inappropriate, for desert is an "essentially backward looking concept."[18] For Arnold to say that the goals of the institution that determine desert claims must be morally good, amounts to saying that a person deserves something because of the good results that emanate from her getting that

---

[18] Feinberg, "Justice," pp. 81ff, also makes this point.

thing. This consequentialist analysis effectively undercuts his claim that receiving accrued profits is something an entrepreneur deserves. It might have good results if she gets them, but this doesn't mean she deserves them. We might say, for example, that if we gave in to the demands of a terrorist organization, it would have the good result of initiating the freedom of the hostages being held, but this would not by any means entail that the terrorist deserved the ransom.

This also is an objection that Arnold mentions, but again his response is unsatisfactory. What he says is that the account may indeed *be* consequentialist, but since it is not *utilitarian*, his argument survives as a valid strategy for justifying desert claims. But this misses the point of the objection, for desert is not just a nonutilitarian concept, it is a nonconsequentialist one as well. As I have pointed out, the idea of deserving something is "backward looking"; its justification cannot be based on the consequences of getting the thing deserved.

Arnold's second response to this objection is that to say that his account of desert is unsatisfactorily utilitarian is to presuppose a previous moral evaluation of the institution. "If utilitarianism is true," he writes, "then all moral claims, including desert claims, are directly or indirectly justified by considerations of utility."[19] No they are not. If utilitarianism turns out to be true, then there would be *no such thing* as moral desert in the traditional sense. All actions will be justified by their consequences, not by whether or not persons deserve what happens to them. If our penal system were justified only on utilitarian grounds, then we would no longer punish people according to what they deserve; we would punish them based on what would ensue from the punishment.

It won't help here to appeal to a kind of two-tiered account of an institution, like Rawls's defense of retributive principles of punishment on higher order consequentialist grounds.[20] On such a view, the particular claims of desert are indeed justified by antecedentalist (i.e., backward-looking) considerations, even though the practice as a whole has its justification in its consequences. But for Arnold, the justification of the particular claims of entrepreneurs to deserve their profits refers to the consequences of their receiving them. This is consequentialist at both levels and thus not a proper use of desert claims at all.

Finally, a closer look at the three ways that the actions of entrepreneurs promote the goals of the market reveal the curious fact that the desert claim is not based on the primary entrepreneurial function of changing

---

[19] Arnold, "Profits," p. 393.

[20] *Cf.* Rawls "Two Concepts of Rules," *Philosophical Review*, vol. 64 (1955), pp. 3–32. *Cf.* also John Kleinig, "The Concept of Desert," *American Philosophical Quarterly*, vol. 8, no. 1 (January, 1971), p. 75.

production strategies after all. For the phenomenon that contributes to the overall goals of the institution of the market is the *receiving* of the profits by the entrepreneurs. That is what provides the incentives for continued investment, keeps money in the hands of those that can use it, and spurs others to act similarly. On Arnold's analysis, the beneficial effect upon which the desert claim is based is not the original activities of the entrepreneur in picking creative new production strategies to meet demand, but it is actually the receipt of the profits that has the beneficial effect grounding the desert claim. What this indicates, I think, is that Arnold has presented the rudiments of an argument for entitlements (to profits) by entrepreneurs based on the incentive effects of that property rights structure. While such an argument might be made (it is one that is of course much discussed), it is not one that has anything to do with desert.

I wish now to zero in on the central reasons why I think entrepreneurs do not deserve their profits. In doing so, I will focus on the benefit that the entrepreneur delivers in developing and producing a new product (or an old one in a different way). And I will assume that it is *this* that would provide the direct basis for a claim of desert.

III. Why Entrepreneurs Do Not Deserve Their Profits

Aside from Arnold's more particular argument, there are two other general strategies for arguing that entrepreneurial profits are deserved. One is to make the claim that, in winning profits, an entrepreneur displays superior traits of character that can themselves be the basis for a claim of desert. This is a position that Rawls attacks. He argues that such traits of character, while they may be noteworthy and valuable, are the inevitable results of natural talents and inborn capacities which are not themselves deserved, and thus cannot be the basis for a claim of moral desert. "[A person's] character depends in large part upon fortunate family and social circumstances for which he can claim no credit. The notion of desert seems not to apply to these cases."[21]

Rawls has been variously criticized for this line of argument.[22] One type of response is to say that our natural talents are in fact deserved if anything is, for eventually all our actions and dispositions can be traced back to either natural capacities or conditions of our upbringing. So if we do not deserve things based on these, how can anything be deserved at all?[23] Secondly, it can be argued that Rawls is too narrow in his focus on moral

---

[21] Rawls, *A Theory of Justice*, p. 310.

[22] Cf., e.g., Robert Nozick, *Anarchy, State and Utopia* (New York: Basic Books, 1974), pp. 213–215.

[23] Cf. Alan Zaitchick, "On Deserving to Deserve," *Philosophy and Public Affairs*, vol. 6, no. 4 (Fall 1977).

character in evaluating the status of moral desert. For a claim that entrepreneurs deserve their profits could be based on the moral worth of the *actions* taken by these individuals, actions that are voluntary and cannot be said to be necessarily the result of natural endowments or upbringing. If anything is the basis for desert claims, it is the free actions of agents. Penal systems are designed according to this very idea. I would now like to consider this line.

The first suggestion I will consider is that entrepreneurs deserve their profits because they have born an undue burden of risk in the development of productive factors and the starting of a firm. That is, the entrepreneur takes a less risk-averse stance toward capital (and time and even reputation) in facing the possibility that the goods she produces will not be met by sufficient demand for consumers. Hence, it is claimed that the bearing of this risk is the basis for the desert of profits which arise if the venture is indeed successful.

The objections to this line of argument, though, are straightforward.[24] First, taking a risk, by itself, would not qualify as grounds for a desert claim unless the point of the risk-taking is in some independent way praise- or blameworthy. This is so despite our proclivity to say "she got what she deserved" when someone loses on a foolhardy risk. We wouldn't say, however, that a mountain climber deserved to fall because of the high risk of doing so that she assumes.

What this shows, I think, is that risk taking is not itself sufficient ground for deserving anything. It depends completely on the *point* of a person's taking a risk. Risking one's life in battle is often thought of as grounds for praise or decoration, but this is true only when the intended outcome of the behavior is itself noble or worthwhile. Taking the same risks for some evil or selfish end, or just "for the hell of it," would not support a claim for deserving anything (except perhaps disdain or ridicule). Whatever is deserved is thus based on the moral quality of the agent's ends, not on the risk taken to achieve those ends. Moreover, it is often the case that the relation between risk-taking and deservingness diverges (and indeed runs the opposite way): when the level of risk a person assumes becomes too high, the strength of the claim to deserve something (like praise) diminishes. We call an overly risky person foolhardy, for example, and hence *less* deserving of the (say) praise that a more cautious individual would merit.

Similarly, the relation between the riskiness of some production venture and the return of a positive rate of profit is a complicated one, and not always reflective of our intuitions about desert. For often, highly risky

---

[24] Arnold, "Profits," p. 395, makes points similar to these.

ventures return relatively low rates of profit, and so-called "sure-things" – where maybe initial venture capital required is low and probability of market success is high – can return a high rate of profit. So it cannot be the mere assumption of the risk that grounds the claim for deserving profits; it must be established that the risk is taken to achieve some beneficial or praiseworthy end.

This, then, brings us to the second proposal. This claim is that the basis by virtue of which entrepreneurs deserve their profits is that a benefit is provided by the production and sale of a good for which there is sufficient consumer demand. After all, those who buy the product in question, at a price that results in a profit for the entrepreneur, must have wanted or even needed that product, since we assume that consumer actions are voluntary. This provision of a benefit, at the cost of the entrepreneur's time, effort, and creative and organizational skills, is the kind of activity which would ground the claim that the entrepreneur deserves any resulting profits returned to the firm. So the claim amounts to this:

> An entrepreneur, E, deserves some profit, P, by virtue of the fact, F, that E has provided a benefit to a set of individuals, and the relation between the values of F and P meets the propriety and proportionality conditions of desert claims.

As I will presently argue, my denial of this claim rests on the contention that the factors which determine the magnitude of the profit returned after a cycle of production and exchange necessarily run afoul of the proportionality requirement for all desert claims set out above. That is, while we are assuming for argument's sake that the entrepreneur performs a service to the community of people that purchase her product, and thus might deserve some positive response, the *profit* she earns cannot be that deserved response. This is because an essential part of what determines the magnitude of profit for the production cycle is the proximity and capacity of potential competitors, and this is independent of the factors upon which the desert claim is purportedly made.

Recall that one of the essential factors in the determination of market prices is the unmet demand for that good in that sector of the market. And what affects that unmet demand are the various barriers to entering the market that face other potential producers, whose competitive presence would drive prices below what could be offered by the original producer-entrepreneur. The profit returned, then, which is a function of the market price, is directly determined by these barriers: such things as monopolies on information or technology (including patents and copyrights) held by the entrepreneur, lack of attractive credit opportunities for new producers, other high transaction costs (like the cost of physical relocation), and the like. And, again, these are conditions that the entrepreneur did not herself create; and more importantly, they are not part of what we have described as the beneficial effects of entrepreneurial activities (the desert's base, F).

Frank Knight has put essentially the same point this way: "Nearly all supplies of goods and services . . . enjoy some degree of monopoly. Each has a monopoly with a certain *market area*, and competition is effective only at the boundary between market areas."[25] My point here is that the size and scope of that limited sectoral monopoly determines the size of the profit margin returned on the sale of the commodity produced. And the various factors listed above determining the profit margin are not part of the value of entrepreneurial activity (which is limited to meeting demand).

That value, after all, amounts to the provision of a beneficial good or service to a group of consumers willing to pay the market price for the commodity. This benefit is not affected by the *source* of the product (except insofar as this affects prices). So whether or not the good is provided by our original entrepreneur or some competitor, the benefit (i.e., the product's being consumed) remains the same. In fact, since the existence of competing producers effectively drives the price down, the benefit of the entire enterprise to individual consumers is increased when profits to producers decrease.

But my point does not rest on the claim that a positive rate of profit represents less of a benefit to consumers (goods at a price which in principle could be lower), but rather that the size of the profit is not *determined* by the magnitude of consumer benefit upon which the purported desert claim is made.

Imagine an analogous case of a criminal who deserves some punishment. For it to be the case that the criminal deserves the particular sentence given to her, its severity must be proportional to the harmfulness of her criminal acts. If, for example, prison sentences were randomly pulled out of a hat, we would not say that the prisoner deserved that punishment, for the severity of the sentence was not *determined* by the harmfulness of the crime. To make the analogy closer to the present case, imagine that the sentence was determined, not by chance, but by the availability of prison space in the area, or the numbers of guards employed by the facility. These factors are not related to the severity of the crime, so if they determine the punishment, then we would not say that the criminal deserves that particular sentence. "Desert" is a fundamentally nonconsequentialist moral notion: what is deserved can only be determined by the value or disvalue of the factors which are the basis for the desert claim.

Rawls makes a similar claim (though his focus is on the moral worth of

[25] Knight, *Risks*, p. xx.

the person as the desert basis). He writes: "the extent of one's contribution (estimated by one's marginal productivity) depends upon supply and demand. Surely a person's moral worth does not vary according to how many offer similar skills, or happen to want what he can produce. No one supposes that when someone's abilities are less in demand or have deteriorated . . . his moral deservingness undergoes a similar shift."[26] I have tried to make a similar claim, but not about the varying moral worth of the character of the entrepreneur, but about the arbitrary relation between the entrepreneur's supposed contribution to the benefit of others and her profit margin.

Now it may be objected here that the presence or absence of other producers of the same product actually does affect the value of the contribution of the initial entrepreneur's product. This is because the marginal value of the product (which, it is assumed, is equal to the benefit received by a purchaser of a single extra increment of it) increases or decreases with the competitive threat posed by other producers. So the benefit provided actually is proportional to the profit.[27] This line, however, goes astray in two ways. First, it can plausibly be argued that the marginal value of a particular product is not a proper measure of the welfare increase in its consumption.[28] It is an economist's fiction that the equation between price, marginal value, and welfare is in fact an equation. The various fluctuations in the relative values of consumable products, from Edsels to Hula Hoops to heroin, most often have little to do with the relative utility gained by consumption of those products, or more generally the "good" consumers receive from them. This is not exactly to deny our earlier assumption about the benefits of consumption, but to say that even if the purchase of the product reflects a welfare increase for the person, that increase is not *measured* in any precise way by its price.

Second, this objection ignores all of the arbitrary ways in which products' marginal values, as well as corresponding profits, can fluctuate due to competitive pressures. Imagine that a particular firm can take advantage of a sudden drop in the price of a single input factor, a price change that competing firms lack access to (e.g., a favorable wage arrangement with a non-unionized labor pool); and imagine that this drop does not induce a price change for the firm's output. (Since competing firms lack access to this cheaper factor, its price will not be bid upward, at least for a while.) Under these conditions, where production prices decrease but market price for the good remains constant, the profit margin thereby rises. And this takes place without a corresponding change in the

---

[26] Rawls, *A Theory of Justice*, p. 311.
[27] I am grateful to Thomas Christiano for help in clarifying these points.
[28] *Cf.* Buchanan, *Ethics*, p. 52, for a point similar to this.

benefit enjoyed by consumers of the product. Examples such as these illustrate the indirect relation between profit margin and benefit, a relation which must be direct if the profits are to be deserved.[29]

If there could be a measure of "pure demand shift," where that refers to a shift in the demand for some product on the part of consumers alone (and profits are directly determined by this), the above objection might have some force. But "demand" can fluctuate because of natural disaster, monopoly formation in a market sector, advertising strategies, and the like. To say that the corresponding shift in marginal product value is proportional to a shift in the benefit received in the product being consumed is flatly implausible. Recall, and this is the crucial point, that the proportionality condition requires that there be a *direct* link between the benefit delivered, upon which the desert claim is made, and the size of the reward deserved. What I am arguing here is that there is no such direct link in the case of profits and consumer benefit. To say that there is ignores the various factors external to the benefit provided to consumers by the purchase of products that determine the profit margins of entrepreneurs.

So my argument amounts to this: entrepreneurs do not deserve their profits because, in a manner analogous to the prison sentences in the example above, they are not determined by virtue of the magnitude of the benefit upon which the claim is based. This is so because, as I have tried to explain, profits are determined by such external factors as the proximity of competing firms, general availability of production technology, and so forth. And since this amounts to a violation of the proportionality condition set out above, it cannot be held that these profits, determined in this way, are deserved.

IV.   DESERVING MARKET SHARES IN GENERAL

So much for entrepreneurs. the extrapolation of the above considerations to apply to allocations of markets generally is actually quite straightforward. Whenever allocations of resources in market settings are the result of competitive forces external to the direct relation between desert basis and reward, then the rewards received (or, perhaps, the costs incurred) are not deserved. Whenever barriers to expanded competition are part of the explanation of the magnitude of market shares received, then the proportionality condition for desert claims I explained above will not be met. Therefore, in such cases, whatever moral reasons can be brought to bear on the question of who gets what, these should not include reasons of desert.

[29] For elaboration on this point, see Nell, pp. 408ff.

Indeed what I have said would also help support a general skepticism about the possibility of evaluating, in morally relevant terms, the benefit that is provided by the producers of resources in a market apart from the price of that resource. Desert requires that such an evaluation can be made, since there must be a relation between that value and the value of the reward returned to those who produce that resource. What I say here might indicate that the evaluation on either side of this relation would be forbiddingly vague, and thus the question of who actually deserves what in a market is useless. To see the force of this skepticism, one need only ask which is of greater magnitude, in morally relevant terms: forty hours of dull and difficult work on an assembly line or the same time spent as a corporate executive in an office, *apart from the market values of these tasks* (i.e., their prices). In order to even begin to claim that the market is allocating to such persons the resource bundles they in fact deserve, one needs to be able to make these evaluations. One must then make the *further* claim that the sizes of these resource bundles are indeed determined by (are proportional to) the effort expended (or benefit produced). I hope to have shown by the forgoing just what an impossibly tall order this is.

To sum up, I have argued that in market economies where profits arise from disequilibrium conditions which determine the size of profits returned to entrepreneurs, those profits are not deserved. The basis of this claim is that a necessary condition for the validity of a claim of personal desert is that a proportionality obtains between the actions upon which the desert claim is based and the mode of treatment or object deserved, where the value of the former determines the latter. And I have argued that, in the case of entrepreneurial profit, this condition is not met because the rate of profit is determined by factors independent of the value of the activities grounding the desert claim. By this more exact argument, I have tried to lend support to the general claim that competitive markets do not allocate goods according to a principle of desert. This is so whenever the rewards allocated by the market are determined by the competitive forces of supply and demand, in ways sufficiently similar to the case of entrepreneurial profits. The relevance of this, if nothing else, consists in dislodging another pillar in the already shaky moral foundations of free market capitalism.

Philosophy, Virginia Polytechnic Institute and University of California at San Diego

LUCK*

BY RICHARD A. EPSTEIN

But come bad chance,
And wee joyne to it our strength,
And wee teach it art and length,
Itself o'er us to'advance.
JOHN DONNE, *Song*

INTRODUCTION: ESCAPING LUCK

John Donne's song was hardly written in the tradition of political philosophy, but it has a good deal to say about the theme of luck, both good and bad, which I want to address. There is no doubt but that bad luck has bad consequences for the persons who suffer from it. If there were a costless way in which the consequences of bad luck could be spread across everyone in society at large, without increasing the risk of its occurrence, then most of us would pronounce ourselves better off for the change. In this sense it can be said, for example, that there is a utilitarian grounding for a moral obligation to care and provide for those persons who suffer the fortunes of bad luck. For the sake of argument I do not wish to contest this particular starting point, although there are many who would. Instead, I want to ask the question of whether this moral obligation should be converted into a legal obligation, backed by public force. The dominant answer to that question today is yes. Even those who think that markets should determine decisions on production find that the state has a proper role to reduce the adverse consequences of bad luck. My cast of mind is more skeptical. In life, or, in this instance, politics, "come bad chance, and we do join to it our strength." In general the effort to use coercion to counter the adverse effects of luck tends only to make matters worse. I believe that this conclusion is especially strong when efforts are made to bend or modify the ordinary common law rules of property, contract, and tort to correct for the undeserved influence of luck. While the position is surely more controversial, I also believe that the practical problems of implementation of any comprehensive social obligation to counter the effects of bad luck are daunting.

* I should like to thank Stephen J. Schulhofer for his helpful comments on an earlier draft of this paper.

In this essay, then, I propose to examine the role that luck, both good and bad, should have in the organization of social and political institutions. The theme, like Donne's Song, is a broad one, because luck is always with us from the time we are born until the time we die. Birth itself, as the phrase "accidents of birth" suggests, is something of a lottery. A person may be born male or female; he may be born of parents of high station or low; he may be smart or dumb, handsome or ugly, healthy or sick. The set of endowments that people bring into this world will shape in very large measure their prospects for success once they are in it. Yet their initial good fortune is not based upon achievement or merit, or indeed any other obvious form of desert.

The role of luck does not end, however, with the fortunes of birth. In its most extreme version, the thesis is that all human accomplishment is the product only of good fortune. Even for those persons who labor diligently, luck is decisive because genetic fortune and a receptive environment give them the wherewithal to make the advances and contributions for which they are rewarded. All gains therefore become in some sense "unearned windfalls," and luck becomes the dominant, indeed, sole determinant of success and failure.

Even more modest accounts have to recognize the powerful place of luck in human affairs. The dominant legal rules for the acquisition of property give the first possessor of an unowned thing complete title to it. In some instances, the acquisition of valuable things is the result of systematic search. In other cases, it reflects the alert responses of attentive individuals. In some cases, acquisition is sheer luck or good fortune. The mixture of luck and planning can vary widely over separate cases, and yet the uniform rule leaves the thing with its founder, without any effort to isolate luck from skill, or to reward the finder only the increment value attributable to his early acquisition of the good.

Luck continues to exert its influence whenever individuals make decisions under conditions of uncertainty. A drunk or careless driver strikes a pedestrian standing on the sidewalk. For the pedestrian, it is a case of bad luck in being in the wrong place at the wrong time, but death is still permanent and injuries still debilitate. The driver himself may have been drunk or careless a hundred times before, yet only this time have his actions resulted in harm. Like his victim, he too is a victim of bad luck.

The problem of luck also reaches ordinary decisions taken in the marketplace. People decide to make investments, to get married, to change jobs. Each of these decisions may be sound ex ante, but the consequences may be dreadful ex post. Conversely, people may make unsound decisions ex ante, and "luck out" in the end. Normal financial calculations speak of expected rates of return on investment. Yet the odds are far greater that the observed rates of return will either exceed or fall short of that figure, and the difference, or some substantial portion of it, is ordinarily attributable to luck. But again the investor must live with the outcomes of his choices, regardless of his original prudence.

Luck, then, exerts a pervasive influence on our lives. But need that be so, or should legal and social institutions take steps to change the balance of fortune that luck itself has created? It is just this question that I want to address in this essay. Answering it, I believe, gives us some insight into the fundamental choices that any society must make about self-governance, including the choice between capitalism and socialism.

The paper is organized as follows. The first section examines the traditional common law approach to the question of luck. The second section examines two conceptions of "redress" for harm: the common law idea of redress for the wrong by a given person, and the broader Rawlsian conception of redress for bad luck generally. Rawls regards as "morally arbitrary" those outcomes that occur when luck is allowed to reign unchecked. One sentence well sums up Rawls's position: "since inequalities of birth and natural endowment are undeserved, these inequalities are to be somehow compensated for."[1] The third section then argues that the narrower common law conception of redress is to be preferred to its broader Rawlsian alternative. The fourth section then asks whether voluntary systems of social support and charitable giving are a suitable social response to the problem of bad fortune. Section five then links the analysis of luck to the treatment of property rights, and the global political choice between capitalism and socialism.

I. LUCK IN THE LAW

The traditional legal system took very little notice of luck in the formation of its legal rules. The original distribution of natural talents and abilities was taken by it as a "given," which the state did not attempt to alter by coercive means. The rules of the natural acquisition of unowned property followed a similar pattern, and turned only on the fact that the finder occupied the land or took the thing in question.[2] The fortune, skill, or alertness that led to acquisition did nothing to either strengthen or

---

[1] John Rawls, *A Theory of Justice* (Cambridge: Harvard University Press, 1971), p. 100. The role of luck in Rawls's thinking is also noted by G.A. Cohen: "They [i.e. Rawls and Dworkin] say that, because it is a matter of brute luck that people have the talents they do, their talents do not, morally speaking, belong to them, but are, properly regarded, resources over which society as a whole may legitimately dispose." G.A. Cohen, "Self-Ownership, World Ownership, and Equality: Part II," *Social Philosophy and Policy*, vol. 3, no. 2 (Spring 1986), p. 79.

[2] For a general discussion, see R. Epstein, "Possession as the Root of Title," *Georgia Law Review*, vol. 13 (Summer 1979), p. 1221.

weaken the title in question. Property once reduced to private ownership was also governed by a set of rules that gave no place to luck. The old legal maxim with respect to property captures the dominant attitude well. *"Res perit domino"* – the thing perishes for its owner – is a Roman maxim, long accepted in the common law. Prima facie, the risk of the destruction of a thing falls to its owner to bear as best he can. That same attitude was carried over to personal endowments or talents, as well. The radical change in fortune or net worth is his to bear as best he can. In order to find some warrant to demand recovery for that loss from some other person, the owner of property has only two recourses, contract and tort, and neither of these reach cases of simple bad luck, or imposes upon the state (and through it, upon other citizens) any comprehensive duty of compensation.

First, the owner may be able to show that the risk of loss that the rules of ownership place upon him had been assumed by someone else through agreement. Risk allocation is done in all sorts of agreements for the sale of labor and goods. But its operation is best understood in connection with the ordinary contract of insurance, whereby the company agrees to compensate the individual for the loss of property in accordance with some formula that the two parties have agreed upon in advance. One purpose of insurance is to allow the insured to equalize income – and (imperfectly) through it, his utility – in all alternative future states of the world.[3] While the premium paid causes some loss of wealth in the periods in which the property remains useful, the contingent protection provided by insurance generates an immediate benefit, even if no payout is made in the policy in the end. The insured's loss only occurs as the coverage is exhausted without the occurrence of a compensable event. At formation, the gain from insurance contracts is great, which is why insurance is routinely sold for property, life, health, and disability. Both sides are made better off through the reassignment of risk.[4]

Second, contract aside, the owner may be able to show that the destruction of the property is the result of some (wrongful) actions by

---

[3] The actual operation of insurance is far more complex. Life insurance, for example, cannot equalize a person's wealth after death, and may not be desired by persons who have no dependents or heirs. Even disability insurance may not be desired by persons who think that they get very little value out of money when sick or injured. But these examples only show that complete insurance need not be desired. They are not inconsistent with the proposition that insurance, when purchased, tends to equalize wealth across different states of the world. See generally, R.A. Epstein, "Products Liability as an Insurance Market," *Journal of Legal Studies*, vol. 14 (December 1985), p. 645; Alan Schwartz, "Proposals for Product Liability Reform: A Theoretical Synthesis," *Yale Law Journal*, vol. 97 (Feb. 1988), pp. 353, 362–367, and the materials cited in note 13, p. 362.

[4] Again, the statement is somewhat incomplete. Some insurance is purchased in order to *bond* the loss prevention services that the insurer provides the insured. Thus, the vast bulk of boiler insurance goes for inspection, not payouts for losses.

someone else. In the early legal systems the type of showing that had to be made was quite specific and limited. Impatient with abstract philosophical speculation about causation, the formative Roman and common law systems both demanded some direct physical connection between the property destroyed and the action of the defendant: the model of causation was the fist in the face, or stated somewhat more elegantly, *corpore corpori* – by the body and to the body.[5] Over time the number of links in the chain were grudgingly expanded to cover certain cases of indirect harm (e.g., the defendant waved a red flag to lure the plaintiff's cow over the side of a cliff, but did not touch her). After all the refinement and shouting was over, however, the level of causal connection at its loosest remained quite tight. Until early in this century, the dominant legal strategy with respect to causation stressed the importance of finding the *single* defendant on whom the loss should be properly placed, usually on the ground that only the "last wrongdoer" could be regarded as the "sole proximate cause" of the loss from whom compensation could be demanded.[6] Even modern proximate cause theories typically only contemplate two, or perhaps three, codefendants in a single lawsuit.

All this is not to say that there were not enormous intellectual disputes over the proper principles of liability within the class of acts causing harm – debates that rage on with undiminished intensity today. But it is important to recognize that *none* of these classical legal disputes challenge the basic principle that luck, good or bad, neither increases nor reduces civil liability. The point can be made in two ways: first as it applies to the losses that occur within the class of harms inflicted upon others; second as it applies to the kinds of losses that are kept wholly outside the tort and compensation system.

Starting with cases where one person has caused harm to another, everyone has long agreed that some compensation must be tendered for those losses that one person had deliberately inflicted upon another. To be sure, there are many learned disputes about the proper scope of self-defense and the like, but those issues rarely arise in the frequent cases of naked aggression that characterize, for example, so much street crime.

[5] See F.H. Lawson, *Negligence in the Civil Law* (Oxford: Clarendon Press, 1950), p. 14: "We know that as late as the classical period and, so far as appearances go, in the time of Justinian an action could be brought on the *lex* [Aquilia] itself only if the death or injury resulted from direct contact between the body of the wrongdoer and thing (*corpore corpori*). Translated into the language of the English law, this means that the *lex* penalized only trespasses." The reference to the "*lex* itself" notes that analogous actions, not explicitly under the language of the statute (here occidere, to kill, literally by force) were allowed for those who furnished a cause of death, e.g., supplied a victim with poison.
[6] See, e.g., T. Beven, *Negligence in Law*, (London: Stevens & Haynes, 3rd edition, 1908), p. 45.

Instead, the basic perception is startlingly simple. If the law were to allow one person simply to take what another owns just because he wants it, then there will never be any security of the person or property. We shall revert to the state of nature from which political organization has provided us some merciful escape. Repeal the ordinary prohibitions against deliberate trespass to person and property, and civilization is at risk. Odd that so small and elementary a point of law should have such momentous social consequences.

While intentional harms are the easiest cases to bring within the legal system, they are not the only ones. From the earliest times there has been well-nigh universal agreement in both Roman and common law that there should be compensation for *some* accidental losses, so long as the losses were done by the defendant to the plaintiff. But which losses? The major battle ground has been the choice between strict liability and negligence. The former, strict, theory holds that a prima facie case for liability is made simply by showing that the defendant inflicted the loss in question. The rival negligence theory insists upon all the causal requirements of damage to person and property found in the strict liability theory, but demands in addition that the loss of the injured party be "wrongful" in the sense that it could have been avoided by the exercise of reasonable (for which read either customary or cost-effective) care by the defendant.[7]

It is quite impossible to trace here the ebb and flow of this debate, but both sides of the debate reject the obligation to make compensation to persons on account of their bad luck *simpliciter*. Under both theories the restricted sense of causation noted above, that is, instances in which the defendant has used force to hurt the plaintiff or has set traps to injure him, remains essential to any recovery by an injured party. In a strict liability system, if you missed hitting someone else, you did not have to pay, but if you hit, then (prima facie) you paid. There was no pooling of losses based,

[7] The literature on this debate is legion. See, e.g., R.A. Epstein, "A Theory of Strict Liability," *Journal of Legal Studies*, vol. 2 (January 1973), p. 223; R.A. Posner, "A Theory of Negligence," *Journal of Legal Studies*, vol. 1 (January 1972), p. 29; S. Shavell, "Strict Liability versus Negligence," *Journal of Legal Studies*, vol. 9 (January 1980), p. 1. See also, Symposium on Causation in the Law of Torts, with articles by Jules Coleman, Robert Cooter, Richard Epstein, Mark Kelman, Judith Thompson, and Ernest Weinrib, *Chicago-Kent Law Review*, vol. 63 (1987), p. 397.

[8] The most extreme illustration of the principle is a variation of the famous case of Summers v. Tice, 33 Cal.2d 80, 199 P.2d 1 (1948), where two defendants shot at a plaintiff in likelihood that each person's bullet hit. The court there held that the loss was joint and several, so that each defendant was liable for the whole, but had an action against the other for 50 percent contribution, if he were solvent. If it could have been shown that defendant A had a 51 percent chance of having fired the bullet, his would have been the total loss, notwithstanding the equal culpability of the two defendants. The same result would hold if the defendant who shot the plaintiff was guilty only of ordinary negligence, while the one who missed had engaged in reckless conduct.

say, upon the dangerousness of the basic underlying actions undertaken by a group, say, of hunters or miners.[8] That same approach applied to negligent persons, whose escape from liability was complete if they did not cause physical harm, no matter how great the level of their carelessness.

The ravages of bad luck show their force not only with regard to cases within the tort system, but also those cases that fall outside it. As I noted, the debate between negligence and strict liability is anchored to a prior causal connection to the defendant's actions.[9] *Nothing* in the dispute seeks to place the consequences of bad luck, pure and simple, into the class of compensable events. The tenacity of this last limitation upon liability is shown by some early cases that indicate the outer limits of liability. If the basic principle is that a defendant can be held responsible only for what he has done, then it becomes strictly necessary to distinguish between Acts of God (the old phrase for natural events) and the actions of the defendant, as causes of an injured person's harm.

Like all distinctions, this one admits of many easy and some difficult cases. On the easy side, it is possible to distinguish between the injured party who is struck by lightning and the injured party who is struck by the defendant's fist. Nonetheless, any distinction of importance to the law will generate over time its fair share of marginal cases in which philosophers delight, and over which lawyers despair. Thus, if an extreme frost causes the best-made water main to burst, it has been held to be an accident for which the defendant is not responsible.[10] If a large gust of wind blows A into B, then while A has been carried away, he has not acted, and therefore cannot be held responsible no matter how strict the rules of legal responsibility. Yet if A, in an effort to escape a raging storm, runs into B, he has acted, albeit under overwhelming external compulsion. We no longer therefore have an act of God, but a coerced action, so that for this narrow class of cases, the question of liability *vel non* will not turn on causation but on the choice between negligence and strict liability.[11]

While the marginal cases give us some clue about the nature of human action and the metaphysics of the will, they should not be allowed to obscure the fact that birth defects, bad family connections, and all the other

[9] There was some liability for omissions, but here too only with respect to breach of some special relationship that linked plaintiff to defendant. See, e.g., Restatement Second of Torts, §323. Kline v. 1500 Massachusetts Avenue Apartment Corp., 439 F.2d 477 (D.C. Cir. 1970).

[10] Blyth v. Birmingham Water Works, 11 Exch. 781, 156 Eng. Rep. 1047 (1856).

[11] Note that it is possible to adopt an intermediate position which recognizes the specific defense of compulsion by acts of God, without committing one's self to the more general principle of no liability without negligence. The compulsion cases are the easiest to identify as situations in which a person's will is overborne by external events. Allowing this defense does not open up all stranger cases to the complex cost-benefit calculations that many rules of negligence invite.

"morally arbitrary" accidents of birth lie wholly outside the realm of any conceivable system of tort compensation.[12] These all fall so clearly on the Act of God side of the line that no litigation is necessary to establish the fact. The common law system is thus sharply circumscribed in its level of ambition and application.

II. REDRESS, BROAD AND NARROW

The concept of redress as it appears in traditional tort law is necessarily linked to the requirements of the ordinary tort action, that is, a suit by an individual plaintiff against the individual defendant from whom redress is sought. The modern philosophical uses of the term represent an important departure from that usage. When Rawls talks about the use of the principle of "redress" to explain the need to provide compensation for the "inequalities of birth and natural endowments," he is not using the idea of "redress" in the same sense as lawyers. Rather, his broader account of redress amounts to an important deviation from traditional philosophical usage stemming from Aristotle, who in speaking about corrective justice wrote as follows:

> It makes no difference whether a good man has defrauded a bad man or a bad man a good one, nor whether it is a good or a bad man that has committed adultery; the law looks only to the distinctive character of the injury, and treats the parties as equal, if one is in the wrong and the other is being wronged, and if one inflict injury and the other has received it.[13]

The examples used by Aristotle in this passage are the typical kinds of wrong that common lawyers have long recognized, cases of fraud, adultery (itself a breach of the marriage contract), and the infliction of injury upon another. Aristotle does not of course develop the precise principles of

---

[12] The recent "wrongful life" cases are not an exception to this general rule. These cases fall into two categories. In the former, parents bring suits against a physician for having a baby at all. The grounds of the action are quite traditional in that it is alleged typically that the physician was careless in an operation designed to sterilize either the father or mother, so that the costs of having the baby were a consequence of the breach of duty. These suits have met with mixed success with normal babies, but have generated some large rewards where the child born suffers from serious birth defects, imposing extraordinary costs of care on the parents. The more exotic class of wrongful birth cases is brought by the defective children themselves. Here courts have been reluctant to reward damages to the injured party because they cannot quite figure out the baseline for compensation when the child claims that he was better off never having been born. The first case in the wrongful birth line was Gleitman v. Cosgrove, 49 N.J. 22, 227 A.2d 689 (1967). See generally, *Prosser and Keeton on the Law of Torts* (W.P. Keeton gen. ed., 5th ed. 1984), p. 370.

[13] Aristotle, *The Nicomachean Ethics*, Bk. 4, Ch. 4, trans. H. Rackham (Cambridge: Harvard University Press, 1926), p. 275.

redress in each of these situations with the detail demanded of a lawyer, and such should not be expected of him, when his own general point is that concrete disputes depend upon the conduct of each party in the immediate transaction, and not upon any detached view of their overall station and virtue. The linkage of this plaintiff with this defendant is the one feature of corrective justice that is clear from his treatment of the issue.

Rawls is aware that Aristotle's account of corrective justice, and hence of redress, is limited to various kinds of wrongful actions, but insists that it is nonetheless consistent with his general approach. He writes:

> Aristotle's definition clearly presupposes, however, an account of what properly belongs to a person and of what is due to him. Now such entitlements are, I believe, very often derived from social institutions and the legitimate expectations to which they give rise. There is no reason to think that Aristotle would disagree with this, and certainly he has a conception of social justice to account for these claims.[14]

Yet Rawls downplays the point that Aristotle's own view of distributive justice (which covers Rawls's original position) is, on the examples given, much closer to the standard common law position than to Rawls's own system, with its very prominent redistributive component. Aristotle's reference to defrauding tallies well with the common law actions for deceit; his concern with adultery is a species of breach of contract to marry, as well as ordinary status obligations; and his reference to the infliction of harm refers to the tort tradition. In each case there is a determinate party against whom the charge must logically be lodged. Nowhere is there any hint that bad fortune in and of itself upsets the prior, appropriate distribution of rights, thereby making some correction or restoration necessary. After all, if general character is irrelevant to the outcome of the case, why is a prior history of good or bad fortune relevant? The common law is closer to Aristotle and the natural rights tradition of Locke than it is to Rawls.[15] The only imbalance that the legal system recognizes stems from human conduct that hurts others. "Mere" differences in wealth or fortune are beyond the scope of the law, at least within the traditional common law conception of corrective justice.

[14] Rawls, *A Theory of Justice*, pp. 10–11.

[15] There can be an extensive debate over whether such philosophers as Locke and Nozick follow this pattern of common law rights. Locke, for example, appears to allow some limited place for redistribution, at least in cases of "extreme want," albeit one that falls short of a robust commitment to some guaranteed level of social support. I discuss some of these issues in R.A. Epstein, "Taxation in a Lockean World," *Social Philosophy & Policy*, vol. 4, no. 1 (Autumn 1986), p. 49, esp. p. 69, n. 36.

III. LUCK BEYOND THE LAW

Which concept of redress should be used? It is one thing to study legal institutions as they have emerged in the private law in order to understand how past and present societies have responded to the major problems of the time. It is quite another to assume that their responses provide sufficient *justification* for the practices that they embody. Here the possible biases are legion. One possibility is that the normal private law systems of responsibility simply do not begin to account for the full range of obligations that people owe one another within society. The informal bonds of association that are created within the family or the church, for example, may involve far greater social obligations than those which are expressed within the legal system, which is, I take it, the point of Robert Frost's famous remark that "Home is the place where, when you have to go there, they have to take you in." Yet even these informal practices by themselves do not create any general duty of redress for bad luck, for they speak only of the status duties that certain individuals owe *limited* others (family, church members) within society. The principle of redress, more broadly conceived (as Rawls, for example, would conceive it), has to operate *generally* from each person in society to every other person in society, just as the principles of tort and property in fact do operate today. On questions of ultimate principle, the common law is a guide but not a taskmaster. Is there some deeper normative position that justifies its customary restrictions on the idea of redress? Or is that practice itself a ready target for immediate reform?

One way to approach the subject is to look more closely at the structural limitations that attend the ordinary lawsuit in which one person claims redress from another. Where the claim is that the defendant has causally wronged the plaintiff, it is easy to conceive of a situation in which one plaintiff sues one defendant. We thus have the two-party relationship (the dyadic connection, as it is often called) established by the underlying facts of the case. Given the assertion of causal connection, we know why this plaintiff has picked on this defendant, and not someone else.

This mode of resolving disputes becomes, of course, wholly inappropriate for the redress of injuries if one function of the legal system is to neutralize the consequences of good and bad luck. The point becomes clear both in the property and tort cases we have spoken of.

(1) Property. Start with the case where someone acquires property by original acquisition. If we wanted to rule out the fruits of good luck, it would be necessary to distinguish the fraction of the private gain attributable to luck, and that which is attributable to systematic investments in labor, and even alertness. Yet even here there is no obvious other

claimant to oppose the finder, so that the only possible course of action is to socialize that "windfall" portion of the private return attributable to luck alone.

Formidable obstacles lie in the path of that endeavor. Apportionment requires the kind of information that is rarely, if ever, available in the individual case, while no general rule of thumb (e.g., the finder keeps half) is apt to have a good fit, given the enormous variations in the amount of luck involved in individual cases. Even if this all-pervasive measurement problem could be gotten around, the effort to distinguish between luck and skill (assuming that skill is not a form of genetic luck)[16] still poses further obstacles to the efficient deployment of the assets that finders acquire. Thus, decisions on how to improve or use assets so found are heavily dependent upon the anticipated return from those investments, but the finder cannot calculate that return unless he knows what portion of the return on investment he will be allowed to keep for himself. The greatest effort will be induced where he keeps the entire return for himself. In the ordinary business partnership or joint venture, detailed divisions of the gains and losses are drafted by contract to cover the case of joint inputs by different parties. No single general legal rule sets the ideal division of the proceeds, even in the simple case where one party contributes capital and the other labor to a common venture. Yet just such a rule must be proposed if the gains from luck are held to be social, and those from labor individual.

Similarly, the ability to sell, mortgage, or exchange the asset in some subsequent transaction clearly is facilitated if the title is not subject to some undefined social claim to part of the asset or to the wealth it generates. The clearer the title, the easier it is to transfer ownership. The point becomes most clear as we move from small to large number situations. In a hypothetical society with only two persons, it might be of little consequence whether it was posited that both were equal owners of external resources, or that each could take claim ownership of that which he possessed first.[17]

---

[16] See, on this point, E. Hoffman & M.L. Spitzer, "Entitlements, Rights, and Fairness: An Experimental Examination of Subjects' Concepts of Distributive Justice," *Journal of Legal Studies*, vol. 14 (June 1985), p. 259. Their experiments show that there is at least some widespread sentiment for the sharing of windfall gains (at least as the Lockean would define them). The finding is of itself great importance, for it helps explain why programs of redistribution have such broad appeal. But the finding accounts for redistribution by voluntary means as well as redistribution by coercion. It helps explain why both these means might be tried, but does not afford a ground to choose between them.

[17] See, e.g., G.A. Cohen's example of a world composed only of Able and Infirm, with joint ownership and external goods and individual ownership of talents. G.A. Cohen, "Self-Ownership," pp. 84–87. Cohen's point is that this ownership structure places very powerful restraints on Able's ability to deal with his own talents, and thereby reveals the awkwardness of having separate systems of ownership for different forms of resources. But once it is granted that a system of property rights has to work in a world with large numbers of persons,

But the relative advantages of the second, private ownership, model become apparent on the more realistic assumption that there are many separate persons in the original position. As that number of parties increases, the holdout and bargaining problems increase dramatically under collective ownership. By the same token, these bargaining problems are reduced under a common law system of individual ownership, because the large number of potential buyers and sellers now facilitates the emergence of a thick competitive market with well-defined prices. The desire systematically to negate luck by establishing initial collective property rights to external objects creates enormous barriers to ordinary transactions, without yielding any identifiable social gains that make the expenditures worthwhile.

In sum, the simple common law rule that ignores luck, both for talents and external resources, works to maximize the total value of any goods and services that are produced. More complicated rules, tied overtly to a system of desert, may have a greater intuitive moral appeal, but they are prey to far greater institutional and practical impediments. Locke's labor theory of acquisition lays too much stress on the element of desert. But it yields its place in practice to the less rigorous requirements of the common law first possession rule, in part because the easy rules of acquisition make it more likely that purposeful labor will be undertaken once title to the things acquired is secure.[18] There is no case for taking luck into account by modifying the common law rules of property.

(2) Tort. A similar conclusion arises when the legal system tries to equalize the consequences of luck in the context of an ordinary property damage or personal injury case. Return for a moment to the case where only one of two negligent drivers has injured a pedestrian. In order to equalize the position of these two drivers, it would be necessary to find some way to charge each of them with some portion of the loss, a matter of no little practical difficulty, as the careless driver who avoided the collision has continued untroubled along his way. Indeed, the problem of pooling would not stop with these simple two-party cases. There are many negligent drivers on the road, and yet only a tiny fraction of them have been involved in an accident. If we are to be systematic and relentless in

---

then the simpler common law system, whereby external things in the original position are regarded as unowned, has the virtue of eliminating the enormous collective action problems that would otherwise arise.

[18] See E. Kitch, "The Nature and Function of the Patent System," *Journal of Law and Economics*, vol. 20 (October 1977), p. 265. Kitch's point is that the system of patent law extends its protection to many sketchy inventions in order to encourage further labor by the patentee. Note that recognizing ownership by first possession improves the likelihood that labor will be expended on external resources, so that in the end the value of most resources will be in fact enhanced by the labor so often thought to justify private ownership.

the desire to nullify the consequences of luck, then all persons who have engaged in conduct equally culpable should bear losses equally great. It is strictly necessary, therefore, to identify all the individuals who have committed culpable actions, and to find some system whereby we could assess each of them the appropriate share of the now common burden. The money collected would then have to be divided up among all those who had in fact been injured by those persons whose negligence had converted itself into harm. Ideally, the amount collected would have to equal the amount paid out, with an allowance for administrative costs, itself no easy administrative feat.[19]

With pooling, what is needed is a constant monitor of all individuals that could assess the severity of their negligence independent of the losses that occurred in particular cases. If we assumed that the costs of getting the relevant information were zero, then there would be no reason to be fazed by this task. We should run our costless computer at very rapid speeds. But transaction costs are positive, and error costs are even larger, and together these exercise a powerful constraint on the range of plausible legal arrangements. Any effort to estimate risk, where it has not materialized, must be done by crude proxies. Is the intellectual sophistication worth the confusion that it brings in its wake? Or are the costs of shifting wealth so great that everyone is better off if the attempt is not made?

One way to look at this question is to ask whether there are any private ways to limit the adverse consequences of bad luck. Here, if we assume that persons are, to some degree at least, risk-averse, there is some clear gain in the pooling of losses from the potential injurers' side. But there is no reason to change the tort system in order to respond to this problem of luck, even when liability is bounded by tight principles of causation. A system of private insurance can better rate persons for their potential for risks, and charge them the premiums to match. The insurance company will, of course, be worried that it will misclassify some individuals and their propensity to cause losses, but its concerns lead to well-defined underwriting and pricing strategies. There are gains from proper classification (i.e., where each person pays a premium that is appropriate given his anticipated liabilities), for now the insurance company will not see its better risks flee the insurance pool because they do not wish to subsidize inferior ones. Still, there are costs in running the classification system,

---

[19] This last point is a problem for Jules Coleman, who wishes to separate, at least analytically, the obligation to pay for wrongdoers from the right to collect for victims. See Jules L. Coleman, "Mental Abnormality, Personal Responsibility, and Tort Liability," B.A. Brody and H. Tristram Engelhardt, Jr., eds., *Mental Illness: Law and Public Policy* (Boston: Kluwer, 1980), p. 107. See also Jules L. Coleman, "Property, Wrongfulness and the Duty to Compensate," *Chicago-Kent Law Review*, vol. 63 (1988), pp. 460–61 ("the central claim I make is that liability and recovery are conceptually and normatively distinguishable").

because the information about the expected behavior of the insured is costly to obtain, both for the insurance company *and* for other prospective insureds.[20] But now the system can reach a stable equilibrium. Each insurance firm will stop where the marginal costs of further risk classification equal the marginal revenues from that classification. If other firms can do the classification better than those already in the market, then they can subdivide the old risk pool, and skim off the better risks by offering them coverage at a lower premium. The tort system thus preserves the causal connection between plaintiff and defendant, while the private insurance system, which piggybacks upon it, socializes by contract from the injurer's side most of the consequences of bad luck.[21] The full assessment of the tort system cannot be made without taking into account the private contractual responses that it tolerates, and indeed invites. With private insurance, luck is less of a problem than before. So long as one stays with the traditional conception of redress for wrongful acts, the question of luck will take care of itself without direct social control.

(3) Bad fortune.   The discussion of luck cannot, however, be limited to cases where bad luck arose within the context of injuries that one person inflicted upon another. If luck itself is morally arbitrary, then we must find ways to redress its consequences even when it is caused by natural events. In this broader context the insurance system can no longer piggyback upon the tort system, as it did above. If A is born with a serious birth defect that is best attributable to cosmic rays, just who is the proper defendant? A (by his next friend) could sue B. But B's obvious response is "why me?" Without any causal connection to link A with B, the selection of B as the possible defendant becomes – to use the traditional expression – morally arbitrary. In order to avoid the problem of uncompensated losses, it becomes necessary to ask: must we tolerate the sins of the arbitrary selection of paying parties?

Not necessarily. Clearly lawsuits will not be practicable if everyone must be joined as defendants in order to compensate needy plaintiffs. The procedural complications thus drive us to a very different, administrative solution, in which state officials have the power to tax the public at large in order to dispense needed payments to persons who have suffered the requisite level of misfortune.

---

[20] This last point is important because it helps explain why the insurance companies have some "give" in their classification system. Overcharged individuals have to pay a price to find coverage elsewhere, or to go it alone. And this will keep them in place, at least for some limited time.

[21] Most, but not all. One element of loss that is not socialized is the insured's time. The standard insurance policy requires the tort defendant to cooperate in the defense with the company, at his own expense. These costs provide a useful break against the greater willingness to engage in risky activities that arises once insurance is in place.

The mechanics of the program of mandatory pooling are, however, more daunting than one might expect. There can be no market mechanism which classifies and pools risks in ways that prevent the cross-subsidization of risks among persons, as with well-functioning markets. Victims are entitled to payments from the common fund even if they have made no contributions to it. In addition, this transfer, like all uncompensated transfers, is very costly to make. The transfer (of cash at least) itself is something of a wash, at least in terms of wealth. The dollar gains to the one party offset the dollar losses to the other. The transfer can only be thought desirable if the victim's need generates a special claim for redress, for now the transfer itself produces a utility gain to the recipient that exceeds the associated utility losses to payors. Or so we could say with confidence if we believed in interpersonal comparisons of utility.[22] Voluntary gifts within families are exceptionally attractive from this point of view. Often these transfers go from rich to poor, and in so doing provide a dual gain, both in the wealth they give to the recipient and the personal satisfaction to the donor.[23] These transactions therefore should not be taxed specially, but freely allowed, because they cost nothing for the state to police and yield clear, identifiable, social gains.

The introduction of coercion, however, changes the picture dramatically. Now the payors are impersonal and have no obvious connection or affection for the payees. The indirect gains of the parties so taxed will be reduced, if not eliminated. To be sure, if the group over whom the coerced transfers is made is small and cohesive, then some element of that dual gain will survive: that is one reason why tithing works in close-knit religious communities, or why systems of redistribution are generally more successful in ethnically homogenous societies, such as the Scandinavian countries, than in a diverse melting pot like the United States. In general, however, most people will take a more skeptical view of transfers to strangers than they do to family or clan. Untouched by the universality and detachment of moral philosophy, ordinary people are more likely to resist the transfer program in question, or seek to minimize its impact upon them. Their task will be made easier because there is so much play in the joints even after it is accepted that persons with bad luck should be "somehow compensated" by their fellow men.

Note some of the obvious contrasts with the tort system. The first is the

---

[22] I do, sort of. That is, I think that it is possible for individuals to make these comparisons in their ordinary lives, which is why marriages and friendships last. But it is quite a different question whether they can be made with similar accuracy in the political context where information is hard to come by, and the power of partisan zeal great.

[23] See D.D. Friedman, "Does Altruism Produce Efficient Outcomes? Marshall versus Kaldor," *Journal of Legal Studies*, vol. 17 (January 1988), p. 1.

sheer volume of the transfers in question. Within tort (even within automobile no-fault systems), most persons will be involved only in a handful of cases during their entire lives, and many of these will be simply handled by an insurance adjuster who knows which driver was in violation of the rules of the road. With the redress of bad luck, the number of instances in which compensation might be required is legion, and someone will have to decide whether all forms of bad health, looks, intelligence, or whatever are events or conditions for which compensation is appropriate. As everyone has some disability, care must be taken to divide the universe in ways that include some individuals with slight misfortune in the class of net payors, for the system cannot work unless the amount taken from the transferors is (allowing for administrative costs) equal to or greater than the amount paid to transferees.

The definition of the "compensable event" only marks the first step. Still to be determined is the level of compensation. Within the tort system there were obvious classes of compensable events, and a sense that compensation could be provided to "make individuals whole." But once the causal link between plaintiff and defendant is regarded as arbitrary, then the ordinary tort signposts for an intelligent compensation system are simply lost. There are not enough resources in the world to provide the victims of bad fortune compensation that approaches that routinely tendered the victims of bad accidents caused |by runaway motor cars, sloppy medicine, and hazardous products.[24] In addition to narrowing the class of compensable events, the formulas for compensation must be tailored to be consistent with some appropriate budget constraint.

The range of options that somehow compensate bad luck is very large. The battles that are fought over which systems will be used, and how, can easily dissipate the gains that one might hope to obtain by transferring dollars from where they are not needed to where they are. The complexity of the situation is such that no comprehensive administrative program to redress bad luck, even one that stopped far short of a move toward perfect income equality, could be in place the moment individuals emerge from behind some Rawlsian veil of ignorance and find themselves in civil society. The information that is needed is quite different from that required for the ordinary system of tort redress. There has to be an explicit account of the resource levels available for the compensation, the criteria for selection, the likely frequency of claims, and the appropriate levels of compensation. It is not possible to mimic the simple tort rule which says that if the defendant

---

[24] See R.A. Schmalz, "On the Financing of Compensation Systems," *Journal of Legal Studies*, vol. 14 (December 1985), p. 807.

is insolvent, then the plaintiff is out of luck, because there is simply no one else whom he can sue. With an expanded conception of redress, there are always additional dollars that could be raised from tax revenues to keep the transfer system alive. The indirect consequences of inflating the currency, starving capital investment, or dulling incentives may not dominate the political discussion, but in principle they cannot be ignored.

There is a sobering moral here. Expand the conception of redress to cases of bad luck, and the gaps of knowledge behind the Rawlsian veil are too large to overcome. Yet once we leave the veil of ignorance, the risks of self-interested decision-making, especially in legislative contexts, can doom the efforts to introduce any social system of compensation. It is easy to see why people might want to redress, or at least temper, the differences from natural fortune. But it is far more difficult to figure out just how these goals can be attained at any time in social life by coercive means, at a cost that people behind the veil would regard as acceptable. The case for social redress of bad luck may seem compelling if the ends are first accepted as fixed without considering the difficulties of implementation. But it is far more problematic when ends and means are considered simultaneously.

The irony should be manifest. The usual defense of the common law rules of property, contract, and tort derives from the natural rights or libertarian position. Yet the case for this lean system of entitlements is only strengthened by explicit resort to Rawls's veil of ignorance technology that is so often turned to other ends. If rational individuals behind the veil of ignorance knew what is known today, then I doubt that they would write into their fundamental law any principle that calls for the coercive redress of losses attributable to natural events or to bad luck.

The point can be taken one step further. Luck need not be regarded only as a difficulty to be overcome. It also has important beneficial uses of its own – precisely because it is morally arbitrary. The critical point is that there is a distinction between those forms of arbitrariness that are the result of *nature* and those forms of arbitrariness that are the result of *human intervention*. Stated in a phrase, the distinction is this: nature does not misbehave, while people do. More concretely, when we deal with the first form of arbitrariness we have a relatively fixed distribution of rights. The individual is the owner of his natural talents and the things that he is first able to reduce to his possession. The state is called upon to protect these entitlements, and thus needs to use its force only to redress imbalances brought about by wrongful acts of others. The rights in this system are definite, and it is possible for them to be exchanged in ways that benefit both parties and which create on average additional opportunities for gain by other citizens in society. As the objectives of the state are modest, they can be financed with relatively low taxes, which ideally should be flat rate, over all economically realizable sources of income.[25]

Let it be decided that these naturally morally arbitrary distributions do not stand, and the entire system of property rights becomes indefinite. There is no presumption that talents should remain where they begin or that individuals can keep what they acquire by first possession. The effort to neutralize the inequalities attributable to natural talent is, as an empirical matter, tied to the creation of a larger state, which in turn is more subject to capture and abuse by dictatorship and faction. The effort to avoid risk of unequal distribution of natural talents therefore increases the risk of political uncertainty. The risk-averse inhabitant behind the veil cannot simply opt for a rule that seeks to counteract the roll of the natural dice. Instead, he has to minimize joint risks – nature and politics – that are inversely related. To seek greater income equality both reduces the available stock of wealth, and runs some risk of itself becoming a source of political division and instability. There is, for example, an evident tension between freedom and equality whenever a high-tax regime has to decide whether to prevent the migration of its most productive citizens to tax havens elsewhere. The Soviet Union often justifies its restrictions on emigration on the ground that the potential *émigré* has not repaid the state for the cost of his education and advanced training.

This skepticism about coerced transfers does not mean that nothing can be done about the probelm of bad fortune. The partial escape from the problem requires us (and that includes lawyers and philosophers) to avoid the insistent trap of legalism, which says that short of legal coercion there is no form of obligation that citizens have toward each other. It is, however, possible to recognize that imperfect obligations of assistance do arise and that these should be supported by family, religious, and social institutions.[26] Initially, these imperfect obligations do count for something within the larger social framework, for universities, hospitals, and religious orders all depend upon voluntary contributions for their support. Over the years they have learned the techniques of fundraising that have permitted them to overcome the assurance and free-riding problems that they so often confront. The organizers of these groups learn to sponsor social events, to obtain in-kind contributions, to build up networks of friends and supporters, to adopt programs of matching grants, to obtain newspaper

[25] See, for discussion, R.A. Epstein, "Taxation in a Lockean World."

[26] I have discussed these at greater length in Richard A. Epstein, *Takings: Private Property and the Power of Eminent Domain* (Cambridge: Harvard University Press, 1985), pp. 314–324; and "The Uncertain Quest for Welfare Rights," *Brigham Young Law Review* (1985), p. 201, reprinted in G.C. Bryner & N.B. Reynolds, eds., *Constitutionalism and Rights* (Provo: Brigham Young University, 1987), p. 33.

coverage and public support, to identify the needy, and to weed out deadbeats. These mechanisms are far from perfect, but the relevant comparison is: are they better than the Welfare Department of the City of New York in housing the homeless?

There is, moreover, no reason to believe that these forms of endeavor would shrink if the level of mandatory social services were reduced further than it is today. Quite the opposite, the removal of public support should increase the level of private support that is forthcoming, as it would be quite unreasonable to believe that in a system of decentralized decision-making, everyone would suddenly decide to ignore the poor and needy once relieved from heavy tax burdens. To be sure, there would be some transitional problems, given the dependency that many individuals have on the welfare system as it is now constituted, but these could be eased by a clear set of transitional rules and other overdue legal changes needed to remove other restrictions on voluntary market transactions.

It may be said that an increased reliance upon voluntary charity is unacceptable because it is an affront to the dignity and self-respect of those who receive it. At best the argument only isolates one possible cost of a system of voluntary charitable behavior. But why should the cost be thought large? Far more than western European countries, the United States today relies heavily upon voluntary charity, not only for the support of the poor, but for educational, religious, and medical services as well. There is little evidence that people refuse to take and share in these benefits because they are not purchased for full value in market transaction, or that they think their dignity is offended. Instead, the appropriate response is often one of gratitude. In any event, making a wide variety of services available to individuals as of right does little, if anything, to remove the sting that people feel who have to ask for help. While people need not ask, or even beg, for help from other persons, they still know that they have received goods and services for which they have not paid. Do current recipients of social security have greater dignity because they receive benefits as of right that far exceed the amount of their contributions to the system? What about the recipients of farm subsidies? The relationship between any pattern of coerced transfer and self-respect is far from clear. In some instances it may have no effect at all, while in others it may increase the cynicism or resignation of those who have learned how to play the system. In general, there will be concerns about dignity no matter how goods and services are dispensed to those who need them. But the best way to control the problem is to reduce the need for dependence, which is hardly done by an expansion of programs of public support.

Do the arguments here lead to a "knock-out" conclusion that any coerced redistribution of income, talents, and wealth from its previous natural state always should be regarded as an impermissible function of the state? That type of categorical conclusion can be reached, I believe, with regard to the substantive rules of property, contract, and tort that regulate discrete, individual transactions. But as regards the larger social duty to "somehow compensate" through collective means, I doubt that the conclusion can be put in so categorical a form. At root the entire issue rests upon a variety of empirical estimates, for which hard data is necessary but difficult to acquire, and about which theoretical inquiry does not yield a pat answer. If one were to start on a blank slate, I should stand with that position, on the ground that I do not know how to design any set of social institutions that can both authorize redistribution by coercive means and then limit that redistribution to some sharply restrained and desirable level. The best approach to the problem that I can devise is a system of federal government, in which the redress of bad luck is done at the state level, and is thus constrained by the ability of individuals heavily taxed to leave. But federalism has its own complications, and in any event did not prove stable, at least in this country, against the demands for comprehensive national regulation of all kinds and descriptions. It is therefore a very open question whether complex institutional safeguards can work when the political system is entrusted with so massive a task as providing redress for bad fortune.[27] But that, too, is a contingent empirical judgment about the way in which the world works, and not how it necessarily has to work. The best that can be said is that the normative case for redress against the accidents of birth and the occurrence of bad luck is far weaker than many political philosophers, with their concern for the morally arbitrary, have understood. The clarity and certainty of the original distribution of rights under the natural law position is an underappreciated utilitarian virtue of the classical natural rights theory.

IV. CAPITALISM AND SOCIALISM

In closing it is useful briefly to state what should be clearer – the connection between the idea of redress for bad luck and the case for socialism. In general, the case for socialism cannot possibly be made on the ground that the collective ownership of goods leads to a better system of total aggregate production. The defects of central planning are too well known to be belabored at any length. Instead, the argument must come from the idea that natural differences in talents are a source of legitimate social concern that require collective and coercive methods of redress. Stated in this way, the case for the redress of bad luck is part of the larger

---

[27] See for discussion, Proceedings of the Conference on Takings of Property and the Constitution, 41 *Miami Law Review* 49, 79–82 (1986).

argument for a systematic drive for income equality. If the remarks I have made about bad luck are correct, then this pillar of socialism falls as well. The effort to redistribute some stock of wealth to aid those in need by coercive means will not do the job. It will only destroy the stock of wealth with which a society begins. The best one could argue for is a case of progressive taxation. That system, in practice, could never generate pure income equality; nor could it provide relief for persons without income to be taxed in the first instance. Even if pressed into service for the more modest task of reducing inequalities of wealth, say, in a manner consistent with Rawls's difference principle, the progressive system also creates both insistent administrative problems (as with income-splitting between individuals or trusts) and unfortunate incentive effects with the increasing marginal rates of taxation. As a political matter, we have retreated sharply from the progressive ideal, as in the United States the 90 percent marginal tax bracket of the 1950s has given way to the top 38 percent marginal tax bracket of 1987 and the 28 percent bracket of today. (English rates have also dropped from a top bracket in the high 90 percent range to about 60 percent today, with still further reductions planned.)

The usual discussions of luck begin from the premise that the end justifies the means: the supposed need to redress the adverse consequences of bad luck and bad fortune are so powerful that they compel the state to undertake extensive programs to counteract its effect. In this paper, my concern has been more with means than with ends. In general, government is relatively good at enforcing common law property rights, and overcoming holdout problems that block the provision of public goods. These surely should not be altered in the effort to reduce the consequences of bad luck. On the other hand, government has never had much success in using coercion as an antidote for luck, as entitlement program after entitlement program – medicare, Social Security, food stamps, welfare – has always shown a marked capacity to outgrow the laudable intentions of its supporters. These failures are often attributed to some given and remediable flaw within the system itself. It may be the third-party payment system for medicare, the taxing provisions of Social Security, or the eligibility requirements of foodstamps. The effort to assign these particular causes overlooks the systematic problems with administration and incentives that manifest themselves in one way or the other with any extensive program of government redistribution. The effort to neutralize the adverse consequences of luck by coercive means is an enormous undertaking that government is ill-equipped to handle. The discussion on redress for luck often recalls the discussions on wage and price regulations of a generation ago. Those in favor of the system of regulation were confident that a history of misadventure could be corrected if better people were hired to design and operate the system. They were wrong, in that the defects of wage and price controls were endemic to the basic enterprise. The same brand of cautious optimism is often heard by those who think that they can restructure a system of social entitlements so as to avoid past failures. My sense is that the optimists again will be proved wrong. In order to compensate for the ill effects of bad luck, it is necessary to resort to a system of centralized planning and control whose practical and administrative difficulties are sometimes obvious – and always tenacious.

Law, University of Chicago

CAPITALIST PERSONS*

BY ANDREW LEVINE

In what follows, "persons" are ideal-typical concepts of human beings, deployed expressly or supposed implicitly in particular theoretical contexts. Thus, the person of Kantian moral philosophy is a pure bearer of moral predicates, bereft of all properties that empirically distinguish human beings from one another: properties that, in Kant's view, are irrelevant to moral deliberation. No man or woman, actual or possible, could be so starkly featureless. But Kant's aim was not to describe human beings in actual or possible deliberations, but moral agency as such. Similarly, *homo oeconomicus*, economic man, is not a composite man or woman, but also a person, a theoretical construct introduced for explanatory purposes in models of economic behavior. My aim is to investigate capitalist persons: ideal-typical concepts of human beings deployed in justifying theories of capitalist property relations.

I shall identify two capitalist persons, and impugn one of them. To situate my position historically, I call the impugned person Lockean, and the other Kantian. It is tempting to designate the Lockean person *"the* capitalist person." However, this characterization would be misleading. Justifying theories of capitalism can employ either concept, and both can serve in accounts of socialist economies. Nevertheless, the Lockean person *is* tendentially procapitalist while the Kantian person is not.

What follows is therefore relevant to the broader capitalism/socialism debate. To fault the Lockean person is not quite to fault capitalism itself. But a case against the Lockean person, if successful, would undermine an important strain of procapitalist argument. More importantly, the considerations I will adduce suggest a way of thinking about distributive justice and, ultimately, an ideal of equality that socialism, but not capitalism, can in principle accommodate.

I

By the end of the eighteenth century, it had become evident that European social, political, and economic life was in the midst of profound

* I am grateful to Sharon Lloyd, Miles Morgan, and Erik Olin Wright for comments on an earlier draft.

transformations. The dissolution of feudal solidarities, the extension of market relations, and the centralization of political authority in nation-states, along with rapid technological innovation and an enormous increase in productivity, were widely acknowledged to comprise a new order – indeed, a new form of civilization. All major social theorists of the nineteenth century took these transformations as chief among their *explananda*, and their explanations were fundamental for the social, political, and economic theories they went on to construct. In Marx's view, the economic structure of the new order was crucial. Thus, capitalism was Marx's principal *explanandum*. Other theorists construed their *explananda* differently. But however the emerging order was conceived, it was universally believed to have profound implications for human life generally, for "forms of consciousness" and therefore for human beings' sense of what they and their fellow human beings are. Implicitly, all major social theories, not only Marx's, converged in holding that the social, political, and economic transformations they sought to account for had given rise to a new person.

To begin at a level of abstraction sufficient for capturing the consensus view, it can be held – uncontroversially, I expect – that the person that emerged with the new order was, if nothing else, an *individual*: an independent center of consciousness and affect, related to other individuals "externally" – just as atoms, the indivisible units of matter in classical atomist theory, relate externally to one another.[1] Needless to say, living human beings were always understood to have distinct minds and bodies. But the individual I have in mind is a kind of person, not a human being. It is an ideal-type concept in a world view consonant with the new, emerging order. It is therefore reasonable, though perhaps false, to hold that the individual appeared with this new order, and to regard the Age of Individuals as a transitory episode of human history.

It might be supposed that this view is distinctively Marxian. But this impression is misleading. Non- or anti-Marxists who have acknowledged the historical particularity of "individualism" include Alexis de Tocqueville and Henry Sumner Maine, Max Weber, Georg Simmel, and Emile Durkheim. Among writers influenced by Marx, but hardly Marxist (in the usual understanding of the term), are Karl Polanyi and Michel Foucault, Harold Laski and C.B. Macpherson. In what follows, however, I encourage the common misconception by adopting a generally Marxian understanding

---

[1] A *non*individualist view, then, would relate persons to one another "internally," as might seem natural (and even obvious) to human beings whose lives are dominated by feudal or other traditional solidarities, and perhaps to communist men and women too, moved by a "general will" in conditions of (relative) abundance. See my *The End of the State* (London: Verso, 1987).

of the emergence and career of the individual. I do so because I believe that Marx's is the most insightful of the several extant accounts of individualism, and because Marx's theory of history, historical materialism, provides the best point of entry into my subject.

II

Historical materialism is a macro-theory of history, an account of the structure and direction of historical change. According to that theory, capitalism is distinguished from other economic structures or "modes of production" by the forms of ownership it prohibits and permits. In contrast to precapitalist class societies, ownership of (other) human beings is disallowed. But, in contrast to socialism (which also disallows ownership of others), capitalism permits private ownership of nonhuman productive assets.[2]

Under capitalism, individuals command their distributive shares largely in consequence of market transactions and other transfers. But for markets to operate, individuals must have an *initial endowment* with which to compete. Theories that assign initial endowments by asserting the existence of presocial entitlements suppose the Lockean person. The Lockean person holds morally fundamental rights to particular assets – claims on resources that others, individually or collectively, cannot rightfully infringe. The alternative, Kantian view construes initial endowments not as matters of presocial right, but as consequences of (hypothetical or actual) social arrangements. One or another of these concepts is at work in all important justifying theories of capitalism.

To own a resource is to have a claim on the income it generates, and also to be able to control and dispose of it as one pleases. Owners' rights are nearly always limited. Typically, the applicable limits are codified in laws. But they may also be recognized in custom, particularly in precapitalist societies with underdeveloped legal codes. In late European

---

[2] Historical capitalisms commonly rely on markets in labor power, means of subsistence, and capital, and also on large-scale factory systems of production. In addition, historical capitalisms are class societies, with a bourgeoisie and a proletariat. Marx did not always use the term "capitalism" in the same way, but for the most part he did regard some (or all) of these features of historical capitalisms as part of capitalism's definition. The definition proposed above is therefore weaker than Marx's definition, though it is suggested by and consonant with historical materialist claims. Peasant societies without relations of feudal bondage would count as capitalist by this definition, so long as peasants own their means of production. Thus, in contrast to standard Marxian usage, the "simple commodity production" sketched in the first volume of *Capital* or Adam Smith's "early and rude state of society" – classless societies of (relatively) independent producers who own their own means of production – would be capitalist societies. On definitions of "capitalism" and "socialism," see my *Arguing for Socialism: Theoretical Considerations* (Boston and London: Routledge & Kegan Paul, 1984; 2nd edition, Verso: London, 1988), pp. 5–11.

feudalism, ownership of persons, though real and economically significant, was constrained by both law and custom. Lords had claims on some, but not all, of the wealth generated by those who owed them fealty, and some, but not complete, control over their vassals' careers as producers. In this sense, lords owned their vassals, though not nearly to the degree that masters owned slaves in systems of chattel slavery. Fundamental to Marx's analysis of the capitalist mode of production – and also to non- and anti-Marxian accounts of the same phenomena – is the recognition that capitalists do not own their workers, but rather compensate them for the labor (or, as Marx would insist, the labor power) they deploy. What capitalists own is nonhuman means of production.

But even when what is owned are things, not persons, absolute control is the limiting case, seldom, if ever, realized completely.[3] However, there is one form of ownership in capitalist societies that some writers do consider absolute: self-ownership.[4] For proponents of this view, persons stand in proprietary relations to themselves in just the way that masters, in systems of chattel slavery, own slaves.[5]

The self-owning individual is a Lockean person,[6] and all Lockean

---

[3] An absolute right to the income generated by deployment of productive assets is also a limiting case. Even libertarian proponents of "minimal states", states that do not redistribute (capitalist) market allocations, acknowledge the right of states to tax individuals to obtain the revenues they require to carry out their (legitimate) operations.

[4] The term, though commonplace, is misleading. Construed literally, "self-ownership" suggests that there is something, the self, that one owns. But "the thesis of self-ownership does not say that all that is owned is a self, where 'self' is used to denote some particularly intimate, or essential, part of the person. . . . The term 'self' in the name of the thesis of self-ownership has a purely reflexive significance. It signifies that what owns and what is owned are one and the same, namely, the whole person . . . ." G.A. Cohen, "Self-Ownership, World-Ownership, and Equality: Part I," Frank S. Lucash, ed., *Justice and Equality Here and Now* (Ithaca: Cornell University Press, 1986), p. 110.

[5] *Cf.* Cohen, "Self-Ownership," p. 109: " . . . each person is the morally rightful owner of himself. He possesses over himself, as a matter of moral right, all those rights that a slaveholder has over a complete chattel slave as a matter of legal right, and he is entitled, morally speaking, to dispose over himself in the way such a slaveholder is entitled, legally speaking, to dispose over his slave. Such a slaveholder may not direct his slave to harm other people, but he is not legally obliged to place him at their disposal to the slightest degree: he owes none of his slave's service to anyone else. So, analogously, if I am the moral owner of myself, and therefore of this right arm, then, while others are entitled to prevent it from hitting people, no one is entitled, without my consent, to press it into their own or anybody else's service, even when my failure to lend it voluntarily to others would be morally wrong."

[6] I am grateful to Joshua Cohen for pointing out that, despite what is widely supposed, particularly after C.B. Macpherson's influential study of Locke in *The Political Theory of Possessive Individualism* (Oxford: Oxford University Press, 1962), Locke himself was not, strictly, a self-ownership theorist. In Locke's view, God is the source of all entitlements, including our rights to our own bodies and powers. Thus, for Locke, insofar as we own ourselves, we do so contingently. However, Nozickean libertarians and other neo-Lockean political theorists wisely eschew divine foundations for rights ascriptions. Lockeans today take self-ownership as fundamental, and go on to use the idea as a point of departure for the elaboration of other, putatively inviolable rights.

persons deployed in historically important justifying theories of capitalism own themselves. To fault self-ownership is therefore tantamount to faulting the Lockean person. To this end, I will show that self-ownership is not, on balance, a tenable idea. Only a few years ago, this appraisal would have gone without saying everywhere but in libertarian circles. Nowadays, it needs to be demonstrated: not least because there is a case to be made for a contrary view from just that quarter where one might have least expected support. It is now clear that many of the objections that were once automatic on the left, especially the Marxian left, cannot hold. G.A. Cohen has shown that self-ownership need not have the inegalitarian implications Nozick and others suppose.[7] And it is also plain that self-ownership is at least *compatible* with socialism. What is essential to socialism in the historical materialist scheme is the deprivatization of ownership of external assets. Self-ownership is not in question. Indeed, in *The Critique of the Gotha Program*, Marx and Engels insisted that, in the early stages of socialism, socialists should support the idea that individuals have claims to the wealth they generate – an idea self-ownership would explain, as Locke had long before shown.

III

In reflecting philosophically on moral, social, and political questions, intuitive judgments are indispensable, though fallible and frequently in need of clarification or correction. In this instance, philosophical vigilance is particularly crucial inasmuch as our raw intuitions about self-ownership are part of what those who derogate the idea purport to explain. In the view once standard among Marxists, self-ownership is an irredeemably "bourgeois idea" that both "reflects" the underlying capitalist foundations of bourgeois society, and supports capitalist institutions against socialism

---

[7] *Cf.* G.A. Cohen, "Self-Ownership," and "Self-Ownership, World-Ownership and Equality: Part II," *Social Philosophy and Policy*, vol. 3, no. 2 (Spring 1986), pp. 77–96, and "Why Marxists Care More About Nozick than Liberals Do," unpublished manuscript. Cohen defends self-ownership from its detractors on the left by arguing that the idea does not imply the inequality of condition that Nozick maintains. He argues too that self-ownership in Nozick's sense is assumed in standard Marxian accounts of capitalist exploitation (where workers are held to have entitlements to the surplus value capitalists extract) and in Marx's account of communism (where the free development of each person's powers, understood as the full deployment of those assets self-owners own, is finally realized). In short, if Cohen is right, self-ownership is compatible with (some) Marxian egalitarian aspirations, and is a even a tenet (some) received Marxian views share with procapitalist libertarian political philosophy. This claim is, to say the least, ironic. Self-ownership has been widely derogated, not only by Marxists, as a "bourgeois" notion *par excellence*. In the end, Cohen claims to agree with this assessment, though for reasons that at present remain obscure. His contention, which serves as my own point of departure, is that traditional dismissals of self-ownership are overly facile, and that if the idea is finally rejected, it will have to be for reasons different from those that Marxists and others on the left have so far contrived.

(or, in an earlier period, against feudalism). Then, since "consciousness arises out of life," self-ownership should seem self-evident in bourgeois societies. But this fact would have no bearing on the rational assessment of the idea. That task requires "criticism" – to emancipate the critic or "class conscious" proletarian from the sway of tendentious and defective "ruling ideas." Then the world can finally be seen as it is, without ideological distortion. Only at that point will the genuine force of the self-ownership thesis become apparent.

However this may be, our intuitions about self-ownership, even without a *prise de conscience*, are not, in fact, of one piece; and neither are they, on balance, as supportive of the idea as proponents of the standard Marxian view might expect. There is intuitive support for self-ownership or, more precisely, for some of its implications. But there are also intuitions, of greater weight, that count against the idea. It will be useful to consider cases that do appear to support self-ownership, the better to clarify what our intuitions are and what their force is.

****

Self-ownership supports a powerful and deeply entrenched intuition about bodily integrity: the idea that our bodies ought to be protected from intrusive (nonconsensual) invasion. Suppose, for example, that the transplantation of one of a healthy individual's kidneys into someone about to die from kidney malfunction is deemed morally right after sound casuistical deliberation in the framework of an accepted moral theory. Perhaps there is some universalizable maxim that enjoins the transplantation of the healthy individual's kidney, or perhaps the transplantation will maximize overall utility. Even so, I would venture that no one would hold that the healthy individual can be rightfully compelled to give up one of his kidneys. His kidneys are his own; and while he may be liable to (moral) criticism for keeping them to himself, it seems blatantly wrong to allow them to be taken from him by force.[8]

I do not think that this intuition is itself ideological in any damaging

---

[8] However, the forced removal of bodily parts is not always offensive to considered intuitions. Forced haircuts, circumcisions, castrations and sterilizations, and also mandatory inoculations, drug and alcohol testing, and testing for infectious diseases, have defenders. It may be that hair and blood and even prepuces and ovaries somehow fall into a different category from kidneys and other organs. But I don't think so. I would suggest instead that in cases where bodily invasions seem warranted, the inviolability of the body is still a pertinent – though overridden – consideration, swamped perhaps by the requirements of citizenship or by a determination to prevent harm to others or for paternalistic reasons. The appropriateness of these countervailing claims is debatable. But their appeal (to some of us) shows that our intuitions about bodily inviolability, though powerful and general, are not so overwhelming that they carry for everyone in all cases.

sense. Some feminists have maintained that bodily violations – ranging from sexual conquest to outright mutilation – are in fact the norm in men's relations with women. They might then conclude that bodily integrity is a "false universal" masking a deeper oppression, just as Marx thought political emancipation under the banner "liberty, equality, fraternity" masked the division of civil society into a bourgeoisie and proletariat. Perhaps so. Nevertheless, our intuitions about bodily inviolability remain. For even if some (or all) women have been fair game for bodily violations throughout most (or all) of human history, it is, as feminists themselves would insist, a consequence of a failure within patriarchal societies to acknowledge the full humanity of women, and also a means for perpetuating the domination of women. The appeal of bodily inviolability holds – for all human beings. It is just that, in practice, the principle is invested with a scope that represents and reinforces patriarchal attitudes.

In view of the many forms of domination and subordination to which humankind has subjected itself throughout its past, it is remarkable how much evidence there is of respect for the inviolability of human bodies. No doubt, the technological impossibility – until quite recently – of putting bodily parts to use outside the bodies of their (original) "owners" accounts, in part, for the respect accorded the integrity of the bodies of otherwise dominated people. But whatever explains the longstanding appeal of the intuition, it is plain that it is deeply entrenched and hardly peculiar to capitalist or postcapitalist societies.

The idea that people are proprietors of their own bodies and powers, that they own themselves, is therefore a good candidate for designation as a universal, moral truth. But its candidacy will succeed only if self-ownership is the best explanation for the intuitions it supports. Other explanations are at hand. One might argue, for example, that overall well-being is enhanced by adopting a rule never to infringe individuals' sovereignty over their own bodies. I would venture that a rule-utilitarian account of this sort, properly elaborated, is probably superior to appeals to self-ownership. But I will not endorse utilitarian explanations either. I will instead propose a generally Kantian grounding for our shared belief in our sovereignty over ourselves. First, though, it will be helpful to introduce yet another intuition that self-ownership appears to explain. This intuition may be less compelling than our sense of our bodies' inviolability. But it is more evidently amenable to the rival justification I will defend.

I have in mind the idea that motivates the distributive principle "to each according to effort," a principle most people would find appropriate in at least some circumstances. When differences in productivity between producers depend upon different technologies or cultural circumstances or societal infrastructures, intuitions will vary over the extent to which efforts expended (however understood) generate claims on wealth produced. Insofar as we stand on the shoulders of others, we toil from different starting points – and this difference is relevant for assessing the outcomes that result. Rival views of justice may construe these disparities differently, but all must take them into account. However, we can abstract away these sources of discordant intuitions by imagining two equally skilled individuals, working in the same circumstances and with the same technologies, but with different intensities or for different periods of time in consequence of different (autonomously formed) preferences for income and leisure. Thus, if Jones works four hours per day while Smith works eight, everything else being equal, most of us will feel that Smith ought to receive more income (indeed, twice as much) as Jones. Actual situations seldom approximate this case. We labor typically with external *and* internal resources that derive, in part, from the efforts of others and from the "free gifts" of nature. But where differences in levels of productivity depend only on (freely undertaken) expenditures of effort, the principle "to each according to effort" does seem unexceptionable.

This conclusion is widely shared. It is compatible with the views of libertarians. It accords with many actual social practices and remunerative schemes. And, as already noted, it is endorsed in *The Critique of the Gotha Program* where the distributive principle deemed appropriate for socialism (in its early stages) enjoins that income be proportional to productive contribution (measured in abstract – homogenous – labor time).

Self-ownership supports this view. Insofar as we own ourselves and labor with our powers alone, what we produce is ours – as an extension of ourselves. Then when everything but what we freely choose to do with the labor we control is equal (or abstracted away), as in the case just imagined, the labor we deploy – as an exercise of our powers – generates differential claims to distributive shares in proportion to the effort we expend.

As in the former case, I concede the appeal of the intuition upon which this conclusion rests. But I would again caution against concluding in favor of self-ownership. In both cases, self-ownership justifies what we intuitively believe. But, in both cases, better justifications are available.

Suppose, for instance, that labor is regarded as a *collective asset* in the sense that the wealth it generates does not attach, prior to social arrangements, to the particular individuals who contribute it. Then we could still accomodate our view that, other things being equal, differential expenditures of effort be rewarded differentially. We might agree to do so in order to boost output by providing incentives for individuals to work longer or more intensively, or to provide means for individuals to satisfy tastes for goods or services that exceed ordinary allotments. Or we might choose to do so because we recognize the value of holding individuals responsible for the (free) choices they make, and we deem the provision of material rewards an appropriate way to do so. The resulting distribution might be the same as in self-ownership accounts. But the underlying rationale would be opposed. On the self-ownership view, expenditures of effort generate entitlements, morally prior to social arrangements. On the alternative view, there are no fundamental entitlements for social arrangements to accomodate. Claims on assets are consequences of (hypothetical or actual) agreements: judgments grounded (presumably) in general facts about human nature, interests, and circumstances.

* * * * * * * *

The collective asset view is effectively endorsed in some influential strains of mainstream liberal theory. Thus, Rawls's account of justice regards distribution as a cooperative – i.e., social – solution to a co-ordination problem, not as an accomodation to presocial rights.[9] In "the circumstances of justice," where cooperation is both necessary and possible, and where it is urgent that cooperation be organized in ways acknowledged to be fair, agreement on principles for assigning distributive shares is in each individual's interest. In Rawls's account, the principles individuals would select are those that implement the idea of pure procedural justice. Rawls's aim is to generalize this idea and render it applicable for regulating "the basic structure" of society. Where what is to be distributed is fixed, fair distributive procedures would result in equal divisions. Thus, in the well-known solution for dividing a pie (where the individual who cuts is the last to choose), the cutter (in order to maximize her share) must divide the pie into equal pieces. Strict equality is the "maximin" solution; and a maximin strategy is rational for any agent whose position in the eventual distribution is assigned by those with whom she is in competition. But, for income and wealth – and perhaps also for other primary goods – the supply is not fixed. Then, still acting on the assumption that one's position will be assigned by those with whom one is in competition, individuals will opt again for distributions that maximize minimal payoffs or, as Rawls concludes, that enhance the distributive shares of representative members of the least well-off group. Thus, just distributions may not be strictly egalitarian. Efficiency considerations can

---

[9] Ronald Dworkin's views on justice also share this feature, though in developing a view of equality that is "ambition-sensitive" by definition – rather than in consequence of an "agreement" to reward (freely undertaken) expenditures of effort differentially and, more generally, to respect the consequences of (free) choice – Dworkin comes perilously close to a Lockean view of desert.

swamp the presumption for strict equality.[10]

In the original position, under a veil of ignorance, we can only advert to general facts about human nature and the human condition to guide us in selecting principles of justice. Under the veil, we know that material inequalities can help augment overall productivity by providing incentives for producers to utilize the assets they control efficiently. Insofar as we are each bent on maximizing our own share of primary goods, as Rawls stipulates, and inasmuch as this concern, under the informational constraints of the original position, enjoins adoption of a maximin strategy, inegalitarian incentive structures will be adopted if and only if they maximize minimal outcomes. Thus, Rawlsian justice can accommodate differential rewards for effort, and also for the use of talents and skills and even for the deployment of (external) capital assets – so long as the inequalities that result work to the advantage of representative members of the least well-off group. Given the facts of the matter, the (Kantian) persons supposed in Rawls's theory of justice will therefore accept inequalities of condition. But unlike Lockean persons, the persons Rawls imagines have no fundamental entitlements to their (unequal) distributive shares, no presocial proprietary rights to which social arrangements must conform. If they can be said to have "entitlements" at all, it is in virtue of a system of rules they have themselves contrived.

In Rawls's account, there is, as noted, a presumption for strict equality, even in the distribution of income and wealth. This presumption is reason enough, I think, to undertake measures aimed at *educating* people away from the material incentives that justify unequal outcomes – provided the requirements of justice (including equal respect for alternative conceptions of the good) are not infringed.[11] Other things being equal, societal benefits

[10] However, in Rawls's view, basic rights and liberties must be distributed equally (and to the greatest extent possible), regardless of efficiency considerations. For Rawls, the principles of justice are lexically ordered. It is only after basic rights and liberties are equally distributed that "the difference principle," which allows inequalities in the distribution of other primary goods, pertains.

[11] It is one thing to use state power to enforce particular conceptions of the good, and something else again to move towards realization of an ideal order through the transformative effects of institutional arrangements. Against the likely rejoinder that political education *per se* inevitably infringes respect for individuals' conceptions of the good, I would therefore assert – following Mill and a host of other political philosophers, both liberal and nonliberal, and also following Rawls himself – that political institutions *necessarily* educate, and that a central task of political philosophy is to articulate a conception of the citizen to educate *towards*. Thus, *On Liberty* is not only a "constitutional" tract, defending principled limitations on societal and state interferences with individuals' lives and behaviors. It is also an investigation of the institutional arrangements best suited for forming *liberal* citizens: individuals disposed to tolerance and the advancement of their own and each others' autonomy. Similarly, for proponents of Rawlsian justice, a paramount task is to contrive a strategy for making individuals more just – that is, more disposed to implement the egalitarian vision Rawlsian justice expresses.

ought to be distributed equally. That doing so might diminish overall productivity, to the detriment even of the least well-off, is a sad consequence of human psychology as we now confront it. But we need not suppose that susceptibility to material incentives is an eternal human foible. We ought, instead, to work to transform our natures, the better to realize the egalitarian vision Rawls's theory of justice articulates.

I would not dare speculate on the fate of the principle "to each according to effort," were we successfully weaned away from material incentives. My point is just that, in a Rawlsian framework, differing expectations follow from disagreements about the likely consequences of effort pooling, not from disagreements about justice itself. Distribution according to effort, whenever it actually is appropriate, can be as well accommodated by Rawlsians as by proponents of self-ownership.

IV

What Lockeans aim to defend by means of self-ownership is human dignity, an ideal they share with Rawlsians and perhaps with utilitarians too. Self-ownership promotes this end by investing individuals with rights that protect against invasive bodily intrusions, but also, more importantly, with rights that implement a certain conception of human freedom. In the Lockean scheme, freedom – understood, roughly as "the absence of externall Impediments" (Hobbes) – is indispensable for human dignity.

Since Lockeans like Nozick are not anarchists, they do not advocate unrestricted freedom. A social order that imposed no external impediments would devolve into a "war of all against all" – to the detriment of our interests as free beings. Thus, individuals cannot be left free to violate the rights of others. Constraints to this end, so far from offending human dignity, are in fact the condition for its realization. But beyond those expressly minimal restrictions necessary for political association, human dignity requires that individuals be unimpeded in pursuit of their ends.

This exigency shapes the Lockean strategy for defending human dignity, just as it captures the Lockean sense of what human dignity is. It is as advocates of principled limitations on the use of public coercive force – in a word, as liberals – that Lockeans set about their central task. The rights that protect individuals' lives and behaviors from state interference insure respect for what we are.

* * * * * * * * *

Self-ownership confers rights against involuntary bodily intrusions, and against coerced deployments of individuals' bodies and powers. It also confers rights to whatever the free exercise of our bodies and powers produce. But, for Locke and his followers, property rights extend beyond self-ownership. Lockean persons also have proprietary claims on parts of the external world. The Lockean defense of human dignity encompasses all of these rights. The idea, in short, is that we be free to do as we please with what we own (provided we do not violate the rights of others or otherwise undermine the basis of political association), and that we be free to appropriate the wealth our assets generate.

However, these claims are separable and of unequal merit. Respect for persons evidently does require protection against involuntary bodily intrusions. It probably also requires that individuals be accorded liberties in as broad an area as is compatible with political association. But it does not then follow, nor is it independently self-evident, that respect for persons requires that we own what our assets produce. Neo-Lockeans confound these claims when they maintain that we own ourselves and then extend self-ownership to parts of the external world. We have seen how self-ownership is, at best, unnecessary for defending the defensible positions it ostensibly explains. We now see that the idea is also misleading. It confounds the defense of freedom with the idea that we are entitled, as a matter of infrangible right, to what we produce with what we own.

This observation suggests another flaw in the Lockean strategy for defending human dignity: its core idea of freedom is vulnerable. But this is not the place to rehearse familiar arguments to the effect that there is more to freedom than unconstrained property rights in the assets we own, nor to insist that freedom can be restricted by institutional arrangements that engender resource inequalities, as well as by deliberate state interventions.[12] There is no need to press Lockeans on their view of freedom because the Lockean person is vulnerable enough, particularly in contrast to its Kantian rival. It is appropriate, then, to turn directly to the Kantian person, specifically to its Rawlsian variant. Again, human dignity provides a perspicuous focus.

V

Even more directly than Locke, Kant made respect for humanity the foundation of the moral order. Treating humanity "whether in oneself or in others only as an end and never as a means only" is, Kant maintains, a categorical imperative, binding on all rational agents.[13] This aspect of

---

[12] See my *Arguing for Socialism: Theoretical Considerations*, Chapter 2.

[13] Kant, *The Foundations of the Metaphysics of Morals*, Part 2. The more familiar version of the categorical imperative would have us "Act only according to that maxim by which you can at the same time will that it should become a universal law." However, Kant insists that all formulations of the categorical imperative, including the formulation alluded to above ("Act so

Kantian moral philosophy motivates Rawls's expressly Kantian reflections on human dignity[14] and the view of the person it supposes.

The Kantian person, like all persons, is an artifact of a theory: in this case, a theory of moral deliberation – an account, from the standpoint of the agent, of what one ought to do when moral considerations obtain. Kant would have agents generalize their maxims, the principles that determine the actions under consideration. A properly generalizable maxim is, Kant holds, an objective "law of freedom." But Kant was not the first to focus on *generality* as essential for "the moral point of view." Generality has been invoked at least since the first enunciation of the Golden Rule. When we are told to do unto others as we would have others do unto us, we are commanded to deliberate by abstracting out everything that distinguishes ourselves from others and to take only what we and others have in common into account. To be sure, Golden Rule deliberations are not quite Kantian deliberations. In the former, we ask with respect to some action we propose to undertake whether we could will that it be done to us. In the latter, we ask whether we could will that everyone do it. But, in both cases, particularities that distinguish ourselves from others are morally irrelevant. What is relevant is what is general.

This idea is key to understanding why Kantian persons do not own themselves. The reason, in short, is that self-ownership valorizes aspects of selfhood that are irrelevant from the moral point of view, the vantage-point from which human dignity stands revealed. The connection between generality and dignity is a central theme of Kantian moral philosophy. This is not the place to trace the connections Kantians draw, but only to underscore their main conclusion: that the capacity for moral agency – pure moral personality, bereft of particularities – is the source of human dignity. Dignity cannot reside, therefore, in what we are empirically, for our "empirical selves" are constituted by morally irrelevant particularities. However, the person who owns himself is a bundle of particularities. Thus, from a Kantian vantage-point, this person cannot play the role Lockeans intend. It cannot serve in a defense of human dignity. For if Kantians are right, dignity resides precisely in what self-ownership fails to capture: the autonomy of the (rational) will. This conclusion, in turn, has important implications for the theory of justice, and therefore indirectly for the choice between capitalism and socialism.

---

that you treat humanity, whether in your own person or in that of another, always as an end and never as a means only") are strictly equivalent.

[14] *Cf.* Rawls, *A Theory of Justice*, passim and esp. pp. 251–257; and "Kantian Constructivism in Moral Theory," *The Journal of Philosophy*, vol. 77 (Sept. 1980).

Rawls's official view is that justice is compatible with either capitalism or socialism – that is, with private or public ownership of external assets.[15] Perhaps it is.[16] But it is one thing for justice to allow social practices that permit individuals to own alienable resources, and something else again to claim that the owners of these resources have presocial entitlements to them and to the wealth they generate. If justice actually is compatible with capitalist property relations, it is in consequence of considered judgments about allocation procedures, based on a view of human society, nature, and circumstance. The considerations that bear on the choice of forms of property are speculative and empirical, not normative. If capitalism or socialism can both be just, it is because, in a certain range of conditions, these economic systems accord with the principles of justice, not because individuals have entitlements one or another system somehow accomodates.

For the same reason, talents and skills and other *inalienable* assets also fail to generate claims on what they produce prior to social arrangements, even if what we know of human psychology makes it reasonable, now and for the foreseeable future, to reward their exercise differentially. Again, the putatively intractable problem is that without differential compensations, talents might not be developed or deployed. This seems to be what led even Marx to the conclusion that distributions under socialism (in its early stages) should accord with productive contributions – which will in general be greater in proportion to the skill of the labor expended. As socialism is transformed into communism, scarcity will diminish – diminishing, in turn, the importance of distributive considerations – and acquisitive dispositions will eventually disappear. Only then, Marx thought, will it become possible for societal benefits to be generated according to ability and distributed according to need.

It may be that Cohen is right in holding that traditional Marxian views of capitalist exploitation unwittingly suppose self-ownership. It is now clear, in any case, that Marx's express account of exploitation, though probably not the core idea his formulations express, is defective.[17] Then Cohen's exposure of self-ownership assumptions is only an additional mark against the received view. This conclusion would not change the fact that Marx was not, except unwittingly and superficially, a self-ownership theorist. The person supposed in Marxian accounts of distribution under capitalism and socialism is Kantian, not Lockean. For Marx, as for Rawls, no one owns anything as a matter of unassailable right. Productive assets, in the final analysis, are collective assets.

[15] *Cf.* Rawls, *A Theory of Justice*, pp. 265–73.

[16] For a contrary view of the implications of Rawlsian justice, see my *Arguing for Socialism: Theoretical Considerations*, Chapter 2.

[17] See, among others, John Roemer, *A General Theory of Exploitation and Class* (Cambridge: Harvard University Press, 1982), *passim* and esp. pp. 8–23.

For Kantians, what distinguishes individuals from one another empirically has no moral relevance and therefore no bearing on distributive justice. But it is precisely these features that *are* relevant for eliciting different levels of productive contribution. If human nature or, more precisely, human psychology in the range of conditions that now exist or can now be imagined, joined with an interest in the cultivation of talents and the deployment of skills, makes it necessary to reward skilled more than un-skilled labor – or, more generally, to remunerate productive contributions differentially – this too is only a sad consequence of the conditions that pertain. I have already suggested that (Rawlsian) justice supports effort pooling, even if it allows and, in likely circumstances, encourages returns proportional to effort. It is clearer still that justice supports talent pooling and pooling the returns generated by alienable assets. In these cases, only efficiency considerations warrant deviations from strict equality. Effort pooling confronts the same problem, but may also conflict with a wish to hold individuals responsible for the choices they make. Then so long as responsibility is represented in distributional shares – roughly, so long as the circumstances of justice pertain – effort pooling may be impossible to implement. Indeed, given pertinent general facts, talent pooling and even (external) asset pooling may be only regulative ideals. The egalitarian vision Rawlsian justice articulates may remain forever elusive.[18] But it neverthe-less remains an outcome towards which justice tends.

VI

Lockean justice is not egalitarian in this sense. It does not tend towards equality of condition. For Locke and his followers, a just distribution is any outcome that results from acquisitions and transfers that violate no one's rights, no matter how inegalitarian that distribution may be. The rights that might be violated, in the Lockean view, in schemes for implementing particular distributional "patterns" – are, of course, property rights. Thus, the Lockean person, the bearer of morally primitive property rights, is indispensable for Lockean justice. To fault the Lockean person is to fault Lockean justice itself: presumably to the advantage of its Rawlsian rival.[19]

---

[18] I do not think we need accede to this pessimistic conclusion, though I cannot claim to be able to defend an optimistic prognostication "within the realm of reason alone." For some elements of an argument supporting the historical feasibility of the egalitarianism implicit in Kantian moral theory, see my *The End of the State*.

[19] Strictly speaking, a successful assault on Lockean justice is not by itself a reason to support Rawls's theory because there are other plausible alternatives. There is, for example, utilitarian justice: roughly, the view that a distribution is just if and only if it has the consequence of maximizing aggregate or average utility (in comparison with alternative possible distributions). But I have already said enough in support of Rawlsian justice or, at least, its Kantian defense of human dignity to justify regarding it as *the* serious competitor to

We have already seen how self-ownership, the essential feature of the Lockean conception, is, at best, a dubious explanation for some appealing intuitions, and also how it is a misleading idea that joins together distinct claims of unequal merit. To conclude, I shall sketch a defense of self-ownership still available to a Lockean. No other sort of defense is, I think, even remotely plausible. I will suggest, however, that the position that emerges casts the very idea of the Lockean person – and therefore Lockean justice itself – into an even deeper quandary.

Locke took self-ownership as a premise in an argument supporting a right to (unlimited) private appropriation of external resources. However, enough has already been said to undermine, if not self-ownership itself, then its status as an uncontested premise. Self-ownership cannot be defended directly by appeal to considered intuitions. And Locke's own justification, essentially an appeal to God, plainly will not do. Self-ownership therefore needs an argument if the Lockean project is to remain viable. Indeed, it needs an argument consonant with and, if possible, drawing on Lockean ideas. The celebrated Lockean proviso can serve as a basis for such an argument.

Locke thought appropriation just only if it is limited by the proviso that there be "enough and as good left in common for others."[20] Construed literally, this proviso can never be satisfied so long as external resources are scarce. Then to appropriate anything at all is to diminish the amount available for others. But the proviso need not be taken literally. Its core idea – refined and developed by Nozick and David Gauthier, among others – is to allow appropriation that diminishes the common stock, but that does not worsen the *welfare* position of others (except insofar as may be necessary for the exercise of one's own prior rights – particularly, the right of self-defense).[21]

This idea can serve as a basis for a theory of original appropriation from which self-ownership may be derived rather than assumed.[22] Supposing that our bodies and powers are initially unowned, it is plain that their self-appropriation will not diminish the well-being of anyone else. Through

---

the position I impugn. It is worth noting that utilitarianism is often faulted precisely for its inability to defend human dignity adequately – for treating human beings as bearers of utility and therefore only as means and not, as Kant would have it, ends in themselves.

[20] John Locke, *Second Treatise of Government*, paragraph 33.

[21] *Cf.* Robert Nozick, *Anarchy, State, Utopia* (New York: Basic Books, 1974), pp. 175–82; and David Gauthier, *Morals By Agreement* (Oxford: Oxford University Press, 1986), Chapter 7.

[22] What follows draws on an idea of Gauthier's, developed in *Morals by Agreement*. Gauthier uses the Lockean proviso in the course of an extended argument for the possibility of grounding moral judgments in (contractual) agreements. Since the use I propose for the proviso is different and more circumscribed, many of the subtleties implicit in Gauthier's own elaboration of the idea are omitted here.

successive interactions, some individuals may become worse off in consequence of the bodies and powers of others. But at the moment of "original appropriation," internal resources can be appropriated by the persons to whom they are attached by nature without detriment to anyone else. The same consideration holds for external assets: whenever they can be seized without diminishing the welfare position of others, they can be appropriated rightfully.

Locke, again, distinguished these cases, taking self-ownership as a premise in an argument for ownership of external things. He held that an individual appropriates justly when she mixes her labor with (unowned) nature, extending self-ownership to the appropriated item by what can be described, unsympathetically, as sympathetic magic. But it is fatally unclear, among other things, how items to be appropriated are individuated (When I pick an unowned apple off a tree, do I lay claim to the apple? the tree? the forest?) and how much labor an individual must deploy to assume possession (Is simply removing an apple enough?).[23] In addition, Locke's labor theory of property is a response to a highly idiosyncratic formulation of the problem of original appropriation – a formulation that takes God's (purported) gift to Man of "the world and all that dwells therein" as a point of departure, and that gives priority to an "inalienable" right of self-preservation. On the other hand, the Lockean proviso supposes none of this, and can do the job Locke intends in its own right. The idea, again, is straightforward: whatever an individual takes from the stock of unowned things without diminishing the welfare position of others, he takes rightfully. By this reasoning, one owns oneself for the same reason one can own external things: because no one is made worse off by the claim.

There is, of course, a difference between alienable (external) and inalienable (internal) assets. Access to external assets is personal-neutral. Internal assets, on the other hand, can only be appropriated directly by those to whom they are already attached. But this difference is a fact of nature, incidental to the theory of justice in acquisition. It is a matter of fact, not of right, that internal assets are inalienable and that access to them is person-specific.[24]

VII

If I am right in holding that the only plausible way for a Lockean to maintain self-ownership is to invest the proviso with the burden of

[23] Cf. Nozick, Anarchy, pp. 174–178.

[24] Technological innovation may ultimately make access to internal assets more nearly person-neutral than has been the case until now – as has already occurred, to some degree, with organ transplantations. It is instructive to reflect on real or imaginable innovations that break down the person-specificity of inalienable assets in order to appreciate the generality, pace Locke, of the Lockean problem of justifying the original appropriation of things.

originating it, then the notion of given rights to which institutions must conform, the core idea of Lockean justice, amounts to much less than is commonly supposed.

In Locke's express view, proprietary rights to one's own body and powers comprise the primitive moral landscape, and political philosophy is the story of their extension. But if the proviso is the source of even these entitlements, everything – including oneself – is initially a collective asset in just the way talents and skills are for Rawls. Everything is part of the common stock of (privately) unowned things. Self-ownership is not given, but is instead derived by a principle that justifies private appropriation – of one's body and powers and of (some) external things.

That principle is, again, satisfaction of the proviso. We must then ask: what motivates this principle? This question is not directly addressed by Locke, nor is its importance recognized by his followers. Nevertheless, it is the central question Lockeans must confront. However, addressing this question casts the Lockean project in an unexpected light. For it is immediately apparent that the proviso is as much a consequence of a hypothetical agreement as are Rawls's principles of justice.

In Rawls's original position, each individual is interested only in maximizing his own share of primary goods. Individuals take no interest in each others' interests. In the Lockean account, as I have recast it, there is, implicitly, an original position too: but, in contrast to Rawls's version, individuals know who they are and what they want; and they are utility maximizers, concerned with primary goods and other resources only insofar as their own welfare is affected.[25] But, like the individuals Rawls imagines, they too take no interest in each others' interests. This is why they claim no right to block appropriations that do not impinge on their own well-being. They agree, in other words, to the principle of *laissez-faire* for appropriations that do not affect their own welfare in order to be unimpeded in the appropriations that do interest them – of their bodies and powers and of as many external things as they can acquire in a world where others are in competition with them for the same scarce resources.

Thus the revised Lockean view stands closer to Kantian positions than first appears. Entitlements, for the Lockeans I imagine, are not, as they were for Locke himself and for many libertarians today, properties of atomic individuals. They are not a point of departure, but a conclusion of a political argument that takes, as its proper starting-point, the need to distribute societal benefits and burdens fairly among individuals who have no prior claims on any part of the world, including even themselves.

---

[25] For the present, I assume, following Nozick and Gauthier, that utility adequately represents welfare or well-being.

There formerly appeared to be two distinct ways of thinking about justice to which defenders of capitalism might appeal, and two corresponding persons. For Lockeans, justice was a matter of accomodation to preexisting property rights, and persons were the bearers of these rights. On this view, a distribution is just if it accords with the rights of Lockean persons, where self-ownership specifies, in large part, what these rights are. Then what persons rightfully get is tied inextricably to what they do with what is antecedently theirs. On the rival Kantian view, property rights were derived from hypothetical social agreements. Contribution and distribution were therefore not intrinsically joined, though they are linked in practice by Rawls and other Kantians in virtue of facts about human nature and the human condition. But if self-ownership can only be sustained by appeal to the proviso, the Lockean position effectively takes on the character of its rival. At bottom, prior to any appropriations, contribution and distribution are disjoined for Lockeans too.

The Lockean quarrel with Kantianism, then, is not really about the existence of morally primitive property rights. Even as they maintain the self-ownership thesis, Lockeans should concede that property in oneself, as in external things, is derived, not given. The dispute, instead, is over the nature of the hypothetical agreement that specifies what justice is. Lockean rights ascriptions, if they are not arbitrary "non-sense on stilts" (Bentham), depend on making a case, in opposition to the case Rawls and other Kantians have made, for ascribing moral relevance to the physical and mental endowments allotted us by nature. For Lockeans, our bodies and powers help generate the distributive shares to which we are entitled – not in consequence of contingencies of human nature and circumstance, but as a matter of infrangible moral right, secured by a hypothetical agreement that invests the proviso with the task of originating entitlements. For Rawlsians, on the other hand, the exercise of the assets the self-ownership thesis assigns us, along with other outcomes of "the natural lottery," bear on justice only in consequence of considerations strictly outside the theory of justice: on human nature and the human condition – in short, on the (perhaps ineluctable) recalcitrance of human beings to rise above the human-all-too-human obstacles in the way of genuine equality.

It is not possible here to pursue the many questions raised by this reformulation of the difference distinguishing the two principal views of justice our era has produced, and the two corresponding persons they suppose. In lieu of a protracted discussion, it must suffice to recall what has already been noted: the greater affinity of the Kantian positon with "the moral point of view" and, in consequence, the evident success of Kantian, but not Lockean, theory in defending what both kinds of philosophical argument aim, above all, to support – the essential dignity of humankind.

VIII

The Lockean person is a capitalist person, a person presupposed in (some) justifying theories of capitalism. If it is an untenable idea, as I have suggested, then so is the genre of justifying theory that supposes it. If I am right, it is no longer possible to maintain, as many procapitalists do, that only capitalism can accommodate the rights persons have.[26]

The case for the other capitalist person implicit in Kantian moral philosophy is evidently strengthened by this result. But the Kantian person, the person supposed in Rawls's theory of justice, is, as it were, less capitalist than its rival. The idea pulls in a different direction: towards dissociation of contribution from distribution and towards equality of condition. This egalitarian vision is possible under socialism; under capitalism it is not. For capitalism, by definition, allows inequalities that follow from private ownership of (external) productive assets. The Kantian person is a capitalist person, then, only as a concession to humanity's inability to date to develop and deploy productive assets without recourse to material incentives.

Thus, a Rawlsian could not defend capitalism over socialism by appeal to justice *per se*. It would be necessary, instead, to speculate about the likely consequences of capitalism – in contrast to socialism – for the satisfaction of the principles of justice: for the equal distribution of basic rights and liberties, for democratic equality of opportunity, and for maximizing the share of primary goods accorded representative members of the least well-off group. If capitalism wins, it is in consequence of these speculations, not because it is intrinsically more just.

It is worth noting that the procapitalist Ralwsian argument just sketched is, very nearly, a Marxian argument. The idea, again, is that people who are susceptible to material incentives and who have a compelling interest in increasing the level of productivity are better served by capitalism than by socialism. But in the historical materialist view, the role of capitalism is precisely to provide an incentive structure that encourages the introduction of new technologies and the efficient allocation of productive inputs, thereby raising levels of development to a point where, on efficiency grounds, capitalism is no longer useful. Where Marxists would differ from procapitalist Rawlsians is in thinking that capitalist development can proceed to a point where this stage is, in fact, achieved.

Thus, Marxists defend the historical possibility of what Kantians already tendentially endorse. For the Kantian person is a capitalist person only in a

---

[26] Strictly speaking, only a full-fledged Lockean person, who owns himself and parts of the external world too, requires capitalist property relations. Self-ownership, as noted, can survive capitalism's demise.

certain range of circumstances, circumstances that historical materialism deems surpassable. Ironically, but suggestively, the capitalist person that survives the demise of self-ownership requires socialism to realize its nature fully.

Philosophy, University of Wisconsin – Madison

CAPITALISM AND SELF-OWNERSHIP*

BY ANDREW KERNOHAN

From the standpoint of libertarian ideology, capitalism is a form of liberation. In contrast to the slave, whose productive powers are wholly owned by his master, and the serf, whose productive powers are partially owned by his lord, the worker under capitalism is presented as possessing the fullest possible self-ownership. That capitalism fosters self-ownership is a false and stultifying myth.[1] Exposing its errors from within capitalism's own conceptual framework requires a careful analysis of the concept of a person's "ownership" both of his or her productive powers and of the means of exercising these productive powers. This analysis will show that, in certain plausible circumstances, the capitalist economic system can make full self-ownership impossible. Since capitalism's supposed nurturing of self-ownership provides one of the major justifications for its moral legitimacy,[2] capitalist ideology has a serious internal inconsistency.

Oddly enough, Marxists are in accord with libertarians in believing that capitalism preserves self-ownership. Marx himself writes:

> The exchange of commodities of itself implies no other relations of dependence than those which result from its own nature. On this assumption, labour power can appear upon the market as a commodity, only if, and so far as, its possessor, the individual whose labour power it is, offers it for sale or sells it as a commodity. In order that he may be able to do this, he must have

---

* I would like to acknowledge the financial support of the Social Sciences and Humanities Research Council of Canada and the hospitality of the University of Toronto Department of Philosophy during the period in which this essay was written. The essay has benefitted from the constructive criticisms of Lois Pineau and Romano Roman.

[1] G.A. Cohen has recently studied the libertarian justification of capitalism from the perspective of self-ownership in "Self-Ownership, World Ownership, and Equality: Part II," *Social Philosophy & Policy*, vol. 3, no. 2 (1986), pp. 77–96; and "Nozick on Appropriation," *New Left Review*, vol. 150 (1985), pp. 89–105.

[2] For example, Nozick presupposes this justification when he writes, "End-state and most patterned principles of distributive justice institute (partial) ownership by others of people and their actions and labor. These principles involve a shift from the classical liberals' notion of self-ownership to a notion of (partial) property rights in *other* people." *Anarchy, State and Utopia* (New York: Basic Books, 1974), p. 172. There are, of course, other ways of trying to justify capitalism, arguments from maximizing utility or moral desert being the most common.

it at his disposal, must be the untrammelled owner of his capacity for labour, i.e., of his person.[3]

In this essay, however, it will be argued that the capitalist economic system can rob at least some workers of their ownership of important productive powers. Under increasingly common circumstances, capitalism separates the possessors of certain types of skills from full legal ownership of these skills. This generates a moral condemnation of capitalism within its own theory of justice.

This problem of the alienation of important powers should not be confused with another problem facing any libertarian defense of private property: in the state of nature all persons have a liberty to use all things and no right to exclude others from a similar liberty. This liberty is grounded in their self-ownership right to use their human powers on things as they see fit. The transition to a regime of private property involves some persons acquiring a claim-right that others not use certain things while themselves retaining their original liberty. The acquisition of private property by some involves the restriction of liberty for others. This restriction of liberty is difficult for the libertarian to justify. But our point is this: no matter how the origins of the property structure might be justified, after the capitalist relations of production have attained a certain degree of development they will begin to interfere with the self-ownership of persons. Our point concerns the injustice of the continuation of capitalism, not of its origins.

We will be concerned here with the productive powers of persons. Examples of productive powers include a skill at knitting, a talent for computer programming, an ability to wheel cement all day in the hot sun, and so forth. A classification of personal powers immediately suggests itself. Some powers one is born with, some are acquired by diligent self-development, and some can only be learned through the efforts of others. For instance, in a hunting and gathering society, an individual might be born with a talent for speedy flight, might acquire accuracy with a bow and arrow only after much lonely practice, and might learn to find edible tubers through lengthy tutelage from the elders of the community. Different justifications for property rights may give different analyses of the ownership of these powers. One could argue that individuals own their speed by right of first possession and their accuracy through their invested labor, but that the community has rights in an individual's gathering ability because its inculcation was a community effort. But in our complex industrial world, with its requirements for correspondingly complex skills,

---

[3] Karl Marx, *Capital*, volume I (New York: International Publishers, 1967), p. 168.

productive powers tend to amalgamate such types. A skill at healing, for example, is acquired through a natural aptitude for study, perseverance in school work, and an investment of hundreds of thousands of dollars worth of society's time and energy. In the case of the would-be doctor, analyzing ownership of personal powers by mode of acquisition will not prove useful.

But is it appropriate to talk about personal powers being owned? Certainly there is a long tradition in political philosophy which says it is. A major premise in Locke's justification for the initial privatization of resources in the state of nature is the claim that:

> . . . every man has a property in his own person; this nobody has any right to but himself. The labor of his body and the work of his hands, we may say, are properly his.[4]

We are also familiar with situations involving the ownership of all the powers of one person by another, that is to say, slavery. On the other hand, it does seem odd to say that Wayne owns his talents as a hockey player. The relation between Wayne and his talents is a stronger one. His talents are constitutive of his very being; he has, after all, done very little else besides playing hockey since he learned to walk. Though the relation between Wayne and his talents may appear stronger than just ownership, we nonetheless want to say that he has certain rights with respect to those talents. If these rights are approximately the same ones that a paradigm owner has with respect to his or her property, we will be inclined to say that ownership is at least part of the story about Wayne's relation to his talents.

For an account of the rights (in a loose sense of rights) that pertain to an owner (in the most complete sense of owner) we can turn to the work of A.M. Honoré.[5] Honoré distinguishes eleven standard incidents of what he calls full "liberal ownership." These are (1) the right to be put and maintained in physical possession of a thing, (2) the right to the personal use and enjoyment of the thing, (3) the right to manage how the thing is used, (4) the right to any income generated by the thing, (5) the right to consume, waste, or destroy a thing and the power to alienate it, (6) immunity from expropriation, (7) the power to bequeath the thing, (8) the right to have no definite term to one's enjoyment of the thing, (9) a duty to forbear from harmful use of the thing, (10) a liability to have the thing taken for payment of debts, and (11) the right to the reversion on termination of lesser interests (like a lease) in the thing. In general, the

---

[4] John Locke, *The Second Treatise of Government*, ed. T.P. Peardon (Indianapolis: Bobbs-Merrill, 1952), p. 17.

[5] A.M. Honoré, "Ownership," A.G. Guest, ed., *Oxford Essays in Jurisprudence* (Oxford: Clarendon Press, 1961), pp. 107–147.

rights mentioned are exclusive rights because they not only curtail the liberty of others to use the thing but also place a duty on others not to interfere with the owner's use. This is what makes such property rights private.

The possession by one individual of all these types of claim-rights, duties, powers, and liabilities with respect to a given thing is the paradigm case of full liberal ownership. Historically this paradigm was perhaps realized for a short time in late eighteenth and early nineteenth century America by the original pioneers – or at least so goes the myth. But full ownership is of little practical importance in the late twentieth century. Contemporary owners make do with a much less robust set of rights in things. Shareholders in a corporation, for example, have some rights from the above list over the property of the corporation (an income right, a very slender management right, rights to security and bequest), but lack many others (the right to sell corporation property or even to possess or use it, and most of the management rights).[6] Modern ownership patterns are typically of this sort. Various owners possess different bundles of rights in one and the same thing. The fact that their bundles are not complete does not stop us calling them "owners," though it does enable us to see how people can own a thing to a greater or lesser extent. Their rights are still private rights since partial owners exercise what rights they do have to the exclusion of others. This does not stop others from having different, but still exclusive, rights in the thing. Nor is it the case that any one of these rights (or a limited subset thereof) is either necessary or sufficient for ownership.

Honoré offered this list as a paradigm of the concept of ownership. It can be judged whether or not other arrangements of rights should be termed ownership by comparing them to this paradigm. We can thus decide on the appropriateness of the concept of self-ownership by examining the list of rights that persons have with respect to their talents and abilities and comparing it with Honoré's. Let us begin with a maximal notion of self-ownership such as might be appealed to by a libertarian. It is clear that most of the incidents apply. With respect to one's powers, one has the rights of possession, use, management, income, alienation (in the sense of selling one's labor or wasting one's talents), security, indefiniteness of term, and reversion. As well, one has a duty against the harmful use of one's abilities. Against this, because of their nature, one cannot bequeath one's talents, nor, because of the relative enlightenment of our times, is one

---

[6] Shareholders, however, do have a full set of ownership rights with respect to their shares. But this might be described as a second order right with respect to the company's property. Shareholders have full liberal ownership of a right to partial liberal ownership of the productive resources of a company.

liable to have one's talents taken in repayment of debts.[7] This collection of nine out of eleven incidents is a closer approximation to Honoré's paradigm than is the bundle of rights of the shareholders of a large corporation. So we may safely use the notion of property rights with respect to a person's productive powers.

Let us now go on to consider the relation between property in personal productive capacities and property in the means of production of the necessities and comforts of life. Productive capacities are more intimately related to the means of producing consumer goods than to consumer goods themselves, so we shall confine our discussion to the former. This point is worth emphasizing. The productive activity of knitting a sweater is far more dependent on the knitting needles used than on the sweater that eventually results. Liberal theorists have generally been concerned with the relation between ownership of the exercise of productive powers (labor) and ownership of the product of the exercise of productive powers (the product of labor). Our attention here will be on the relation between ownership of productive powers (labor power) and ownership of the means of exercising productive powers (means of labor, means of production).

Our discussion is complicated by the fact that the product of labor, though sometimes a consumable, is frequently itself a means of production. Some factories produce things people can use directly, like cars, while other factories produce the machinery which will be used to make the cars. Because of this, our conclusions about the relation between ownership of powers and ownership of the means of their exercise will interestingly contradict traditional conclusions about the relation between ownership of labor and ownership of its product.

Nozick has defended the sort of libertarian justification of capitalism we want to look at, a theory in which:

(a) through the exercise of one's productive powers (labor) one can justly acquire private ownership of the products of this labor, provided one does not thereby worsen the situation of others, and

(b) through the exercise of one's private rights in one's justly acquired property (particularly the rights to manage and to sell) one can justly acquire further private property.[8]

On the face of it, our interests and Nozick's appear different: clause (a) discusses ownership of the product of labor, while we have been interested

---

[7] This latter does not seem strictly entailed by the liberal concept of self-ownership. A strict view of contractual obligation does not seem to rule out forced labor or indentured servitude in satisfaction of a contract.

[8] Nozick, *Anarchy*, pp. 151–153, 160–164, and 174–182.

in ownership of the means of labor. However, in most situations of interest, what are the means of production at one time are the product of the exercise of productive powers on different means of production at another, earlier time. Many things can be described both as the products of the exercise of powers and as the means for the exercise of powers. It is important not to focus on the first of these descriptions to the neglect of the second.

The private property rights of some persons to the exercise of certain personal powers are not consistent with the private property rights of others in the means of exercising these powers. Suppose that, through the mechanisms postulated in clause (b) of Nozick's theory of entitlement, it comes to pass that all the means of production in society become the private property of very few individuals or of one collective entity (e.g., the state). Under these conditions some, nonowning, individuals will be legally denied the exercise of their productive powers since they will be legally denied access to the means of exercising their powers. Admittedly, they can buy access to the means of exercising their powers from the owners of the means of production, but this does not give them any legal rights with respect to the means of production or, by implication, to the exercise of their powers. The mere fact that Mary can buy John's car gives her no rights in either it or the exercise of her ability to drive it.

It could be objected, based on clause (b) above, that people can lose their property rights in things through a series of just transactions. So if John sells his car to Mary, after the transaction he no longer has property rights in the car. In a similar fashion, people could come to lose their property rights in their labor. But notice that if John sells "his" car to Mary and in the transaction Pat loses her property rights in the car without her consent (perhaps Pat is John's partner and a co-owner of the car), then John has defrauded Pat. Persons cannot justly lose their property rights through the actions of others. Now, for simplicity, consider the position of a new graduate of a college or technical school. If all the requisite means of production are the property of others, he or she will be prevented from exercising his or her powers by ownership structures that have grown up through transactions which can only be the work of others. Yet the transactions of others should not be able to remove the new graduate's self-ownership.

The example of the new graduate may not seem to be an example of self-ownership being denied in any obvious fashion. On the contrary, it may seem ridiculous to suppose that the new graduate suffers any loss in legal or moral rights with respect to his or her newly acquired skills. Suppose A has a hammer and B has the nails. Even though B's nails are the means by which A can use the hammer, B's ownership of the nails does not deny A's ownership of the hammer. By analogy, the ownership by others of the means by which the new graduate can use his or her skills does not curtail the new graduate's ownership of the skills. Even if the new graduate is denied the use of his or her skills, he or she still has possession of the skills themselves. Ownership of these skills does not give the graduate a right to exercise them on means of production already owned by others any more than someone's ownership of a hammer permits its use on other people's nails.

Rather than illustrating self-ownership denied by capitalist ownership, the new graduate example presents us with a challenge. To make our case, we must do three things:

(1) We must point out the intimate connection between a skill and its exercise, a connection so close that it does not make sense to talk of owning one and not the other.

(2) We must point out the disanalogies between owning a hammer and owning a productive skill.

(3) And we must show how the historical priority of the property rights of capitalists must bow to the moral priority of the new graduate's self-ownership.

The first point concerns the distinction between owning a capacity and owning the exercise of a capacity. With this distinction, a libertarian defender of capitalism could claim that self-ownership, and the liberties it is equivalent to, requires private ownership only of capacities and not of their actual exercise. If the new graduate can have full self-ownership without being able to exercise his or her capacities, then capitalist ownership structures pose no threat to self-ownership. Suppose, then, that we have someone who does not own the exercise of a skill. Can this person be said to fully own this capacity to produce? If we look back at Honoré's list of incidents as they pertain to just the skill or capacity itself, the answer is no. Three of these incidents involve rights to the *exercise* of the skill or capacity: the right to use or exercise it oneself, the managerial right to decide who else may exercise the skill and when, and the income right to any benefits flowing from the exercise of the skill. The person who does not own the exercise of the skill clearly lacks these rights to use, manage, or gain income from the skill. In other words, he or she loses rights with respect to the skill itself and not just to its exercise. His or her ownership of just the skill itself, as opposed to its exercise, must be less than full ownership. Someone who owns a skill but not its exercise owns that skill to a lesser degree than someone who owns both the skill and its exercise. This is analogous to the difference between someone who has legal title to a piece of land, but does not own the leasehold, and someone who owns land in fee simple. The former cannot use, manage, or produce income on his or her land and thus has a lesser degree of ownership than the latter. If someone does not own the exercise of his or her productive powers, then he or she must have less than full ownership in the powers themselves.

Leaning hard on the distinction between owning powers and owning their exercise is inconsistent with other claims which a libertarian justification of private property needs to make. If self-ownership just guaranteed ownership of the capacity to labor but not of labor itself, then the labor justification of private property loses whatever credibility it might ever have had. There are problems afflicting the argument that by mixing something one owns (labor) with something one does not own, one begins to own the latter.[9] How much worse, then, are the problems for an argument that by mixing something one only partially owns with an unowned thing, one can somehow appropriate it. The ownership of a skill is a much weaker premise than is the ownership of its exercise in labor from which to argue for the justified ownership of labor's product. Nor would the libertarian diatribe against taxation as forced labor[10] have much force if one had no right to one's labor but only a right to one's capacity to labor.

Let us go on to the purported analogy between the ownership, on the one hand, of a skill and of the means of its exercise and, on the other hand, of a hammer and some nails. The crucial point about the hammer is that it has a myriad of alternative uses besides banging in nails. It can be used for tearing down boards, driving in tent pegs, killing insects, or whatever. So B's ownership of the available nails only denies A one particular use of the hammer; it does not deny A the right to use the hammer in general. A's ownership is reduced in the weak sense that one possible use of the hammer is ruled out, but not in the strong sense that all possible uses of the hammer are ruled out. A still retains Honoré's incidents of the rights to use, manage the use of, and draw income from the use of the hammer, though these rights are slightly attenuated. This slight attenuation does not offend one's intuition that A still fully owns the hammer.

Contrast this with an imaginary case in which A is somehow denied all use of the hammer. Not only can A not bang in nails with the hammer, A cannot even pick it up or move it around. A cannot permit others to use the hammer, or draw any income from its use. A no longer has the right to use the hammer, to manage the hammer, or to the income from the hammer. In such a case we would be inclined to say that A has suffered a reduction in ownership of the hammer. A's *type* of ownership has changed. Similarly,

---

[9] These problems are canvassed by Nozick, *Anarchy*, pp. 174–175.
[10] For example, *ibid.*, pp. 169–172.

if one could imagine a thing that had only one use, and if that one use became somehow legally denied to its owner, then we would have to say that its ownership was not merely attenuated, but had been reduced in type. Some productive powers are just like this. They are so specialized that they have no other use than to be exercised on a particular kind of means of production, and cannot be exercised without it. For instance, a skill at computer programming cannot be exercised without access to a computer. If such a skill cannot be used, its possessor no longer has full ownership of it, but only some lesser interest. It is not enough that the bearer can still sell the use of the skill to the owners of the means of its use, though not to anyone else. This fact is based on the bearer retaining the right to exclude others from the exercise of the skill without his or her consent. But this partial management right in no way mitigates the absence of any right to use or exercise the skill.

We can now characterize more precisely the circumstances under which capitalism will only permit less than full self-ownership. Some skills can be exercised without any means of exercise, for instance, a skill at whistling or singing. Some skills, though requiring a means of exercise, have many uses; physical strength is an example. But A's ownership of a skill S will be less than full liberal ownership when:

1. S needs some means of exercise P.
2. S has no other outlet than P.
3. P is totally owned by persons other than A.
4. No other P's, except those owned by people other than A, are available in any practical way.

Such circumstances can easily occur in capitalist societies. They can also occur in a state capitalist society, the sort of socialism in which all the means of production become the private property of the state. Quite possibly they are not completely preventable in any society.

One could still feel uneasy with the notion of a skill having only one use and one outlet. This likely stems from the notion that even a complex and specialized skill is nothing more than a collection of simpler subskills and aptitudes which do have other applications. A computer programmer, for instance, must have an aptitude for problem solving, some mathematical skills and aptitudes, a knowledge of programming languages, some typing skills, and so forth, all of which can be used to do other things. To look at this point theoretically, consider the following definition of "labor-power" from Marx:

> By labour-power or capacity for labour is to be understood the aggregate of those mental and physical capabilities existing in a

human being, which he exercises whenever he produces a use-value of any description.[11]

The key question is how we understand a skill to be aggregated out of its subskills. If we understand "aggregation" in its distributive sense, in which the whole is nothing more than the sum of its parts and the skill is simply a haphazard collection of subskills, then the uneasiness is justified. But surely the way subskills are aggregated makes a difference; how the collection of subskills is organized into the specialized skill is important to the constitution of that skill. The specialized skill is more than the sum of its parts. So if a person loses the use of a specialized skill but retains the use of its component subskills, then there is something that he or she has lost.

It might still be replied that one cannot exercise one's property rights, even in one's personal powers, in such a manner as to infringe the property rights of others. This is, in fact, number (9) in Honoré's list of standard incidents, the prohibition of harmful use. Since the new graduate cannot exercise his or her private property rights to the exercise of his or her productive talents without violating the private property rights of the capitalists, then the new graduate's rights have not, in fact, been interfered with. But this reply is a double-edged sword. It is also the case that the capitalists cannot exercise their rights to exclude the new graduate from the means of exercising his or her talents without violating the new graduate's rights. The two conclusions are inconsistent.

To remove the inconsistency a libertarian would need to argue that the rights of the capitalists take precedence over the rights of the new graduate. In a historical sense this may be true. But in a moral sense, on the face of it, the very opposite is true; self-ownership of labor is a foundational right while the capitalists' rights to things are merely derived from it. For example, all of us are both the product of the child-rearing labors of our parents and the self-owners of our powers. Surely the latter takes precedence.[12] But it could be replied that the skills and capacities of the new graduate are very sophisticated products of a particular historical development and not the skills that he or she would have owned in the state of nature. If all one's self-ownership amounted to was ownership of the exercise of one's "natural" skills, the new graduate would not have a case. However, a libertarian could not possibly rest happy with this assumption. It would not be consistent with the labor justification of appropriation which implies that self-developed talents, at least, must be

[11] Marx, *Capital*, p. 167.
[12] See L.C. Becker, *Property Rights: Philosophical Foundations* (London: Routledge & Kegan Paul, 1977), pp. 37–39, for a discussion of this argument.

the property of their possessor.[13] It would imply that anyone who used a highly other-developed talent to invent something[14] would not own the invention since the talent used to invent it was not his or hers to begin with. It would also raise the question of who, if not their bearer, does own nonnatural talents. Are they the collective property of the community at large? Or are they the common property of all the individuals in the community? Or are they unowned and just waiting for the first person to come along who wishes, with a little work, to appropriate them?

It might be replied that the capitalists' ownership satisfied what Nozick calls the "Lockean proviso."[15] Both transactions and appropriations must satisfy the condition that they do not worsen the situation of others. Nozick interprets the idea of worsening the situation of others as not reducing their supply of consumer goods from some baseline.[16] The baseline is, of course, the state of nature, which makes it fairly easy for even monopolistic capitalism to satisfy the constraint. But this interpretation of the Lockean proviso accepts a picture of persons as essentially consumers of the products of the productive process. This unexalted vision of humanity presupposes that the only interests of persons which need protecting are passive desires to consume. And this is simply false. Persons are essentially producers as well as consumers. Contrast the vision of C.B. Macpherson:

> Whether the Western tradition is traced back to Plato or Aristotle or to Christian natural law, it is based on the proposition that the end or purpose of man is to use and develop his uniquely human attributes or capacities. His potential use and development of these may be called his human powers. A good life is one which maximizes these powers.[17]

If we were to focus on the exercising of their productive powers as the urgent interests of people which need protecting by the Lockean proviso, we would get an entirely different version of it. Transactions and appropriations must not diminish from some baseline the abilities of persons to exercise their productive powers. What baseline? By the arguments presented above, it cannot be the exercise of only "natural" powers. So it must be the exercise of powers as historically developed in the society in question. And this is inconsistent with any endowment structure which legally denies persons the means to exercise these powers.

---

[13] See Nozick's reply to Rawls, *Anarchy*, p. 214.
[14] Like Nozick's medical researcher; *Anarchy*, p. 181.
[15] *ibid.*, pp. 178–182.
[16] *ibid.*, pp. 174–182.
[17] C.B. Macpherson, *Democratic Theory: Essays in Retrieval*, (Oxford: Oxford University Press, 1973), p. 8.

There may still be room for an *ad hominem* objection. Under the conditions of scarcity that will prevail in any foreseeable future, any society, be it socialist, egalitarian, welfare maximizing, or whatever, will have to have rules which regulate and restrict access to the means of production. Therefore, any society, not just a capitalist one, stands to be in a position of reducing the self-ownership of some of its members. But this point about other societies should not detract from the importance of the fact that capitalism, which prides and justifies itself on preserving and nurturing self-ownership, can permit the development of situations in which self-ownership is restricted. Other theories, not committed to both unrestricted thing ownership and unrestricted self-ownership, may find consistency easier to attain.

A libertarian might wish to defend capitalist private property rights by insisting that these rights are founded in basic liberties. In his book, *Anarchy, State and Utopia*, Robert Nozick seems to give an argument leading from the principle of liberty to the justice of unrestricted private property rights. What Nozick has produced, however, is an argument for unrestricted private property rights using unrestricted private property rights as his premise, and thus he begs the question he tries to answer. Other critics of Nozick have made this point before,[18] but the distinctions we have developed allow us to set out the argument in an especially perspicuous way.

Nozick's argument, which stars the great basketball player Wilt Chamberlain, is well-known, but we shall quote it for reference. Nozick contrasts his entitlement theory of distributive justice with theories of justice which assess distributions according to how well they realize just patterns. Patterned theories can make various claims as to what a just end-state distribution might be: egalitarian, socialist, utility-maximizing, or whatever. But, in Nozick's theory, justice has got nothing to do with what pattern of distribution results from a historical process. Justice is concerned only with what sort of historical process took place. A process is just if, and only if, it satisfies the two principles that we mentioned above:[19] one, private property rights may be acquired in unowned things in accordance with a Lockean labor theory of property; and two, private property rights in unowned things may be transferred in any manner that does not violate the rights of some other person, including his or her property rights. His argument against all possible patterned or end-state conceptions of justice

---

[18] E.g., J. Reiman, "The Fallacy of Libertarian Capitalism," *Ethics*, vol. 91 (1981), pp. 85–95; and C.C. Ryan, "Yours, Mine and Ours: Property Rights and Individual Liberty," J. Paul, ed., *Reading Nozick* (Totowa: Rowman & Littlefield, 1981), pp. 323–343.

[19] Nozick, *Anarchy*, p. 151, together with pp. 174–182.

(and thus, by exclusion, in favor of private property) proceeds by counterexample.

> For suppose a distribution favored by one of these non-entitlement conceptions is realized. Let us suppose it is your favorite one and let us call this distribution D1; perhaps everyone has an equal share. Perhaps shares vary in accordance with some dimension you treasure. Now suppose that Wilt Chamberlain is greatly in demand by basketball teams, being a great gate attraction. . . . He signs the following sort of contract with a team: In each home game, twenty-five cents from the price of each ticket of admission goes to him. . . . Let us suppose that in one season one million persons attend his home games, and Wilt Chamberlain winds up with $250,000, a much larger sum than the average income and larger even than anyone else has. Is he entitled to this income? Is this new distribution, D2, unjust? If so, why? . . . If D1 was a just distribution, and people voluntarily moved from it to D2, transferring parts of their shares they were given under D1 (what was it for if not to do something with?), isn't D2 also just? If the people were entitled to dispose of the resources to which they were entitled (under D1), didn't this include their being entitled to give it to or exchange it with Wilt Chamberlain?[20]

A page later, after a few similar examples involving the accumulation of the means of production, he concludes:

> Here I wish merely to note how private property even in means of production would occur in a socialist society that did not forbid people to use as they wished some of the resources they are given under the socialist distribution D1.[21]

We are meant to infer that any society which abolishes private property must also abolish liberty. In order to maintain whatever pattern of distribution a theory judges just, a society would need to constrain the liberty of its members. Given the centrality of liberty as a value, this is undesirable. Only an unrestricted right to private property in the capitalist mode is compatible with liberty.

This counterexample depends, as counterexamples do, on the force of certain of the reader's intuitions. These are brought out in a succeeding paragraph:

[20] *ibid.*, pp. 160–161.
[21] *ibid.*, p. 163.

The general point illustrated by the Wilt Chamberlain example and the example of the entrepreneur in a socialist society is that no end-state principle of justice can be continuously realized without continuous interference with people's lives.[22]

This is a powerful intuition indeed; no one wants others continuously interfering in his or her life. But the intuition has a certain vagueness. Just exactly what sorts of interference in people's lives are wrong and why? Not all interferences are as unjustified or as unnecessary as they may seem at first sight. Two things that Nozick might think wrong with interference in people's lives are: one, interference is immoral because it violates people's rights; and two, interference is impractical since enforcing a pattern of distribution is too difficult to actually do.

Let us take these two cases in turn. In the former, the only rights that would be violated in preventing the sort of transactions envisioned in the Wilt Chamberlain example are private property rights. To make this apparent, one has to remember that there is no unitary ownership right as such.[23] Instead, what we call the right of private ownership is in fact a collection of claim-rights, powers, duties, and immunities with respect to the thing owned. Recall Honoré's analysis of full liberal ownership into eleven incidents. We can use these incidents to analyze the transaction in which fans each give Wilt Chamberlain twenty-five cents to see him play basketball. Nozick claims that both the fans and Wilt have a basic liberty to engage in this transaction. Looking closely at the liberty involved in such a transaction, one can see that it involves:

(a)   the unrestricted power of each fan to alienate from him or herself the sum of twenty-five cents, and

(b)   the unrestricted right of Wilt Chamberlain to accept this benefit that his skills have brought him.

These two rights, which guarantee the liberty of the fan and of Wilt to engage in this transaction, should seem familiar. They are just two of the rights of ownership in Honoré's list: the private property right of the fan to alienate his or her capital and the private property right of Wilt Chamberlain to the income from his skills. If the participants have a freedom of some special moral status to engage in such transactions then this status is justified, not by any basic liberty but by two private property

---

[22] *ibid.*, p. 163.

[23] The idea of using an analyzed notion of private ownership in the discussion of Nozick's argument is due to Ryan, "Yours, Mine." Ryan points out that some holdings, e.g., the entitlement to a university teaching job, do not carry with them a right to be transferred at will. So Nozick should not just assume this right of transfer pertains to the fan and his or her 25 cents.

rights. The liberties on which Nozick's argument is based turn out, on analysis, to be property rights whose justification is the very issue in dispute between Nozick and his opponents. So this attempt to argue from the special moral status of such transactions to the justice of private property adds nothing new to the discussion. Using an unanalyzed notion of private property hides from view the fact that the freedom Nozick extols is not a separate right to liberty but is a component of the concept of ownership.

Our analysis has revealed that the liberty to engage in such "capitalist acts between consenting adults"[24] as the transaction between Wilt and his fans is protected by two rights, an unrestricted self-ownership right to income on the part of Wilt and a thing-ownership power of alienation on the part of the fans. It cannot be denied that self-ownership is an important part of what we mean by personal liberty. The notion of self-ownership captures some of what is attractive about the notion of personal liberty or freedom of the person. The nine rights mentioned as applying to a person's productive powers protect people against the interference of others with the use, enjoyment, employment, and so forth, of their human capacities. But self-ownership is still only a component of liberty. Our conception of liberty includes political and constitutional liberties, freedom of conscience, freedom of thought, and so forth. Nozick's argument trades on an ambiguity. What he seems to promise is an attack on nonentitlement theories of distribution based on a wide concept of liberty that does not presuppose the legitimacy of private ownership. What he actually delivers is an attack on nonprivate property-based distributions that utilizes only the self-ownership component of liberty. His attack would be more interesting if it could be based on other, independent components of personal liberty.

Moreover, Nozick's attack utilizes only the most contentious component of the self-ownership component of liberty, the right to charge what the market will bear for the exercise of a power. But nothing he has said about liberty gives this component any claim to moral absoluteness. Recognizing this, an opponent could equally propose that a just notion of self-ownership consisted in Honoré's incidents except with a cap of, say, $40,000 per year on the right to the income from the exercise of one's skills. Without taking this proposal to be a recommendation about a full-blown theory of egalitarian justice, let us imagine the consequences. Wilt's ownership of his skills does not include the right to accept any income in excess of the above amount. Wilt's rights are not infringed when he gets no more than this amount because, by hypothesis, he has no such right. The fans have no freedom to give him more than this amount because he has no right to receive it. One is not free to give people things if they have no right to own

---

[24] Nozick, *Anarchy*, p. 163.

them. For example, a developer who had dealings with the government of a small Canadian province once gave a week's room and board in his Caribbean hotel to the premier of this province. The developer no doubt had the right to alienate the hotel room for a week, but there is a serious doubt as to whether the premier had the moral right to accept it. So it is not clear that the developer was at liberty to give the premier the room. It should be noted that Nozick's argument does not depend just on Wilt's self-ownership. If it did, it might be possible to construe his argument as another form of the labor justification of private property. His argument requires, as well, the fans' right to alienate the sum of twenty-five cents. The latter is definitely a private property right to things.

Nozick's claim that continuous interference in people's lives is wrong because it violates rights or liberties does not advance the discussion, but there are other interpretations of his point. Continual interference is a disutility, though such a utilitarian justification of property rights would not appeal to Nozick, nor is it the concern of the present paper. This point need not detain us here, except that we should note how his appeal to our intuitions on this point may presuppose our utilitarian biases. He might also be thinking that continuous interference is not possible in practice. What good is a patterned system of distributive justice if such a systme cannot be enforced?

This point cuts both ways. Certain property rights that were once relatively easy to enforce have become, through the development of technology, unenforceable in practice. For instance, think of copyright laws and the development of photocopy machines. Without a Mountie standing over each of the nation's photocopy machines it would be impossible to prevent a situation such as the present writer's possession of an unauthorized copy of Chapter 7 of *Anarchy, State and Utopia*. Property rights in printed materials, computer software, and the like are rapidly becoming unenforceable, and, on this interpretation of Nozick's point, would thus cease to be property rights.

A deeper moral can also be drawn. To a large degree the extent of "continuous interference in people's lives" that is necessitated by a particular conception of property rights is determined by the development of technology. The unlimited right to the income of a thing, that is, the freedom to accumulate unlimited capital, only became possible with the invention of money. Only the existence of money makes a Wilt Chamberlain example possible. Suppose, for example, that his fans could not use money but instead had to pay Wilt with candy bars or other objects of similar value. It is less than obvious that he could, in practice, accept the creative attempts of his million fans to give him objects of the requisite value. The sheer volume of candy, fruit, vegetables, lumber, sausages, and so forth would be overwhelming, if not a hazard to health.

Just as the invention of money creates the problem of limiting Wilt's income without continuously interfering in the lives of his fans, other inventions could solve it. It is no longer difficult to imagine a society which used debit cards and computer memories instead of money as we now know it. In such a society it would be relatively easy to limit Wilt's income without interfering with his fans. When Wilt's income reached its $40,000 limit the computer could either stop accepting money on his behalf, or accept it for later redistribution in equal portions to all his donors, or accept it to be used for the common benefit, or whatever. No impractical interference need be involved. There is no need to endorse or defend any particular scheme of computerized money at this juncture. Suffice it to show that, on this interpretation, Nozick's point has some force only at a particular stage in the development of technology.

Our discussion has revealed a deep-seated inconsistency in the theory of ownership grounding the libertarian justification of capitalism. Capitalist ownership requires the existence of two virtually unrestricted rights: the right to use one's property however one wants and the right to acquire ownership of whatever results from this use. These rights are restricted only by a duty not to harm others. As well, they must apply both to things and to powers; thing ownership is grounded in self-ownership, and thus self-ownership must be at least as unrestricted as thing ownership. Assuming unrestricted self-ownership, from its income right the libertarian can justify private property. The unrestricted rights of private property justify capitalist accumulation of the means of production. But this can lead to the situation described earlier on, a situation in which persons do not have the right to use certain types of powers because the means of using them are the property of others. In these circumstances, persons no longer have unrestricted self-ownership of their powers. Self-ownership is led to justify its own negation, and this contradiction presents a serious problem for the libertarian justification of capitalism. We must search elsewhere for an adequate synthesis of people's interests in their productive powers with their interests in the means of production.

Philosophy, Dalhousie University

AGAINST COHEN ON PROLETARIAN UNFREEDOM*

BY JOHN GRAY

In a series of important papers, G.A. Cohen has developed a forceful argument for the claim that workers are rendered unfree by capitalist institutions.[1] His argument poses a powerful challenge to those (such as myself) who think that capitalist institutions best promote freedom. Yet, formidable as it is, Cohen's argument can be shown to be flawed at several crucial points. It is not one argument, but three at least, and one of the goals of my criticism of Cohen on this question is to distinguish and assess the various separate lines of reasoning that together make up his case for the unfreedom under capitalism of workers as a class. Cohen argues of workers that they are rendered unfree by *the institution of private property* on which the capitalist system depends, that they suffer *a form of collective unfreedom under capitalism*, and that they are *forced to sell their labor power under capitalism*. Against Cohen, I will maintain that every sort of unfreedom which he shows to exist under capitalism has a direct counterpart under socialist institutions. For that reason, Cohen's arguments establish nothing about the distinctive bearings of capitalist institutions on freedom. Indeed, the upshot of Cohen's arguments is a set of conceptual truisms about individual and collective freedom and unfreedom, force and justice, which have application wherever these concepts themselves find a foothold. Within the framework of Cohen's reasoning – in which an obsolescent philosophical method of conceptual analysis is applied to the

* For their comments on an earlier draft of this paper, I am indebted to Scott Arnold, Gerry Cohen, Jon Elster, David Gordon, Andrew Melnyic, David Miller, Ellen Paul, Jeffrey Paul, G. Pincione and Andrew Williams. Responsibility for this paper, including its interpretation of Cohen's argument, remains mine. Research for this paper was conducted during a period of residence as Distinguished Research Fellow at the Social Philosophy and Policy Center, Bowling Green State University, Bowling Green, Ohio. I am grateful to the Center and its Directors for providing me with ideal conditions for thinking and writing.

[1] "Capitalism, Freedom and the Proletariat" in *the Idea of Freedom*, ed. Alan Ryan (Oxford: Oxford University Press, 1979); "Illusions about Private Property and Freedom," J. Mepham and D. Ruben, eds., *Issues in Marxist Philosophy*, vol. IV (Hassocks, Sussex: Harvester Press, 1981); "Freedom, Justice and Capitalism," *New Left Review*, vol. 125 (1981); "The Structure of Proletarian Unfreedom," J. Roemer, ed., *Analytical Marxism* (Cambridge University Press, 1986); and "Are Workers Forced to Sell Their Labor-power?" *Philosophy and Public Affairs*, vol. 14, no. 1 (1985).

terms of liberal discourse – these truisms are incontestable. At the same time, they tell us nothing of substance about the impact of capitalist and socialist institutions on the freedom of workers. Most particularly, Cohen's arguments tell us nothing about the *comparative freedom* of workers under capitalist and socialist institutions. I shall myself advance a number of arguments for supposing that workers as a class under socialism are likely to be less free than they are under capitalism. But even if my arguments for the greater freedom of workers under capitalism are inconclusive, Cohen's argument for proletarian unfreedom demonstrably fails.

I. PRIVATE PROPERTY, CAPITALISM, AND LIBERTY

   Cohen argues first that capitalism cannot constitute or be equated with liberty (even economic liberty) because capitalist institutions rest upon, or comprehend, private property. Private property, Cohen maintains, necessarily restricts liberty. (For the purposes of my argument, I shall follow Cohen's example in treating "liberty" and "freedom" as synonyms. I do not intend to endorse any *general* thesis of their synonymy.) He asserts: "free enterprise economies rest upon private property: you can sell and buy only what you respectively own and come to own. It follows that such economies pervasively restrict liberty. They are complex structures of freedom and unfreedom."[2] Or, as Cohen put it in a later essay: "private property pretty well *is* a particular way of distributing freedom *and unfreedom*. It is necessarily associated with the liberty of private owners to do as they wish with what they own but it no less necessarily withdraws liberty from those who do not own it. To think of capitalism as a realm of freedom is to overlook half its nature."[3] In the latter paper Cohen spells out his point more systematically: "For consider," he urges, "if the State prevents me from doing something I want to do, it evidently places a constraint on my freedom. Suppose, then, that I want to perform an action which involves a legally prohibited use of your property. I want, let us say, to pitch a tent in your large back garden. . . . If I now try to do this thing I want to do, the chances are that the State will intervene on your behalf. If it does, I shall suffer a constraint on my freedom. The same goes for all unpermitted uses of a piece of private property by those who do not own it, and there are always those who do not own it, since 'private ownership by one person presupposes non-ownership on the part of other persons'."[4] Cohen in his earlier piece uses a similar example to make the very same point: "Let us

---

[2] Cohen, "Capitalism," p. 12.
[3] Cohen, "Illusions," p. 227.
[4] *ibid.*, pp. 226–227.

suppose that I wish to take Mr. Morgan's yacht, and go for a spin. If I try to, then it is probable that its owner, aided by law-enforcing others, will stop me. I cannot do this thing that I wish to do, because others will interfere. But liberty, as Narveson (has) reasonably said, is 'doing what we wish without the interference of others.' It follows that I lack a liberty here."[5]

Cohen's argument, then, is that private property institutions restrict liberty, because their existence or enforcement involves interferences with some persons doing as they wish. He adopts here Jan Narveson's rough account of liberty as "doing what we wish without the interference of others," saying that "when a man cannot do what he wishes, because others will interfere, he is unfree."[6] For the purpose of assessing this argument of Cohen's, I shall follow him in adopting Narveson's definition.

If this argument of Cohen's aims to show that the liberty-limiting effects of private property institutions are peculiar to or distinctive of private property, it fails. In part it trades on the truism that one person's freedom, like one person's private ownership, always entails another's restraint or unfreedom: if anyone has a freedom to do something, this means at least that others do not prevent him from doing it. But this thesis of the correlativity of freedom with unfreedom – the theory that having or exercising freedom always presupposes or entails restraint of freedom – has no special connections with the notion of property. One person's freedom to do something has as its shadow the unfreedom of other persons to prevent him from (or interfere with him) doing it, just as one person's owning something has its shadow in others' not owning it. These are perfectly formal truths within a certain discourse of freedom. They tell us nothing about the weight or importance of the unfreedoms generated by private property institutions.

This last remark may be stated in another way. *All* property institutions – capitalist, socialist, feudal, or whatever – impose constraints on the liberties of those who live under them. It is true of every system of property that there will be many things that persons wish to do that they will be interfered with (or prevented from) doing. This is only an entailment of the evident truth that all systems of property are embodied in legal and moral rules which create opportunities and limit the options of those who live under them, where these opportunities and options will have a significant impact on the freedoms of the various social groups affected by them. Most obviously, insofar as the moral and legal rules that go to make a system of property are enforced, those who wish and attempt to act

[5] Cohen, "Capitalism," pp. 11–12.
[6] *ibid.*, p. 11.

in ways prohibited by these rules will be restrained from doing so, or at
least be under threat of such restraint. Their liberty will thereby be
curtailed. This is manifestly true of *any* institution of property. Only a
Hobbesian state of nature, in which no one owns anything because there
are no enforceable rules about property, might appear to form an exception
to this truth. Even there, where there is no system of property but only the
fact of possession, persons will often be prevented from doing as they wish
by others' possession of things the former need in order to implement their
plans. There is then a restraint of liberty, not only under any institution of
property, private or collective, but in any society in which anyone possesses
anything – that is to say, in almost any imaginable condition of social life.

This exceedingly obvious truth may be illustrated with an example.
Consider a society which holds its means of production in common
ownership and whose citizens have only use-rights as individuals over
them. Think of a coastal tribe which lives by fishing and whose means of
production are canoes. The canoes are owned by the tribal community as a
whole, but each individual tribesman has use-rights in them. How does
such an institution of communal ownership bear on the freedom of the
tribesmen who live under it? It is clear that there are many things that
individual tribesmen may wish to do which they will be interfered with in
or prevented from doing. They cannot use them any more frequently, or
for longer time periods, than the usufructuary rules allow. No tribesman
can (without threat of sanction) take a canoe for his exclusive and
permanent use, or give a canoe away as a gift, or sell or rent a canoe to a
non-tribesman. If a tribesman tries to do any of these things, the property
rules of this system of communal ownership will be enforced against him.
He may be ostracized, or punished by loss of his use-rights in the canoes.
Again, if the property system in the tribe is truly communal ownership in
the means of production, and not one of corporate ownership, the
tribesman will have no "share" in the means of production which he can
take with him if he chooses to leave the community. The tribe might allow
use-rights in canoes to be sold, but to the extent that it did, its system of
communal ownership of the canoes would be attenuated. For this reason, a
system of true communal ownership has clear implications for the liberty of
migration from the community. Tribesmen might not be prevented from or
interfered with in leaving the community, but it would be harder for them
to do so, since they would leave with little or nothing. Investing in a new
means of production would be similarly difficult, or impossible, for the
tribesmen as individuals. These last points aside, it is transparently clear
that, even as such a system of communal ownership creates and enlarges
freedom in some respects, it restrains and curtails it in others. Communal
ownership, one might say, pretty well *is* a distribution of freedom *and*

unfreedom. Like any system of property rules, communal ownership is a complex structure of freedom and unfreedom. To think of communal ownership as a realm of freedom is to miss half its nature.

This point may be further illustrated by a consideration of Cohen's own example of communal ownership: "Neighbors A and B own sets of household tools. Each has some tools which the other lacks. If A needs a tool of a kind which only B has, then, private property being what it is, he is not free to take B's one for a while, even if B does not need it during that while. Now imagine that the following rule is imposed, bringing the tools into partly common ownership: each may take and use a tool belonging to the other without permission provided that the other is not using it and that he returns it when he no longer needs it, or when the other needs it, whichever comes first. *Things being what they are* (an important qualification: we are talking, as often we should, about the real world, not about remote possibilities), the communising rule would, I contend, increase tool-using freedom, on any reasonable view."[7]

Cohen's confident judgment that communal ownership of tools enhances tool-using freedom on any reasonable view is hard to accept. He acknowledges that "some freedoms are removed by the new rule. Neither neighbor is as assured of the same easy access as before to the tools that were wholly his. Sometimes he has to go next door to retrieve one of them. Nor can either now charge the other for use of a tool he himself does not require. But these restrictions will likely be less important than the increased range of tools available."[8] It seems plain that other, more important freedoms will also be lost by the communising rule. There is, first of all, the freedom to engage in long-term planning about the use of tools. Since the tools can be taken without permission at any time when they are not needed for use, neither household can effectively engage in long-term planning of their tool-use. (The inability under Cohen's scheme of households to form and implement plans for long-term tool use may be an implication of a simpler difficulty of his scheme. This is the difficulty that it says nothing about what will be done under it when households "need," or wish to use, tools at the same time.) It is precisely this loss of freedom resulting from the inability to make long-term plans that has in many societies led to usufructuary rules of property being supplanted by ones based on individual ownership, which allow for contractual arrangements for the renting of tools and other capital assets. There is, in addition, the freedom, which each tool user hitherto enjoyed, of determining the rate of depreciation of the tools. For, in the real

7 *ibid.*, pp. 16–17.
8 *ibid.*, p. 17.

world – and it is the real world we are talking about, not remote possibilities – tools are worn out by the jobs they do. Different jobs wear out tools at different rates and in different ways, as do different ways of using tools. Under the communizing property rule, no one has the freedom to decide on a rate of depreciation or to implement the policies needed to secure it. Nor – and this is a distinct point, though one that follows from the preceding one – does anyone have the freedom to decide when the tools are to be replaced, whether because they are worn out or because new tools have become available which do the job better. These are freedoms possessed and exercised under private property institutions which wither or disappear under the communist rule. They are not unimportant freedoms for tool users. Their loss under the communist rule must diminish tool-using freedom in important respects not mentioned in Cohen's account of it.

It might be objected that these criticisms depend on interpreting Cohen as hypothesizing a system of full communal ownership, whereas what he sketches is one of only partial common ownership. I am unsure how partial common ownership of tools is to be understood, but, most naturally, it would seem to mean that, when the need of the owner to use the tool competes with that of his neighbor, the owner's need trumps that of the neighbor. The owner does not have an unencumbered right of liberal ownership in the tool, then, but he can always retain or retrieve the tool from his neighbor when he needs to use it. Against this interpretation of Cohen's scheme, I maintain that it does not describe any system of property rights that is workable in the real world. Who is to decide when the owner needs the tool, and who is to arbitrate disputes as to when it is needed by him? If the owner refuses to hand over the tool to the neighbor, because he believes the neighbor's use of it will depreciate the tool to the point that his own future needs for it will go unmet, is he acting within his rights under the scheme of partly communal ownership? Would he be doing so if he retained the tool on the ground that he is uncertain how long he will need it for a job in which he is currently engaged, or about to start? In the real world, it is reasonable to suppose, these questions would be answered by the scheme of partly communal ownership collapsing into full private property or full communism in tools. The scheme of partly communal ownership is, for this reason, an unviable halfway house, and cannot be invoked to answer the criticisms I have developed earlier. I accordingly disregard this interpretation, and proceed on the assumption that, if Cohen's scheme is to be a genuine alternative to private ownership in tools, it must encompass fully communal ownership of them.

It might further be objected that the sense of freedom has shifted here from freedom as noninterference with what one wishes to do to a sense in which it designates the options available.[9] The objection is not an absurd one, but it is baseless. If each tool user wishes to plan long-term use of the tools, determine their rate of depreciation, or implement a decision as to their replacement, he will be prevented from doing so unless all the other tool users accede to his wishes. Just as under private property institutions an owner has a veto over nonowners as to the uses to which his property is put, so under communal ownership every participant in the communal ownership scheme has under the rules constituting the scheme a veto over the uses to which the common assets are put. In Cohen's example, any member of the communal ownership scheme can invoke the communist rule against any of the uses I have mentioned. To be sure, there is a logical possibility that all the co-owners will come to agreement on the uses to which I have referred, so that no one will in fact be prevented from doing as he wishes. In the real world, given that persons have different purposes, values, and rates of time preference, this is a most remote possibility, but even if – granting a socialist transformation of human nature and a correspondingly greater conformism in values among the co-owners – it is irrelevant to the issue at hand. For, as Cohen himself appears to think,[10] freedom as noninterference is curtailed not only when a person cannot in fact act as he wishes (because of interferences by others), but also, counterfactually, when it is true that he *would* be interfered with if he acted on desires he does not in fact possess. Thus, in Cohen's example, tool users are denied freedom to determine rates of depreciation of tools, and so on, even if they never in fact wish to so determine them. They are denied that freedom because, *if* they so wished, the communist rule could be invoked and enforced against them. They would then be prevented from doing as they wished to do. It is incontrovertible that this is a real and important set of freedoms that has thereby been lost. Moreover, these are freedoms that would be attenuated or diminished, if (in response to the problems I have adduced) the communist rule were qualified by another rule – a majoritarian rule, say – for the adjudication of issues of capital depreciation and investment. Even if it were so qualified by majoritarian decision procedures, the communist rule would still extinguish tool-using freedoms possessed under private property institutions. True, if all accepted the outcome of a majority decision, even where it went against the preferences of some, it could not be said that any had been coerced. The freedom of some would still have been reduced, however, since (as we have

---

[9] The "negative" view of freedom as noninterference shifts easily into a view of freedom as nonrestriction of options. On this see John Gray, "Negative and Positive Liberty" John Gray and Z.A. Pelczynsi, eds., *Conceptions of Liberty in Political Philosophy* (London and New York: Athlone Press and St. Martin's Press, 1984), pp. 321–348.

[10] Cohen, "Structure," p. 250, footnote 21.

noted in the case of unanimous agreement) they would have been coerced in the counterfactual case in which they did not accept the majority decision. It is a nice question for Cohen's account, though not one I can address here, whether tool-using freedom is greater under the unqualified communist rule, or under a communist rule qualified by majoritarian (or other) procedures. What is unambiguously clear is that important tool-using freedoms are lost in either case.

It is hard, then, to understand Cohen's confidence in asserting that, in this example, freedom for tool users has on any reasonable view been expanded. For myself, I incline to the contrary view: on any reasonable view, freedom has been diminished for tool users in Cohen's example. I will not press this last point, however, since I will return to the question of judgments of on-balance freedom in Section VI of this paper. Certainly, I do not deny that there are cases where it is reasonable for reasonable men to disagree in their judgments of on-balance freedom. Perhaps Cohen's example is such a case. It remains indisputable that private and communal property systems each generate and distribute freedoms and unfreedoms and that Cohen has said nothing which has a tendency to show that communal ownership has the advantage from the standpoint of liberty.

II. COHEN'S CONCEPTION OF FREEDOM: A DIGRESSION

It is worth pausing at this point to remark that the conception of freedom that Cohen deploys throughout his writings on proletarian unfreedom is not Marx's, but instead one derived from liberal discourse. As Cohen theorizes it, freedom is noninterference with individuals acting as they wish to act (or might wish to act). This is a conception of freedom defended forcefully by Bentham and developed with great power in our own times by Isaiah Berlin.[11] In the context of Cohen's argument, this liberal conception of freedom has several salient features. In it, freedom is sharply distinguished from other values. Freedom is freedom, not justice, welfare or whatever: it is one value among many. (Each thing is what it is, and not another thing.) In general, in fact, Cohen seems to want to work with a conception of freedom that is value-free and morally neutral, so that judgments about freedom will be empirical rather than normative claims. This is a point to which I shall return in Section IV of this paper. Again, freedom is attributed primarily to individuals, and not to groups, collectives, or classes. This is so (or appears to be so) even when the freedom Cohen is theorizing is a form of collective freedom. Finally, freedom as Cohen conceives of it is a matter of degree. This is so, inasmuch as some persons may typically be interfered with less than others

---

[11] On Berlin's conception of freedom, see Gray, "Negative."

in doing what they want. In a capitalist society, for example, according to Cohen, owners of property are typically freer than nonowners. It is precisely Cohen's thesis that in capitalist society owners of property have freedoms which proletarians lack.

It is clear enough that this is a distinctively liberal conception of freedom that is being invoked by Cohen. It would not be endorsed by critics of liberalism such as Arendt or Marcuse,[12] and, if it accords with ordinary usage, it is with the ordinary usage of liberal societies. It is no less clear that the conception of freedom that Cohen employs is not Marx's. It has been argued persuasively elsewhere that Cohen's view of freedom is not only distinct from but incompatible and incommensurable with Marx's.[13] I will not rehearse these arguments here, but a few points, unavoidably brief and dogmatic in character, are worth making about the many points of contrast between Cohen's liberal notion of freedom and the conception employed by Marx. It is, to begin with, important to note that Marx's conception of freedom is on any plausible view not value-free but value-dependent: it embodies or expresses a distinctive view of the human good. Very roughly, this is the view that the good for man is found in conscious, cooperative productive activity (and not, for example, in the individual pursuit of pleasure or in contemplation). Again, freedom is not on Marx's view to be attributed primarily to individuals. It is predicated of the human species itself and of individuals only as instances of it (or, perhaps, as members of the various social classes which constitute the historic self-disclosure of the species in its precommunist manifestations). For this reason, it is wholly unclear that one person's freedom can in the Marxian account (as it plainly does in Cohen's liberal account) conflict with another's. In class society, the freedom of a proletarian to do something may indeed conflict with that of a capitalist, but in communist society, as Marx sketchily conceives of it, it seems that there will be no important instances where freedoms conflict. Finally, it was not Marx's view that, whereas proletarians were rendered unfree by capitalist institutions, capitalists themselves were free (or even freer) under them. Marx's view, surely, was that *both* capitalists and proletarians are unfree under capitalism, even if (or precisely because) the freedom of a proletarian to do something is rendered nugatory by a conflicting freedom of a capitalist. For Marx, freedom is a collective good rather than an attribute of individuals,

[12] See H. Marcuse, "Repressive Tolerance," in *A Critique of Repressive Tolerance* (Boston: Beacon Press, 1968), and H. Arendt, "The Revolutionary Tradition and its Lost Treasure," M. Sandel, ed., *Liberalism and Its Critics* (New York: New York University Press, 1984), pp. 239–263.

[13] George G. Brenkert, "Cohen on Proletarian Unfreedom," *Philosophy and Public Affairs*, vol. 14 (1985), pp. 93–98; John Gray, "Marxian Freedom, Individual Liberty and the End of Alienation," *Social Philosophy and Policy*, vol. 3, no. 2 (1986), pp. 170–174.

and (at any rate in communist society) it is otiose to consider how conflicts among individual liberties are to be arbitrated or resolved. It is because Marx conceives freedom in this way that he can claim to be developing a genuine critique of bourgeois notions about liberty.

Cohen's argument, by contrast, aims to be an immanent criticism of the liberal understanding of freedom. He wishes to show that capitalist societies contain important unfreedoms by the *standard of liberal freedom itself.*[14] The principal burden of my criticism of Cohen is that his argument issues in claims of an entirely formal sort, which give no strength to a case for the specific disadvantages of capitalism in terms of freedom. Accordingly, save for the arguments of Section VI, in which I attempt a *substantive* assessment of capitalist and socialist institutions in terms of workers' freedom, my own critique of Cohen is also an immanent criticism. For the purposes of my argument I accept the liberal conception of freedom. Whether it is an adequate conception is another question, which I hope to address on another occasion.

III.   INDIVIDUAL LIBERTY AND COLLECTIVE UNFREEDOM

Cohen's second argument for proletarian unfreedom turns on the claim that any member of a group may be free to do something that every member of the group is not free to do. Thus, whereas it may be the case that any worker can become a capitalist, it does not follow that workers as a class are free so to do. (I am here following Cohen's conception of capitalism, which in turn follows Marx's. For them, a capitalist society is not simply one exhibiting private property in the means of production – since many societies, including societies of yeoman farmers, say, exhibit this feature – but one in which a propertyless majority must sell its labor to a capital-owning minority. At this stage, I will not dispute this understanding of capitalism, since I will question its adequacy later in my argument.) For Cohen, the unfreedom of workers under capitalism is in the fact that "each is free only on condition that the others do not exercise their similarly conditional freedom,"[15] so that "though most proletarians are free to escape the proletariat, indeed even if all are, the proletariat is an imprisoned class."[16] In other words, if the freedom of any worker to leave his class depends on the fact that most others do not also attempt to leave it, then the class of workers is unfree even if every worker has the freedom to become a capitalist.

These arguments, first stated in Cohen's paper of 1979, are developed

---

[14] I do not mean to suggest that Cohen's is the best statement of a liberal negative view of freedom, but only that it is Cohen's that I shall deploy in my argument against him.
[15] Cohen, "Structure," p. 244.
[16] *ibid.*, p. 245.

in his paper of 1983. There he cites Marx's remark that "in this bourgeois society every workman, if he is an exceedingly clever and shrewd fellow, and gifted with bourgeois instincts and favored by an exceptional fortune, can possibly convert himself into an *exploiteur du travail d'autrui*. But if there were no *travail* to be *exploite*, there would be no capitalist nor capitalist production."[17] Cohen develops the thought contained in Marx's remark by way of an example:

> Ten people are placed in a room the only exit from which is a huge and heavy locked door. At various distances from each lies a single heavy key. Whoever picks this up – and each is physically able, with varying degrees of effort, to do so – and takes it to the door will find, after considerable self-application, a way to open the door and leave the room. But, if he does so, he alone will be able to leave it. Photoelectric devices installed by a jailer ensure that it will open only just enough to permit one exit. Then it will close, and no one inside the room will be able to open it again.
>
> It follows that, whatever happens, at least nine people will remain in the room.[18]

Cohen argues from this analogy that

> Each is free to seize the key and leave. But note the conditional nature of his freedom. He is free not only *because* none of the others tries to get the key, but *on condition* that they do not. . . . Not more than one can exercise the liberties they all have. If, moreover, any one were to exercise it, then, because of the structure of the situation, all the others would lose it.
>
> Since the freedom of each is contingent on the others not exercising their similarly contingent freedom, we can say there is a great deal of unfreedom in their situation. Though each is individually free to leave, he suffers with the rest from what I shall call *collective unfreedom*.[19]

Cohen's argument here is, perhaps, a more substantive version, or a concrete application, of the thesis of the correlativity of freedom with unfreedom: the freedom of the few workers who become capitalists presupposes the collective unfreedom of the many workers who do not. Now it is worth observing that there is so far nothing very determinate in this relationship of individual liberty with collective unfreedom under

[17] *ibid.*, p. 242, footnote 7.
[18] *ibid.*, p. 242.
[19] *ibid.*, p. 244.

capitalism. We do not know *how many* workers becoming capitalists would overturn Cohen's argument. Suppose most workers had a period as capitalists during their lives. Would this render Cohen's attribution of collective unfreedom to the proletarian class invalid? Cohen might allow that collective proletarian unfreedom no longer exists in a society in which most workers spend part of their lives as capitalists, but deny that the economic system in which this can occur is any longer clearly a capitalist system. Such a denial seems unreasonable. In our supposition of a society in which most workers are capitalists for part of their lives, the constitutive institutions of capitalism – private ownership of the means of production and market allocation of capital and income – are by hypothesis fully preserved. (That is the point of hypothesizing that most workers spend part of their lives *as capitalists*.) Admittedly, Cohen might object that capitalism necessarily presupposes a propertyless proletarian majority, and, if he did, his objection would be an authentically Marxian one. That is not a sufficient reason for accepting Cohen's objection, however, since it amounts to identifying capitalist institutions with that nineteenth century variant of them studied by Marx and, thereby, ruling out *a priori* the possibility of the proletarianless capitalism. I shall return to this last point later. Against my criticism, Cohen might further argue that whether or not workers are free in a system in which they spend part of their lives as capitalists depends crucially on *how much* of their lives workers spend as capitalists. This seems to be part of the force of Cohen's assertion that "the manifest intent of the Marxist claim is that the proletariat is forced at (time) t to *continue* to sell his labor power, throughout a period from t to $t + n$, for some considerable n."[20] The point here is not unreasonable. If most workers had to sell their labor power for only a small part of their lives, if (in other words) they spent most of their lives as capitalists, they would no longer be proletarians. In this circumstance, indeed, the proletariat – and with it proletarian unfreedom – would have all but disappeared. In the hypothetical case I have invoked, however, the near disappearance of proletarian unfreedom comes about in virtue of the spread of capital among the workers rather than by the abolition of capitalist institutions.

It is, of course, a standard position in Marxian political economy that the kind of society I have envisaged cannot exist, or cannot exist for very long. Processes of market concentration and proletarian immiseration will prevent the diffusion of capital among workers which alone could raise them within capitalism from the status of proletarians. This is an empirical claim in economic theory which is open for us to dispute: developments such as the growth of pension funds and of labor unions with significant capital assets might be seen as giving evidence of a trend towards the sort

[20] *ibid.*, p. 241.

of capitalism-without-a-proletariat to which my hypothetical example points. Cohen's model of capitalist property institutions, in which the capitalist is the sole proprietor of the means of production, is an anachronistic one, best suited to economic life in England in the early nineteenth century. It has little relevance to the late twentieth century reality, encompassing employee shareholding, management buy-outs, and profit-related pay. It may be premature or speculative to suggest that these developments attest to a trend to a proletarianless capitalism. Nevertheless, even were my example to remain entirely hypothetical, it would demonstrate that, as a matter of its structure or logic, proletarian unfreedom as Cohen conceives of it may be overcome, abolished, or reduced in a variety of ways, of which socialism is (at best) only one.

The indeterminacies in the relation between individual liberty and collective unfreedom under capitalism have implications of another sort for Cohen's argument. Cohen allows that "collective unfreedom comes in varying amounts, and it is greater the smaller the ratio of the maximum that could perform it to the total number in the group."[21] (It seems to be an implication of Cohen's view that collective unfreedom is a variable magnitude that collective freedom likewise comes in varying amounts. Whether it follows from this that a circumstance of complete collective freedom is impossible, since one collective freedom entails another collective unfreedom, is a question I cannot here pursue.) If collective unfreedom is thus a matter of degree – and not, for example, a condition in which individuals simply are or are not – then it matters vitally how large, *and how variable*, are the opportunities of individual emancipation by the acquisition of capitalist status. Perhaps the more proletarians there are who seek to become capitalists, the more opportunities there will be for them to do so. The possibility certainly cannot be excluded *a priori*, and, as I have already argued, the empirical theory which would deny it is at least controversial and disputable. Cohen's argument seems to depend on the assumption that, no matter how large the number of proletarians seeking to become capitalists, the number of opportunities to do so will remain fixed, or at least not expand significantly. He makes explicit this assumption when he discusses another example of collective unfreedom:

> Suppose, for instance, that a hotel, at which one hundred tourists are staying, lays on a coach trip for the first forty who apply, since that is the number of seats on the coach. And suppose that only thirty want to go. Then, on my account, each of the hundred is free to go, but their situation displays a collective unfreedom.[22]

[21] *ibid.*, p. 248.
[22] *ibid.*, p. 250.

Cohen goes on:

> The coach case is a rather special one. For we tend to suppose that the management lay on only one coach because they correctly anticipate that one will be enough to meet the demand. Accordingly, we also suppose that if more had wanted to go, there would have been an appropriately larger number of seats available. If all that is true, then the available amount of collective freedom non-accidentally accords with the tourists' desires, and, though there is still a collective unfreedom, it is, as it were, a purely technical one. But if we assume there is only one coach in town, *and some such assumption is required for parity with the situation of proletarians*, then the tourists' collective unfreedom is more than merely technical.[23]

Cohen's assumption of fixity in the range of opportunities for workers' escape from proletarian status, which he admits is essential to the argument for proletarian unfreedom, seems entirely arbitrary. It is defensible, if at all, only by reference to propositions in Marxian economic theory, which are nowhere argued by Cohen. These are propositions having to do with the systemic scarcity of capital under the capitalist system. It is this alleged scarcity, presumably, which explains the claim that there are so few points of access from the proletariat to the capitalist class. I do not think it can fairly be said that there is any plausible contemporary statement of Marxian economic theory which supports the claim that capital is subject to a sort of endemic scarcity under capitalism. Much empirical evidence would in any case count against such a claim. Indeed, there is evidence that suggests a conjecture directly opposed to that of Marxian theory – the conjecture that, the more workers succeed in becoming capitalists, the greater are the opportunities of the remainder so to do. This is to say that the analogy of the locked room from which only one person can escape may be wholly misleading. A better analogy might be that of a group seeking to climb a mountain, where the more members of the group succeed in doing so, the easier it is for those left behind to be raised up by the strength of those who have gone on before. There is nothing to say that such an analogy does not fit the case of modern capitalism better than Cohen's. In any event, in the absence of a plausible theory which gives to the relation between individual liberty and collective unfreedom under capitalism the determinacy or fixity which Cohen admits to be necessary to his argument, we have no reason to think proletarian unfreedom a necessary feature of capitalism. Or, to put the matter in different terms, the indeterminacies of

[23] *ibid.*, p. 250.

the relationship that Cohen postulates between individual workers and their class situation are abated only by invoking an empirical theory he gives us no reason to accept.

The most fundamental objection to this argument of Cohen's is an altogether different one. It is one that focuses on the condition of simultaneous or joint access to some opportunity, action, or status which Cohen specifies as a necessary condition of freedom in respect of it. Cohen specifies this condition, negatively and by implication, when he specifies the necessary and sufficient condition of collective unfreedom. He tells us: "Collective unfreedom can be defined as follows: a group suffers collective unfreedom with respect to a type of action A if and only if performance of A by all members of the group is impossible."[24] He clarifies further: "A person shares in a collective unfreedom when, to put it roughly, he is among those who are so situated that if enough others exercise the corresponding individual freedom, then they lose their individual freedom."[25] Cohen's definition of collective unfreedom seems radically at variance with much of our standard thought. We do not usually suppose that, unless any subscriber to a telephone system can use it at the same time as every other or most other subscribers, then the entire class of telephone users is rendered unfree by the system. Perhaps Cohen would maintain that this example, though technically a case of collective unfreedom, is not an interesting one. Let us concede the point. I do not think that that could be said of many social institutions of which his definition would yield a description in terms of collective unfreedom. Consider, in this regard, the institution (proposed by C.B. Macpherson[26] and others as a device for diminishing risks to individual liberty under socialism) of the guaranteed minimum income. The guaranteed minimum income, like many other socialist institutions, depends for its existence on its being used at any one time by only a few. The freedom of any worker to take up his guaranteed income, and to live on that alone, depends on the unfreedom of most others, whose labor sustains the guaranteed income scheme.

On Cohen's definition, all workers in the socialist society are rendered unfree by the guaranteed income scheme. Recall in this connection his statement that "a group suffers collective unfreedom with respect to a type of action A if and only if performance of A by all members of the group is impossible."[27] We may go further. Each socialist worker is free to live on the guaranteed income not only *because* most others do not, but *on condition* that they do not. Then *each socialist worker is free (to live on the guaranteed*

---

[24] *ibid.*, p. 248.
[25] *ibid.*, p. 248.
[26] C.B. Macpherson, *Democratic Theory* (Oxford: Clarendon Press, 1973), p. 154.
[27] Cohen, "Structure," p. 248.

income) only on condition that the others do not exercise their similarly conditional freedom. Not more than a few workers can, at any one time, exercise the liberty they have. If, moreover, more than a few were at any time to exercise it, then, because of the structure of the situation, all the others would lose even this conditional freedom. Since the freedom of each socialist worker is contingent on the others not exercising their similarly contingent freedom, we can say that there is a great deal of unfreedom in their situation. Though each is individually free to live on the guaranteed income, he suffers with the rest from a form of *collective unfreedom.*

Like the collective unfreedom suffered by proletarians under capitalism, the collective unfreedom of socialist workers in respect of the guaranteed income is suffered by them as individuals. It is not a group unfreedom. "A person shares in a collective unfreedom when, to put it roughly, he is among those who are so situated that if enough others exercise the corresponding individual freedom, then they lose their individual freedoms."[28] By contrast with genuine collective unfreedom, the unfreedom of the proletariat to overthrow capitalism is a group unfreedom, since "no individual proletarian could ever be free to overthrow capitalism, even when the proletariat is free to do so."[29] By this criterion, the unfreedom of the socialist worker in respect of the guaranteed income is a genuine one and not a group unfreedom. Structurally, it is no different from proletarian unfreedom under capitalism.

I am leaving aside here the important question of whether, when collective freedoms are lost by individuals, what is lost are individual freedoms. For Cohen's argument to go through, it must be the case that collective freedoms are not only freedoms possessed or lost by individuals, but also instances of individual freedom as he conceives of it. This is to say that collective unfreedom and freedom may be analyzable in terms of interference and noninterference with individuals' opportunities to act as they wish. Yet there is in Cohen no systematic argument for the reducibility of collective freedom and unfreedom to individual freedom and its absence. (Perhaps Cohen thinks that collective and individual unfreedoms are extensionally equivalent, but not collective and individual freedoms, but he does not argue this, and it is hard to see how such an asymmetry could be sustained.) Nor is this surprising, since the two sorts of freedom seem on the face of it categorically distinct, and possibly even incommensurable notions of freedom. I mention this gap in Cohen's reasoning, not in order to try to demonstrate that there are indeed two notions of freedom at stake in his argument, but simply to remark that his

[28] *ibid.*
[29] *ibid.*, p. 249.

argument founders unless one kind of freedom (or unfreedom), the collective sort, is reducible without remainder to the other, individual sort of freedom and unfreedom.

The analogy between proletarian unfreedom under capitalism and worker unfreedom under socialism (in respect of the guaranteed income), though close, is not exact. In the case of proletarian unfreedom, as Cohen conceives of it, there are a few that are free in capitalist society – the capitalists (including those proletarians who succeed in becoming such). The reference group of those suffering a collective unfreedom to become capitalists cannot encompass the capitalists themselves. In the socialist society, all are unfree with regard to the guaranteed income. (There is an asymmetry here between the collective unfreedoms at issue if, as I have earlier argued, a capitalist society might exist in which all are capitalists, and if, as seems self-evident, there can be no socialist society in which all live on the guaranteed income and nothing else.) This brings out again an important point – that collective unfreedom, no less than individual unfreedom, is for Cohen a matter of degree. Individuals, as members of societies or groups, may suffer varying degrees of collective unfreedom. In Section VI of this paper, I will argue that socialist institutions may generate more collective unfreedom for workers than do capitalist institutions. This is so even if collective unfreedom is (as I have argued earlier) a pervasive feature of social institutions generally. At this point, I want to observe only that, whereas not all are unfree under capitalist institutions (to become capitalists), there is at least one collective unfreedom which all suffer under socialism – that relative to the guaranteed income. It is unclear to me whether Cohen would consider this a lesser degree of collective unfreedom than that which obtains for workers in capitalist societies.

In fact, Cohen appears to think that not all collective unfreedoms are undesirable simply on account of the unfreedom they contain. He tells us that "some collective unfreedom, like some individual unfreedom, is not lamentable." And, crucially, he goes on: "It is what this particular unfreedom forces workers to do which makes it a proper object of regret and protest. They are forced to subordinate themselves to others who thereby gain control over their, the workers', productive existence."[30] This is a crucial passage inasmuch as it aims to specify what is bad or wrong in the collective unfreedom of proletarians under capitalism. It is an extremely unsatisfactory passage, at the same time, since subordination to others and control by these others of workers' productive life is not peculiar to, or even distinctive of capitalist institutions. Workers may, as I shall later argue, be forced to work for others in a socialist system, thereby losing

---

[30] *ibid.*, p. 251.

control of their productive lives. What is distinctive of, or peculiar to capitalism, is that workers *sell* their labor – an option denied them under feudal and socialist institutions. Cohen has said nothing, however, to show the special evil of such selling of workers' labor. If, on the other hand, the lamentable aspect of proletarian collective unfreedom is in the fact that the option of not working at all is an undesirable one, so that workers are forced to work, then it must be observed that this is a collective unfreedom found in all societies, albeit in crucially variable degrees. Cohen here in fact comes close to conceding my argument that collective unfreedom is a pervasive property of social institutions[31] and is to be found as clearly in the institutions of a socialist society as it is in those of capitalism. Thus, nothing of importance appears to follow from Cohen's arguments about the collective unfreedom of proletarians. In the absence of further considerations, there is nothing to say whether their unfreedom is lamentable or not, or, in general, to show that it is a proper object of moral concern. He achieves the result that proletarian collective unfreedom is an interesting and lamentable unfreedom, rather than a technical or trivial one, only by invoking the altogether independent claim that workers are forced to subordinate themselves to others who thereby gain control over their productive lives. Without this further consideration, the argument that proletarians suffer a collective unfreedom, though perhaps valid, is uninteresting and indeed trivial.

This conclusion follows inexorably from the logic of Cohen's argument. Like any other sort of unfreedom, collective unfreedom is not for Cohen necessarily an evil. For, like the concept of freedom in general, the concept of collective freedom is supposed to be value-free. Accordingly, the badness, wrongness, or moral importance of a specific collective unfreedom must depend on other considerations. (Presumably, it is these other considerations that are invoked *when we make comparative judgments of collective unfreedom*.) In Cohen's account, the importance of collective proletarian unfreedom is explained by reference to the claim that workers are forced to work for capitalists. It is therefore to Cohen's arguments about force and freedom in the workers' situation that I turn for illumination.

IV. LIBERTY, FORCE, AND JUSTICE

Cohen believes, with Marx, that workers are forced to sell their labor power to capitalists, and are thereby rendered unfree. He thinks that workers under capitalism may be in some important respects freer than

---

[31] Cohen coments approvingly ("Structure," p. 245, footnote 10) on Elster's perceptive observation that "such structures [of collective unfreedom] pervade social life."

Marx supposed.[32] But he defines workers (under capitalism) as "those who are forced to sell their labour-power." He stipulates that "a man is a proletarian if and only if he is forced to sell his labour power." He asks: "Is the stated condition necessary and sufficient? Certainly not all who sell their labour power are proletarians, but the condition is that one be *forced* to sell it. Still, it must be admitted that plenty of salaried non-proletarians are as much forced as many workers. So the condition is not sufficient." He goes on further to ask "whether the condition is a necessary one: *are* proletarians forced to sell their labour power?" He informs us that "Robert Nozick answers negatively," but that "Nozick's objection to our condition rests on a false because moralised account of what it is to be forced to do something."[33]

Let it be noted that Cohen has not so far given us any reason *in favor of* supposing that proletarians are forced to sell their labor power, and thereby are rendered unfree. He has adduced instead an argument *against* Nozick's claim that their having to sell their labor power fails to render them unfree – the argument that Nozick's conception of freedom is "moralised" and so "false." Cohen spells out this argument against Nozick by asserting that "to prevent someone from doing something he wants to do is to make him, in that respect, unfree: I am unfree whenever someone interferes, *justifiably or otherwise*, with my actions. But," Cohen goes on "there is a definition which is implicit in much libertarian writing, and which entails that interference is *not* a sufficient condition of unfreedom. On that definition, which I shall call the *moralised* definition, I am unfree only when someone does or would *unjustifiably* interfere with me."[34] He further develops his argument against Nozick in a later piece, contending that:

> Robert Nozick might grant that many workers have no acceptable alternative to selling their labour-power. . . . But he denies that having no acceptable alternative but to do A entails being forced to do A, no matter how bad A is, and no matter how much worse the alternatives are, since he thinks that to have no acceptable alternative means to be forced only when unjust actions help to explain the absence of acceptable alternatives. . . . Nozick's objection to the thesis under examination rests upon a moralised account of what it is to be forced to do something. It is a false account, because it has the absurd upshot that if a criminal's

[32] Cohen, "Structure," p. 244.
[33] Cohen, "Capitalism," pp. 18–19.
[34] Cohen, "Illusions," p. 228.

imprisonment is morally justified, then he is not forced to be in prison. We may therefore set Nozick's objections aside.[35]

Nozick's argument that workers are not forced to sell their labor power is to be rejected then, according to Cohen, because the idea of unfreedom or forcing which it deploys conflates interference with justifiable interference, which in turn has the absurd result that the justifiably imprisoned man is not forced to remain in jail.

Cohen's argument against Nozick is sloppy and fails for several reasons. To begin with, Nozick's argument is *not* that *justifiable* interferences are not interferences with liberty. It is that the domain of liberty is specified by principles of justice, so that a *justicizable* interference with liberty is an impossibility. What Nozick's view excludes as a possibility is not, then, justified restraint of liberty, but justicizable restraint of liberty – that is to say, restraint of liberty justified in terms of justice. Accordingly, *justified* violation of the liberty demanded by justice remains a violation of liberty. Nozick's account of violating side constraints which protect liberty so as to avert a moral catastrophe[36] tells us this: when we violate side constraints and thereby commit an injustice, we do indeed curtail liberty, but we justify doing so by invoking the larger morality within which justice is usually (but not in this case of potential moral catastrophe) paramount. So, whereas justice and liberty cannot compete with one another, moral considerations may in extremity justify a violation of the liberty demanded by justice. (I pass over the possibility that the scope of justice is bounded or limited by circumstances of moral catastrophe in such a way that rights violations are impossible in such circumstances, since this seems plainly to be a possibility which Nozick does not wish to envisage.) For these reasons, it is mistaken to hold, as Cohen does, that Nozick conflates restraint of liberty with justified restraint of liberty.

It remains true, nonetheless, that Nozick's is a normative conception of liberty. In Nozick's account, the demands of liberty are given by a theory of justice – by the theory of entitlements he sets out in his book. By contrast, Cohen wishes to use only a "neutral" or "non-normative" conception of freedom. Thus he tells us that "whatever may be the correct analysis of 'X is free to do A', it is clear that X is free to do A if X would do A if he tried to do A, and that sufficient condition of freedom is all that we need here."[37] It is this "non-normative" account of freedom[38] that Cohen invokes against Nozick. What are we to make of it? Cohen argues that

---

[35] Cohen, "Structure," p. 238.
[36] Robert Nozick, *Anarchy, State and Utopia* (Oxford: Basil Blackwell, 1974), p. 30.
[37] Cohen, "Structure," p. 243, footnote 8.
[38] *ibid.*

Nozick's view is "unacceptable" because it yields the "absurd" conclusion that "a properly convicted murderer is not rendered unfree when he is justifiably imprisoned."[39] The absurdity of this result is, presumably, in the fact that it conflicts with ordinary-language uses of terms such as "force" and "freedom." Cohen's argument itself rests on a confusion. Consider the case of the would-be rapist who is forcibly prevented from raping his victim. On Nozick's account, it is indeed true that forcibly preventing a rapist from committing the act of rape deprives him of no freedom, since the act of rape encompasses an unjust assault on another person's body and liberty, and is therefore an act which no one is entitled to perform. I, for one, do not find this result particularly counterintuitive. It seems to me to square better with our ordinary linguistic and moral intuitions than the Benthamite view which conceives of laws against rape as restricting the liberty of rapists (if only a worthless or disvaluable liberty) for the sake of protecting the liberty of their victims. I will not press this point, however, since Cohen's confusion arises elsewhere. It is plain to all of us that justice demands the restraint of rapists. Now, on Nozick's account, there is no liberty to commit rape, and so no rapist liberty to be restrained. The rapist is forcibly prevented from committing rape, but *he is not thereby rendered unfree*. At the same time, the rapist's liberty may yet be restrained if he is imprisoned for his crime. To think otherwise is to move illegitimately from the injustice of the act of rape to the justice of the penalty of imprisonment. The mere fact that rape is an injustice, taken by itself, has nothing to tell us as to the just punishment for rape. It does not even tell us that punishment is called for in justice. If it is, then perhaps, as in Islamic law, the just punishment of rape is not loss of liberty but, instead, loss of life. Only a full theory of retributive and corrective justice can tell us what justice demands as the legal remedy for rape. Nozick's entitlement theory of justice makes no claim to comprehend the demands of justice addressed in retributive and corrective theory: its subject matter is a different one. For this reason, it might very well be that imprisonment for the crime of rape constituted a restraint of the rapist's liberty, even if forcibly restraining him from the act of rape did not.

In Nozick's account, liberty has primacy among the demands of justice (as it does in Rawls's theory of justice as fairness). Liberty and justice are linked in Nozick's theory, inasmuch as forcibly restraining A from unjustly restraining B is not to restrain A's liberty. A may be forced to do something, or to refrain from doing something, then, and still not be rendered unfree by that forcible restraint. One must *have* a liberty before it can be restrained. One may be restrained, without it being true that it is

---

[39] Cohen, "Freedom," p. 10.

one's *liberty* that has been restrained. This Nozickian view that forcible prevention of an unjust action is not a restraint of liberty is an entirely general thesis which in no way presupposes Nozick's own account of justice. It is a feature, also, of Rawls's theory, in which private ownership of the means of production is not among the requirements of justice. Against this view of liberty or freedom as a moral notion, Cohen invokes his "neutral" or "non-normative" conception, stated earlier. Cohen's conception of freedom as a value-free notion seems to me unacceptable for a number of reasons. I will not consider these here, however, since I will address them later in this section. Also, they arise from a position in philosophical method held by Cohen which I shall expound and criticize in the next section of this paper.

What are Cohen's arguments *for* the claim that workers under capitalism are forced to sell their labor power? Cohen does not deny that they are unfree so to do, only that they are not free not to do so. Indeed, he insists that workers are free to sell their labor power inasmuch as one is in general free to do what one is forced to do. Being forced to sell their labor power *entails* that workers are free to sell it. He argues:

> before you are forced to do A, you are, at least in standard cases, free to do A and free not to do A. The force removes the second freedom, but why suppose that it removes the first? It puts no obstacle in the way of your doing A, and you therefore remain free to do it. We may conclude, not only that being free to do A is compatible with being forced to do A, but that being forced to do A entails being free to do A. Resistance to this odd-sounding but demonstrable result reflects failure to distinguish the idea of being free to do something from other ideas, such as the idea of *doing something freely*. I am free to do what I am forced to do even if, as is usually true, I do not do it freely, and even though, as is always true, I am not free with respect to whether or not I do it.[40]

Thus, workers in a capitalist society, unlike slaves in a slave society, are free to sell their labor, even though they are forced to do so (and so are unfree not to do so).

The unfreedom in workers having to sell their labor power is for Cohen in the fact that they have no acceptable alternative. They may in a pure capitalist society choose to beg, or starve, but those are not acceptable alternatives: they are accordingly forced to sell their labor power. On the other hand, Cohen allows that, objectively speaking, most proletarians could (as some immigrant groups have done) acquire sufficient capital to

---

[40] Cohen, "Illusions," p. 224.

rise from proletarian status: "Proletarians who have the option of class ascent are not forced to sell their labour power, just because they do have that option. Most proletarians have it as much as our counterexamples (the immigrants) did. Therefore most proletarians are not forced to sell their labour power."[41] Cohen here allows that most proletarians are *not*, in objective fact, forced to sell their labor-power. As he admits: "One would say, speaking rather broadly, that we have found more freedom in the proletariat's situation than classical Marxism asserts."[42] His argument that, though most proletarians are not forced to sell their labor power, they are nevertheless unfree, *is one that appeals solely to the collective proletarian unfreedom created by the conditionality of each proletarian's freedom to leave the proletariat*. This is demonstrated by the fact that, having discussed the case of the people in the locked room, Cohen concludes "by parity of reasoning, that although most proletarians are free to escape the proletariat, and, indeed, even if every one is, the proletariat is collectively unfree, an imprisoned class."[43] This is to make his argument circular. We saw at the end of the last section that the proletariat suffered an interesting, lamentable collective unfreedom, only if it could be shown that it is forced to sell its labor power. We find now that, since most proletarians admittedly are not forced to sell their labor power, the argument for their being unfree not to do so depends on their suffering collective unfreedom as an imprisoned class. We find, in short, that Cohen advances no argument (apart from the weak argument from collective freedom) for the thesis that workers are forced to sell their labor.

The point may be put in another way. The claim that workers are forced to labor under capitalism, because they are not free not to sell their labor power, has a corresponding application to the situations of workers under socialist institutions. Under a pure capitalist system, according to Cohen, the worker has no acceptable alternative to working for the capitalist. The proletarian may choose to beg or starve, but, anciently, it is only an irony at his expense to say that he is free to do so. It is ironical to suggest that the proletarian is free to do these things, since we all know them to be undesirable (and, indeed, unacceptable) alternatives. However, note that, on Cohen's own conception of freedom as being value-free, the proletarian in truth *is* free to beg or starve, even though the statement that he has these freedoms may have an ironical flavor. The proletarian is free to beg or starve because no one in a pure capitalist system will interfere with him in or prevent him from doing these things. In Cohen's account, therefore, *the proletarian is free to leave the proletariat by refusing to sell his labor to the*

[41] Cohen, "Structure," p. 242.
[42] *ibid.*, p. 244.
[43] *ibid.*, p. 241.

capitalist. He has this freedom so long as he may without interference beg or starve.

Though he is free to refuse to sell his labor power to the capitalist, the proletarian is nonetheless forced to do so, since he has no acceptable alternative. He is free to do what he is forced to do, Cohen has already told us, because being free to do something is a necessary condition of being forced to do it. The logic of Cohen's argument requires him to go further than this. It requires him to accept that the proletarian is forced to sell his labor power even though he is free to refuse to do so. This is so, at least in part, because "force," unlike "freedom," is for Cohen a normative concept. It embodies standards of desirability and acceptability. It is only the conjunction of the value-free notion of collective unfreedom with the value-laden notion of force that gives Cohen his conclusion that workers are nontrivially unfree under capitalism.

His argument, then, turns on the claim that workers are forced to sell their labor power under capitalism. (Some may well think that Cohen's account *of freedom* is unacceptable because it has the absurd upshot that proletarians are free to leave the proletariat by turning to beggary or submitting to starvation. I let this pass.) But is it true that they have no acceptable alternative? It would be true, if their only alternatives were beggary or starvation. As we have seen, however, Cohen admits that, objectively speaking, most proletarians are in the same position as immigrant groups – they can become capitalists by accumulating capital. Like immigrants, then, most proletarians have another exit from their proletarian status. They need not become lumpenproletarians, but may become capitalists. Having made this admission, Cohen's only argument for proletarian unfreedom is the claim that most workers cannot exercise this freedom at the same time. This is the argument from collective unfreedom I have already criticized, and it is the only argument Cohen has to offer. If workers have other, acceptable alternatives to leaving the proletariat apart from becoming beggars or starving, then the collective unfreedom which the argument establishes is only a trivial one.

Let us, though, in a spirit of charity, set these arguments aside, and allow that there is a sense that the worker is forced to sell his labor power to the capitalist. Let us proceed to compare the proletarian's situation with that of the worker in a socialist state. By hypothesis, the latter cannot acquire private capital and live off that, and, since beggary will presumably be illegal, he cannot live by begging. Unless he is disabled or ill, and so in receipt of government benefits, his only source of regular livelihood is his income from his work. Perhaps family or friends can support him for a while, but let us suppose that, like beggary under capitalism, this is an unacceptable alternative – always supposing, contrary to the historical experience of actually existing socialist states, that it is an alternative that is not legally forbidden. Since the socialist worker has no acceptable alternative to working for the socialist state, he is *unfree* not to do so. Because he is not free not to work for the socialist state, he is *forced* to do so. This is true whether the political form of the socialist state be democratic or authoritarian, and whether the economic unit of the socialist state is a public corporation or a worker cooperative. All that is required is that state or public authorities be the sole permissible source of employment. The unfreedom of proletarians not to work for capitalists has as its mirror image the unfreedom of socialist workers not to work for the state – or, more precisely, for those who exercise power through the state. Like proletarians, socialist workers find themselves in a situation in which their productive lives are subject to control by others. It is ironical to suggest otherwise.

V.   THEORIES, CONCEPTS, AND PHILOSOPHICAL METHOD

The upshot of my argument is that every charge of unfreedom that Cohen can intelligibly make against capitalism may be made just as well against socialist institutions. If workers are rendered unfree by the system of private property on which capitalism depends, they are also rendered unfree by a communal property system. If they suffer collective unfreedoms under capitalism, they suffer other collective unfreedoms under socialism. If they are not free not to sell their labor power under capitalism, if they are *forced* to sell their labor power under capitalism, they are not free not to work under socialism. This is to say that, in every one of the three respects in which capitalism renders workers unfree, there is a clear parity with a feature of socialist institutions in virtue of which they are rendered unfree. Nor is the reason for this parity hard to find. Insofar as they establish anything, Cohen's arguments give support to a series of conceptual truisms. This is, indeed, the manifest character of Cohen's arguments, which all of them consist in an application of a method of conceptual analysis.

For several reasons, Cohen's adoption of this method in political philosophy is misconceived. In the first place, as I have already argued, it can yield only conceptual truths, if it yields anything at all. Such truths can tell us nothing substantial about the fate of freedom under rival institutional arrangements. To find out about that, we must look to a theory of the real world. As things stand, Cohen appears to suppose that, by eliciting conceptual truths, he is in fact saying something about freedom in the real world. It is hard to explain otherwise his recourse to such portentous expressions as "complex structures of freedom and unfreedom." It is a delusion, however, to suppose that conceptual analysis can tell us the way things are in the world.

The philosophical method which Cohen adopts is in any case superannuated. The "analysis" of "concepts" would be defensible as a strategy in philosophical inquiry if it were the case, as Kant supposed, that the categories of the human understanding were invariant and universal. Otherwise, the object of analysis can only be *words*, in all the miscellaneous diversity of their usages. Among us, at any rate, there is no clear uniformity of usage in respect of the key terms of moral and political discourse. Consider, for example, Cohen's idea of liberty. The notion of freedom within which he works is not an unequivocal deliverance of ordinary language, which contains "normative" as well as "descriptive" uses of "freedom" and "liberty" and their associated expressions. As its most sophisticated exponents have long recognized,[44] a neutral or value-free definition of liberty is a term of art, a technical expression developed as part of a reconstruction by stipulation of the terms of ordinary discourse. Further, even if ordinary usage were consistent, it is wholly unclear that it would have authority for political thought. As Joseph Raz has observed, "linguistic distinctions . . . do not follow any consistent political or moral outlook. . . . What we need is not a definition nor mere conceptual clarity. Useful as these always are they will not solve our problems. What we require are moral principles and arguments to support them."[45] And further: "It is . . . important to remember that that concept [the concept of political freedom] is a product of a theory or a doctrine consisting of moral principles for the guidance and evaluation of political actions and institutions. One can derive a concept from a theory but not the other way round."[46]

Because ordinary language embodies no consistent outlook, the appeal to ordinary language cannot even begin the task of developing a theory of freedom. Even if ordinary usage did disclose a coherent conception of freedom – say, a conception of the liberal species which Cohen deploys unreflectively and without criticism – the conceptual truths derivable from an analysis of such usage would amount only to local knowledge of our current linguistic practices. It is wholly unclear to me why Cohen supposes that local knowledge of this sort should or could be authoritative in moral and political philosophy. Many ordinary-language usages, or "concepts," embody and express repugnant moral judgments. (Consider the rich terminology of popular racism.) Why should the deliverances of ordinary thought and practice have any claim on reason, or any weight at all in

---

[44] For example, Felix Oppenheim. See his "'Constraints on Freedom' as a Descriptive Concept," *Ethics*, vol. 95 (1985), pp. 305–309, and *Political Concepts: a Reconstruction* (Chicago: University of Chicago Press, 1981).

[45] Joseph Raz, *The Morality of Freedom* (Oxford: Clarendon Press, 1986), p. 14.

[46] *ibid.*, p. 16.

philosophical inquiry? How, in particular, are they supposed to be able to support *principles* for the assessment and regulation of acts and institutions? They might do so, if (once again with Kant) it were supposed that only one set of practical maxims would emerge from an application of the categories of our understanding. So far as I am aware this heroic supposition is not one that Cohen has endorsed, but without it, the results of the analysis of ordinary language are likely to be inconclusive or merely conservative. Finally, even if such criticisms could be countered, the archaic Rylean methodology which (at least in his work on proletarian unfreedom) Cohen practices fails to address the powerful skepticism about meaning voiced by many recent philosophers, such as Quine and Kripke.

What moral and political philosophy demands, instead of the pursuit of illusory concepts, is the construction of theories – theories which at once latch on to features of the real world and track our dominant moral concerns. Granted, such theorizing should be conducted with as much clarity as we can achieve. It should also, and crucially, help us to understand why freedom is restrained in the real world. The philosophical method which Cohen employs encompasses a disseveration of concepts from theories and theories from values in political thought. Now it may well be that there are some terms in our discourse, such as "power,"[47] which are best theorized in value-free terms, but I doubt that freedom is such a term. Everything suggests we are on firmer ground if we think of freedom as a moral notion.[48] The task of a theory of freedom is to give freedom a definite content by reference to a larger moral and political theory. Most particularly, it is to specify the liberty that is demanded by justice. The demands of justice are, further, to be explained in terms of the requirements of the well-being of individuals – which need to be spelled out in terms, not only of their basic human needs, but also by reference to their cultural traditions and historical circumstances.[49] The structure of liberties demanded by justice will vary according to these aspects of individual well-being. The task of theorizing freedom is, then, one which necessitates a close familiarity with the actual needs of human beings and with the cultural and historical contexts in which these needs are shaped. This task is not advanced by a bankrupt philosophical method in which descriptions of local linguistic behaviors masquerade as fundamental truths of moral and political life.

[47] For an argument that power is best theorized value-neutrally, see John Gray, "Political Power, Social Theory and Essential Contestability," D. Miller and L. Siedentop, eds., *The Nature of Political Theory* (Oxford: Clarendon Press, 1983).

[48] The idea of a moral notion is explored in J. Kovesi, *Moral Notions* (London: Routledge and Kegan Paul, 1971).

[49] See, on this, Raz, *The Morality of Freedom*.

A theory of freedom, accordingly, will treat freedom as a moral notion. It will embed that notion in a larger theory. That larger theory will have to do, in significant part, with what human beings are like and with the way things are in the world, but it will also express our evaluation of human beings and the world. A theory of freedom should have explanatory power as well as moral force. It should help us to understand the world as much as it equips us to assess it. In particular, it should do what Cohen's account signally fails to do – help us to assess the on-balance freedom achieved by rival institutional frameworks.

VI.   CAPITALISM, SOCIALISM, AND ON-BALANCE FREEDOM

How, then, are the rival institutions to be assessed? As Cohen himself acknowledges, making such an assessment is no easy matter. "Each form of society (capitalist and socialist) is by its nature congenial and hostile to various sorts of liberty, for variously placed people. . . . Which form is better for liberty, all things considered, is a question which may have no answer in the abstract. Which form is better for liberty may depend on the historical circumstances."[50] As Cohen again acknowledges, there are two distinct questions about capitalism, socialism, and freedom. "The first, or *abstract* question, is which form of society is, just as such, better for freedom, not, and this is the second, and *concrete* question, which form is better for freedom in the conditions of a particular place and time."[51] In respect of the first, abstract question, Cohen offers "the following intractably rough prescription":

> Consider, with respect to each form of society, the sum of liberty which remains when the liberties it withholds by its very nature are subtracted from the liberties it guarantees by its very nature. The society which is freer in the abstract is the one where that sum is larger.[52]

Cohen's prescription, as it stands, is not easy to apply. There is no mechanical way of individuating liberties, and so no mechanical way of computing which society has the greater sum of liberties. If by "liberties" Cohen (in consistency with his general conception of liberty as noninterference) means acts which persons are not interfered with by others in doing, such liberties are very different in the importance they have to those who possess and exercise them. Even if a mechanical procedure were available whereby we could individuate and count liberties, such a procedure would for this last reason (that it could not attach weights to the

[50] Cohen, "Capitalism," p. 15.
[51] Cohen, "Illusions," p. 232.
[52] *ibid.*, p. 233.

liberties so specified) fail to tell us what we want to know – namely, *how much liberty* each society contains. This is only to state once again a result of recent liberal thought – that judgments of degrees of freedom on-balance cannot as a rule be made without invoking standards of importance in respect of the liberties being evaluated.[53] This is to say that, even though there are central cases where we have no difficulty in making assessments of on-balance or comparative liberty, a libertarian calculus is an impossibility.

This is not to say we are left without resources in the attempt to weigh capitalist and socialist institutions as to the comparative freedom they contain, whether in general or for workers specifically. We have in fact several methods of proceeding. One is to make the move of disaggregation or decomposition of liberty into basic liberties which John Rawls does in his *A Theory of Justice* and subsequent writings.[54] For the most part, Rawls's basic liberties are the civil liberties to which Cohen refers when he tells us that these freedoms of speech, assembly, worship, publication, political participation, and so forth are not necessary concomitants of capitalism.[55] If we accept Rawls's list of the basic liberties, we *can* assess capitalist and socialist societies in respect of them. In the real world, though it is true that capitalism is not always accompanied by the basic liberties, it is no less true that the basic liberties have never been found in the absence of capitalism. There is not a single historical example of a socialist or, in general, a noncapitalist society in which these basic liberties are respected. In the historical circumstances with which we are familiar, there is no doubt which form of society is better for liberty. And, insofar as workers value the basic liberties, there is no doubt which form of society is better for workers and their liberty.

Against the Rawlsian move, which seems entirely unambiguous in its results, Cohen may make a number of objections. He may object that, however true it is in our current historical circumstances that socialist societies fail to protect the basic liberties, the argument from the basic liberties against socialism is nevertheless inconclusive. Perhaps we ought to regard our current historical predicament as something to be rejected or overcome, rather than simply accepted, and perhaps a socialist society is achievable in which the basic liberties *are* protected. This is an objection I

---

[53] On this see John Gray, "Liberalism and the Choice of Liberties," T.A. Hig, D. Callen, and J. Gray, eds., *The Restraint of Liberty: Bowling Green Studies in Applied Philosophy*, vol. VII (1985), pp. 1–25.

[54] Cohen, "Illusions," p. 233.

[55] With reference to Rawls's later writings, I refer especially to "The Basic Liberties and Their Priority," *Tanner Lectures on Human Values* (Salt Lake City: University of Utah Press, 1981).

will not address, though there are powerful reasons in positive political theory[56] for rejecting it, since my own argumentative strategy on this question is satisfied if it is admitted that our present historical context answers the question of on-balance freedom decisively in favor of capitalist institutions.

Cohen might make another, different objection to the Rawlsian move I have made. The Rawlsian move depends on excluding entitlement to property in the means of production from the set of basic liberties. Since property rights in the means of production, individual or communal, do not figure among the basic liberties as Rawls theorizes them, the choice between capitalism and socialism cannot turn on how their respective property institutions create and sustain liberty. (The choice may be, and should be, informed by a theoretical conjecture about the causal role of capitalist and socialist property institutions in sustaining the basic liberties. That is another question.) If we bring the property system back into the assessment of on-balance liberty, it may be that the unequivocal result we earlier obtained no longer holds. A society might curb some of the basic liberties and yet, because its property institutions extended liberty in important ways, do better from the standpoint of liberty than a society in which the basic liberties are perfectly protected. This is the view of many Leninists about the Soviet Union. I do not say that that is Cohen's view of the Soviet Union, but it does give him a way of resisting the upshot of the Rawlsian move.

Such a countermove does not save Cohen's case, however. Let us forswear the idiom of the basic liberties and adopt the conception of freedom as non-interference which Cohen deploys. Let us accept the result which Cohen derives by applying that notion of freedom to capitalist institutions – the result that capitalists are freer than proletarians. They are freer in the sense that, because they have resources in the means of production, they are less often (or less significantly) interfered with in doing as they wish, and so (let us say) have more or better options at their disposal than proletarians do. Accepting Cohen's conception of freedom and the resultant inequality of liberty under capitalism, how does workers' freedom fare under socialism? There seem to be clear respects in which workers' options will be severely diminished under socialist institutions. It is an important argument against socialism that, in transferring the control of employment from a diversity of competing employers to a single public authority, it will unavoidably curtail the options of workers. The point has been well put by Hayek:

[56] See John Gray, "Marxian Freedom, Individual Liberty, and the End of Alienation," *Social Philosophy and Policy*, vol. 3, no. 2 (1986), pp. 180–185.

That the freedom of the employed depends upon the existence of a great number and variety of employers is clear when we consider the situation that would exist if there were only one employer – namely, the state – and if taking employment were the only permitted means of livelihood . . . a consistent application of socialist principles, however much it might be disguised by the delegation of the power of employment to nominally independent public corporations and the like, would necessarily lead to the presence of a single employer. Whether this employer acted directly or indirectly he would clearly possess unlimited power to coerce the individual.[57]

Or, as Leon Trotsky, one of the chief architects of the Soviet system, put it pithily: "In a country where the sole employer is the state, opposition means death by slow starvation. The old principle, who does not work shall not eat, has been replaced by a new one: who does not obey shall not eat."[58] Cohen has told us that, under capitalism, workers "face a structure generated by a history of market transactions in which, it is reasonable to say, they are *forced* to work for some or other person or group. Their natural rights are not matched by corresponding effective powers."[59] It is an implication of Hayek's argument that, in a socialist economy, workers will face a structure generated by political power in which, it is reasonable to say, they are *forced* to work for the state. Their legal rights are not matched by corresponding effective powers.

Against Hayek's argument, it might be objected that it fails to take account of the possibility of a form of market socialism, in which there is a diversity of worker cooperatives and so a variety of employment opportunities for workers. It is not to be doubted that such a decentralized socialist system would likely do better for liberty than any centralist system could. Still, there will be important respects in which workers' liberty will be curtailed under market socialism. The problem is clearest when we consider workers who belong to a minority group. Communal systems of ownership of productive resources may be expected to find it hard to

[57] F.A. Hayek, *The Constitution of Liberty* (Chicago: Henry Regnery, 1960), p. 121. The central content of Hayek's argument is stated in somewhat Marxian fashion by Jeffrey Reiman, *Philosophy & Public Affairs*, vol. 16, no. 2 (Winter, 1987), p. 41: "The space between a plurality of centers of power may be just the space in which freedom occurs, and conflicts between the centers may work to keep that space open . . . as a material fact, state ownership might . . . represent a condition in which people were more vulnerable to, or less able to resist or escape from, force than they are in capitalism. It follows that, even if socialism ends capitalist slavery, it remains possible, on materialist grounds, that some achievable form of capitalism will be morally superior to any achievable form of socialism."

[58] Leon Trotsky, *The Revolution Betrayed* (New York: Pathfinder Books, 1937), p. 76.

[59] Cohen, "Capitalism," p. 258.

permit such minorities to advance, perhaps most particularly when they are operated by democratic procedures. Consider, by way of example, what would likely have been the fate of immigrants of alien cultural traditions, in Britain and the United States, if they had had to gain access to productive resources solely through a democratic political process. Whenever there is a prejudiced majority, such minorities are likely to have narrower options even under market socialism than they do under market capitalism, where a few self-interested capitalists are sufficient for them to be able to borrow or rent resources on the basis of which they can build up capital of their own.

Even when discriminating majorities are lacking, workers' options are limited by the necessity each faces of having in his cooperative to secure the agreement of his fellows for the introduction of any novel practice. As Hayek has again put it, "action by collective agreement is limited to instances where previous efforts have already created a common view, where opinion about what is desirable has become settled, and where the problem is that of choosing between possibilities generally recognized, not that of discovering new possibilities."[60] This point is reinforced when we realise that, because of the fusion of capital ownership with job occupation under market socialism, the dependency of the individual worker on his cooperative will be considerably greater than his dependency on his employer in a capitalist society.

As for the worker cooperative itself, it too will be in a circumstance of dependency. If market socialism is to remain a form of socialism, productive capital will have to be subject to political allocation rather than private provision. Workers will have access to capital only through the agencies of the socialist state. Because private capital is forbidden, no worker can individually acquire enough capital to live. Even as a member of his collective, he is always dependent on the capital that is allocated him by government. Perhaps worker-cooperators will have discretion over how much of their profits they set aside for investment in the enterprise and, to that extent, a part of their capital might be self-generated. But it seems clear that start-up capital and capital needed to stave off bankruptcy, or permit large-scale expansion, will have to be politically allocated. Workers under a market socialist system will confront a situation in which sources of capital are concentrated in one, or a few, state investment banks. They will have far fewer sources of capital than existed under capitalism. It is hard to see how this fact can avoid restricting workers' options.

The general point behind these arguments is that the freedoms generated by capitalist institutions are not only those enjoyed or exercised

[60] Hayek, *The Constitution of Liberty*, p. 126.

by the owners of capital.[61] This is a point recognized by Cohen when he notes that capitalism is a liberating system by contrast with its predecessor systems, such as slavery and feudalism.[62] He omits to note that many of these freedoms, depending as they do on a multiplicity of buyers of labor and sources of capital, would be extinguished by state socialism and diminished under market socialist institutions. Capitalist institutions may, then, be defended as institutions that promote workers' freedom better than any realizable alternative. This may be so even if it be conceded that workers are less free than capitalists. For it is still arguable that they are freer than they would be under any other institutions. All forms of socialism, in particular, appear to diminish that control over the disposition of his own labor and person which the worker gained with the advent of capitalism. It remains unclear on Cohen's account what are the freedoms conferred on the worker by socialism which might compensate for this loss.

If I am right in arguing that workers, even as a class, are better off in terms of liberty under capitalist than under alternative institutions, this supports a defense of capitalism that is to be conducted strictly in terms of its liberty-promoting effects. This argument is that the inequalities in liberty which Cohen finds in capitalist institutions are those which maximize the freedom of workers. Capitalism might then be defended as an economic system which satisfies a variation on Rawls's difference principle – a variation in which it applies only to liberty (and not to the other primary goods). Unlike Cohen, I do not suppose that an argument for capitalism from freedom can or should be severed from one that invokes justice. Nor, indeed, do I imagine that the demands of justice can be specified independently of an account of the well-being of those concerned – though I have not tried to give any account of well-being myself. The considerations I have advanced suggest that capitalism may nevertheless be defended by reference to an argument of freedom alone. The result of these considerations as to substantive liberty on-balance under capitalism and socialism is that capitalism does best for liberty, even for those within capitalism who have the least liberty.

The comparative assessment in terms of freedom of socialism and capitalism may take a third form – by considering collective unfreedom under each set of institutions. Let us, in this connection, go so far as to concede that most proletarians are collectively unfree to become capitalists, thereby putting aside the posibility of a capitalism-without-a-proletariat which I mentioned in an earlier section. If we do this, we may say (in

[61] For the argument that private property maximizes the liberty even of those who have none, see John Gray, *Liberalism* (Milton Keynes: Open University Press and Minnesota: University of Minnesota Press, 1986), pp. 66–68.

[62] Cohen, "Illusions," p. 224.

another idiom than Cohen's) that being a capitalist is in a capitalist society a *positional good*[63] – one that cannot be possessed or enjoyed by all. It is just in virtue of its positionality that Cohen argues for the collective unfreedom of proletarians in respect of it. Now perhaps, in the real world, being a capitalist *is* a positional good, as Cohen and other Marxists suppose. A real collective unfreedom is thereby generated for workers. This tells us nothing, however, as to the *relative* or *comparative* collective unfreedom of workers under capitalist and socialist institutions. It does not even adequately explain the moral significance of the collective unfreedom of the proletariat under capitalism. It shows only that under capitalism workers suffer a collective unfreedom – the unfreedom to become a capitalist – which, it is supposed, socialism would abolish. I have argued earlier that socialism would, in effect, universalize and entrench this unfreedom. Let us accept Cohen's argument to his conclusion, though, and see how workers fare as to their collective freedom under socialism.

Under socialism, then, we shall allow, workers will be rid of the collective unfreedom to become capitalists. At the same time, it is likely that a good many other collective unfreedoms would be spawned under socialism. It is a feature of all forms of socialism that some resources which are allocated by market processes under capitalism are subject to political allocation instead. This is true even under market socialist institutions, in which at least investment capital is politically allocated. In the real world, however, political power is itself a positional good. It cannot be had or exercised by all equally. The positionality of political power entails that, when resources are subject to political control and allocation, they too acquire the attributes of positionality. Thus in "actually existing" socialist societies, education, housing, and health services exhibit a degree of positionality which likely surpasses that possessed by analogous services in Western capitalist nations. Workers in such socialist states suffer a degree of collective unfreedom in respect of the communist elite's access to good apartments, hard-currency stores, higher education for their children, adequate medical care, and so forth, which plausibly exceeds any similar positionality in capitalist societies.[64]

Attempts to explain this fact and which rely on ad hoc claims about historical backwardness, illiberal traditions, or inauspicious circumstances in the societies concerned neglect systematically the role of political allocation

---

[63] On positional goods, see John Gray, "Classical Liberalism, Positional Goods and the Politicization of Property," Adrian Ellis and Krishnan Kumar, eds., *Dilemmas of Liberal Democracies* (London: Tavistock, 1983), pp. 174–184.

[64] A mass of evidence exists as to the extent of politically enforced social stratifications in the USSR. A useful survey of some of it is to be found in K. Simis, "The Machinery of Corruption in the Soviet Union," *Survey*, vol. 23, no. 4 (Autumn 1977–8).

of resources in shaping the incentives of individuals in such societies. By contrast with societies in which resources are primarily allocated by markets, individuals in socialist societies have an almost irresistible incentive to seek positions of power in the party apparatus from which they can assure benefits to themselves and their offspring. Hence the predictable transfer of command positions and their associated benefits across generations of *nomenklatura* in the socialist states. By contrast, insofar as access to goods is in capitalist societies mediated via the market, it is inherently likely to display less positionality than in socialist states. This is so because, except where they are highly monopolistic, markets tend to redistribute resources unpredictably across economic agents and, most especially, across generations.

In general, we may expect that, with the politicization of resource allocation that socialism brings, goods which hitherto had not been positional will become so. In so doing, they will generate collective unfreedoms in respect of them which had not existed before. The pattern of collective unfreedoms in society will mirror that of the possession of the supreme positional good, political power. In this situation, socialist workers will be imprisoned as a class, even if (dubiously enough) each of them is free to join the ruling elite. The collective unfreedom which they will suffer in respect of the positional good of political power will, in its turn, spawn collective unfreedoms in respect of all of the goods that political power allocates – that is to say, most of the goods of economic and social life. It is difficult to resist the conclusion that workers under socialist institutions will suffer a degree of collective unfreedom unknown in capitalist societies.

CONCLUDING REMARKS

The arguments Cohen adduces as to proletarian unfreedom are mostly formal. They support truisms which tell us nothing of substance about the advantages in terms of freedom of capitalist over socialist institutions. When we turn from conceptual analysis to realistic considerations, we find powerful reasons for supposing that socialist institutions will do worse than capitalist institutions from the standpoint of workers' freedom. We find that the parity of unfreedoms between the two systems that is supported by Cohen's atavistic philosophical methodology is, in fact, entirely delusive. In other words, if the goal of Cohen's argument is to demonstrate the existence of unfreedom under capitalism, it succeeds – but only because the unfreedom he discusses exists in every institution of property (and probably in every imaginable society). It seems decidedly improbable that Cohen should devote five papers, which develop a novel and implausible conception of collective unfreedom and contrive to make a host of minute distinctions in the discourse of freedom, to establish so banal a result. If, on the other hand, Cohen's goal is the more interesting one of showing that worker's freedom, or freedom in general, is greater under socialist institutions than within capitalist institutions, his argument to this result demonstrably fails. When we consider the substance of things, we have every reason to think that workers' freedoms will flourish best under capitalist institutions. Oddly enough, this supposition is amply confirmed by historical experience. And that is another argument in favor of a form of theorizing which, unlike Cohen's, seeks to explain and assess the freedom and unfreedom we find in the real world.

Philosophy, Oxford University

CAPITALISM, CITIZENSHIP AND COMMUNITY*

BY STEPHEN MACEDO

INTRODUCTION

The authors of *Habits of the Heart* (Robert N. Bellah, Richard Madsen, William M. Sullivan, Ann Swindler, and Steven M. Tipton; hereafter, simply Bellah) charge that America is losing the institutions that help "to create the kind of person who could sustain a connection to a wider political community and thus ultimately support the maintenance of free institutions."[1] Bellah fears that "individualism may have grown cancerous – that it may be destroying those social integuments that Tocqueville saw as moderating its more destructive potentials, that it may be threatening the survival of freedom itself."[2]

Proponents of the liberal free market order should, I will argue, take seriously the concerns that motivate Bellah and company: citizens of a liberal regime cannot live by exchanges alone. Liberal constitutionalism depends upon a certain level and quality of citizen virtue. But while the need for virtue is often neglected by liberal theorists, it is far from clear that the actual workings of liberal institutions have drastically undermined virtue in the way Bellah's dire account suggests. That analysis serves, moreover, as the springboard for a radically transformist argument that seeks, not so much to elevate and shape, but to transcend and deny, the self-interestedness that the free market exercises. Having argued against Bellah's analysis and prescriptions, I shall attempt to show how the phenomena he describes are open to an interpretation that is happier from the point of view of a concern with virtue. I shall end by using Tocqueville to suggest that combining liberal capitalism with intermediate associations like voluntary groups and state and local government helps elevate and shape self-interest, promoting a citizenry capable of and insistent upon liberal self-government.

* For their helpful comments on an earlier draft, I would like to thank Jack Crittenden, Hannes Gissurarson, Rob Rosen, Jeremy Shearmur, Shannon Stimson, my fellow participants in the Liberty Fund seminar on "Capitalism and Socialism," and the editors of this journal.
[1] Robert N. Bellah, Richard Madsen, William M. Sullivan, Ann Swindler, and Steven M. Tipton, *Habits of the Heart* (Berkeley: University of California Press, 1985), p. vii.
[2] *ibid.*

I. TOWARD A COMMUNITARIAN CRITIQUE OF CAPITALISM

Much of the normative apparatus deployed by Bellah is lifted directly from Alasdair MacIntyre, Michael Sandel, Charles Taylor, and other communitarians.[3] *Habits*, for example, is a lament about "modernity" that often sounds like MacIntyre at his most dire: "Progress, modernity's master idea, seems less compelling when it appears that it may progress into the abyss."[4] And, echoing the "atomistic" complaint of Taylor and Sandel, *Habits* warns that "in our day . . . separation and individuation have reached a kind of culmination."[5]

While *Habits* develops several important communitarian themes, it also helps us see that some elements of the communitarian critique of liberalism are misguided. MacIntyre, for example, claims that modern Western societies are characterized by basic moral disagreement. "The most striking feature of contemporary moral utterance," says MacIntyre, "is that so much of it is used to express disagreements. . . . "[6] And this is, in part, because all we have are "fragments" of genuine morality: the "language and appearances of morality" without the "integral substance."[7] MacIntyre's main evidence for his disintegration thesis is the rampant disagreement among moral philosophers and others about how to justify correct positions on issues such as just war and abortion. These disagreements seem to come to a head in metaethical disputes among "incommensurable" moral paradigms: "deontology," the varieties of consequentialism, perfectionism, and so on.[8] If MacIntyre is right, the problem for a polity like America must be to acquire rather than revise a moral identity.[9]

The evidence presented in *Habits* suggests that it would be hard to

---

[3] See Alasdair MacIntyre, *After Virtue* (Notre Dame: University of Notre Dame Press, 1981); Michael Sandel, *Liberalism and the Limits of Justice* (Cambridge: Cambridge University Press, 1982); Charles Taylor, *Hegel and Modern Society* (Cambridge: Cambridge University Press, 1979), and Taylor's two volumes of *Philosophical Papers: Human Agency and Language* and *Philosophy and the Human Sciences* (Cambridge: Cambridge University Press, 1985).

[4] Bellah, *Habits*, p. 277.

[5] *ibid.*, p. 275; and see Taylor, "Atomism," in *Papers*, vol. 2.

[6] MacIntyre, *After Virtue*, p. 6.

[7] *ibid.*, p. 5.

[8] *ibid.*, pp. 8–21.

[9] MacIntyre's claim is doubly odd. Only philosophers argue about methaethics, yet philosophical communities appear to thrive on such debates. Few in broader political communities are even aware of the distinction between deontology and consequentialism. The practical consensus that sustains actual political communities probably draws on both "rights-based" and "goods-based" considerations (as well as interests, apathy, and other attitudes that have nothing to do with morality). For an interesting discussion of the plurality of ultimate sources of moral value see Thomas Nagel, "The Fragmentation of Value," *Mortal Questions* (London: Cambridge University Press, 1981).

sustain the claim that incoherence is the leading characteristic of political culture in America. The authors of *Habits* find that "beneath the sharp disagreements" animating our politics, "there is more than a little consensus . . . [Americans] all to some degree share a common moral vocabulary . . . the 'first language' of American individualism." We share, as others have put it, an "American ethos," a vision of what, in the abstract, we stand for at our best, a vision centered around liberal/capitalist values.[10]

The concern of *Habits*, then, is not with the existence of a coherent political culture, but with its substance and sustainability. Is materialism bred by economic freedom destroying the "civic culture" that supports liberal democratic institutions?[11]

One leading complaint shared by many communitarians and Bellah is that ends and purposes tend to be regarded as matters of choice, matters about which our liberal public morality provides little guidance. And so, Sandel complains that liberalism posits an "unencumbered self": "the values and relations we have are the products of choice, the possessions of a self given prior to its ends."[12]

MacIntyre, likewise, bemoans what he terms the "emotivist" moral character of our age: "the self as presented by emotivism . . . cannot be simply or unconditionally identified with *any* particular moral attitude or point of view (including that of those *characters* which socially embody emotivism) just because of the fact that its judgments are in the end criterionless."[13] Lacking any ultimate criteria of choice, "the self is 'nothing', is not a substance but a set of perpetually open possibilities."[14] Without "objective and impersonal" criteria of morality, people come to hold that any moral principle is "in the end an expression of the preferences of an individual. . . . "[15] And so, even when Americans are bound up in valuable associations and personal relationships, according to *Habits*, they tend to regard these as basically "arbitrary."[16]

Because they consider the ends of purposes of life to be arbitrary, Americans pursue mere "means" such as material prosperity.

---

[10] See Herbert McClosky and John Zaller, *The American Ethos: Public Attitudes Toward Capitalism and Democracy* (Cambridge: Harvard University Press, 1984), esp. chapter 1.

[11] On the connection between a participatory civil culture and the health of liberal democracy see Gabriel A. Almond and Sidney Verba, *The Civic Culture: Political Attitudes and Democracy in Five Nations* (Princeton: Princeton University Press, 1963), chapter 11; Sidney Verba and Norman H. Nie, *Participation in America: Political Democracy and Social Equality* (Chicago: University of Chicago Press, 1987), *passim*.

[12] Sandel, *Liberalism*, p. 176.

[13] MacIntyre, *After Virtue*, p. 30, emphasis in original.

[14] *ibid.*, p. 31.

[15] *ibid.*, pp. 20–21.

[16] Bellah, *Habits*, p. 21.

Americans tend to think of the ultimate goals of a good life as matters of personal choice. The means to achieve individual choice, they tend to think, depend on economic progress. This dominant American tradition of thinking about success does not, however, help very much in relating economic success to our ultimate success as persons and our ultimate success as a society.[17]

But consider the example of Brian Palmer, discussed in *Habits*, who threw off his frenetic careerism to embrace a "devotion to marriage and children." This is, to Bellah, all for the good, but Palmer is incapable of explaining why,

> his current life is, in fact, better than his earlier life. . . . Both are justified as idiosyncratic preference rather than as representing a larger sense of the purpose of life. . . . What is good is what one finds rewarding. If one's preferences change, so does the nature of the good.[18]

Lacking in substantive justification, Bellah further suggests, personal commitments rest on a "fragile foundation. . . . [Brian Palmer] lacks a language to explain what seem to be the real commitments that define his life, and to that extent the commitments themselves are precarious."[19] The stability of shared commitments and associations requires, for Bellah, articulateness about real human goods.

A couple of points should be noted here. First, the alleged precariousness of Palmer's commitments is not the problem of detachment complained of by Sandel.[20] Brian Palmer cannot easily cast off his old values and ways by a sovereign act of unencumbered choice. His commitments partly constitute his identity. But his wife's decision to divorce him provokes a personal crisis and a good bit of soul-searching and hard thinking: he reads, reflects, reexamines, and only painfully alters and revises his sense of priorities.[21] Palmer's case is typical of those discussed by Bellah: middle-class Americans are, apparently, capable of reflecting upon and revising their moral values and commitments, but they are not "unencumbered selves" choosing in abstract isolation.[22]

Brian Palmer is not unencumbered by his values and ends, but he does

---

[17] *ibid.*, p. 22.

[18] *ibid.*, pp. 5–6.

[19] *ibid.*, 6 and 8.

[20] See Sandel's discussion of the "voluntarist notion of agency," *Liberalism*, p. 59.

[21] Bellah, *Habits*, p. 4.

[22] The point that liberalism does not depend upon an unencumbered conception of the self is developed at greater length in my *Liberal Virtues: A Liberal Theory of Citizenship, Virtue, and Community* (Oxford: Oxford University Press: forthcoming).

lack an articulate account of ultimate human goods. Does this imply that he lacks any sense of real goods, as Bellah suggests? Simon Weil and Iris Murdoch (among others) argue that apprehending the good is more a matter of "seeing" than "saying," a matter of loving attention to "a magnetic but inexhaustible reality."[23] Inarticulateness is not necessarily a sign of the arbitrariness of one's commitments: real human goods may be hard to articulate.

If inarticulateness is not necessarily a sign of arbitrariness, neither is it obviously a sign of the fragility of commitments, or clearly the reason why Palmer's commitments may have become more fragile. Fragility may be a consequence of any number of things: recognition of the plurality of ways of participating in human goods, greater tolerance of diversity, or a greater tendency to think critically about traditional patterns of life. People have become more willing to divorce, for example, rather than live with an unhappy marriage. Bellah does not show that such changes are either bad or the consequence of an inability to articulate what the components of a good life are.

It seems clear that Brian Palmer has learned something from the experiences and reflections surrounding his divorce: "That exclusive pursuit of success now seems to me not a good way to live. . . .I have just found that I get a lot of personal reward from being involved in the lives of my children."[24] Palmer seems to have come to appreciate the real value of family life, and it is simply not clear that his inability to articulately account for his moral progress renders his new commitments more fragile or arbitrary than they would otherwise be.

Bellah, like communitarians generally, tends to avoid objective moral claims, favoring instead the local route to community provided by our shared "social identity."[25] And so he argues that our preferences are "detached from any social or cultural base that could give them broader meaning."[26] Our problem, apparently, is that "American cultural traditions" leave individuals "suspended in glorious but terrifying isolation."[27]

The isolation of the self is exhibited in our public life by the dominance of managerial expertise, and in private by a therapeutic model of relationships. In public the question is what means will most effectively realize ends arbitrarily chosen by individuals. In private the question is how

---

[23] Iris Murdoch, *The Sovereignty of the Good* (London: Ark, 1986), p. 42, and see *Simon Weil: An Anthology*, ed. Sian Miles (New York: Weidenfeld and Nicholson, 1986).

[24] Bellah, *Habits*, p. 6.

[25] Especially Michael Walzer, *Spheres of Justice* (New York: Basic Books, 1983), and "Philosophy and Democracy," *Political Theory*, vol. 9 (Aug. 1981), pp. 379–399.

[26] Bellah, *Habits*, p. 7.

[27] *ibid.*, p. 6.

to get in close touch with your own "feelings" so that you do what you "really" want to do, where what you really want to do is arbitrary, personal, and not discussable; it is discovered "down deep" inside yourself rather than in some form of "reason-giving moral argument" or social "conversation."[28] Modern liberalism's moral condition is, as another communitarian has put it, a "mixture of private Romanticism and public utilitarianism."[29]

Relationships, Bellah finds, are modelled on a "therapeutic" quest for self-clarification, self-acceptance, and self-expression: the therapist takes "each person's values as given or self-defined," as "self-set values."[30] The task of therapy is simply to achieve "clarity" about one's "personal preferences" so that they can better be realized.[31] Bellah worries that this conception of "healthy" personal relationships implies an ultimately isolated self-reliance. "In the end," according to Margaret Oldham (another Bellah interviewee), "you're really alone and you really have to answer to yourself. . . ."[32]

Both MacIntyre and the authors of *Habits* are concerned to emphasize the importance of understanding our choices as choices among options defined by inherited ideals and traditions. Perhaps our culture does elevate self-expression at the expense of tradition, but traditionalism becomes mere conventionalism unless it is supported by a critical account of which among our many inherited practices have real value.

Neither liberalism nor capitalism depends on keeping personal choices detached from inherited ideals and traditions. The defense of liberal freedom supposes that we are inheritors of many ideals and traditions, and that mature persons have a right to choose among a plurality of conceptions of the good life. Liberals would also want to emphasize that persons are quite properly critical interpreters of inherited ideals and traditions, and that this process of criticism properly leads to the rejection of patterns of life based on mere habit, prejudice, or stereotype (patterns based on maxims such as "a woman's place is in the home"). Indeed, it is not clear how one would go about distilling a valuable tradition from the welter of our inherited practices without the capacity for critical judgment of the sort that liberalism elevates.[33]

[28] *ibid.*, p. 140.

[29] Taylor, *Hegel and Modern Society*, p. 126. But for a more positive view of Romanticism, see Nancy Rosenblum's excellent study, *Another Liberalism* (Cambridge: Harvard University Press, 1987).

[30] Bellah, p. 127–128.

[31] *ibid.*, p. 15.

[32] *ibid.*

[33] Sotirios A. Barber develops the notion that reasoned criticism is central to the task of distilling a tradition from mere history; see his *On What the Constitution Means* (Baltimore: Johns Hopkins University Press, 1984), pp. 84–5. I develop the argument that liberalism does not depend upon an instrumental notion of rationality in *Liberal Virtues*.

What Bellah tends to portray as a general value skepticism in America appears actually to be carefully focused and embedded in a set of substantive values. Brian Palmer, for example, is not skeptical about the value of giving everyone the equal right to pursue their choices. Palmer praises California:

> By and large, the rule of thumb out here is that if you've got the money, honey, you can do your own thing as long as your thing doesn't destroy someone else's property, or interrupt their sleep, or bother their privacy, then that's fine.[34]

Palmer's vision of tolerance, for Bellah, implies that freedom is a matter of being left alone, of "freedom as freedom *from* the demands of others [which] provides no vocabulary in which . . . Americans can easily address common conceptions of the ends of a good life. . . . "[35] And liberal justice, for Bellah as for Sandel, yields a public preoccupation with mere "procedures."[36] But Palmer's statements could equally well be interpreted as a set of ultimate substantive commitments which are partly, though not completely, constitutive of the good of all: liberal freedoms place a premium on peace, choice, and prosperity, the resolution of differences through persuasion rather than coercion, the value of reflectiveness and self-control, and an openness to change. And Palmer's freedom is not the freedom of an isolated individual: the self-examination provoked by his divorce leads him to read, reflect, and talk things over with his children, to whom he is devoted.[37] Liberal freedom of choice can, in general, be understood as the freedom to choose among associations and communities.

Bellah himself does not really press the charge, in any case, that our public life is wholly given over to the pursuit of material gain, or that our politics is merely procedural, or that freedom stands for isolation. *Habits* is a profoundly ambivalent book: its authors, despite their misgivings, recognize that many Americans continue to participate in politics and various voluntary associations and to affirm that a wide range of common involvements is crucial to living a good life:

> If there are vast numbers of a selfish, narcissistic "me generation" in America, we did not find them, but we certainly did find that the language of individualism, the primary American language of self-understanding, limits the ways in which people think.[38]

[34] Bellah, *Habits*, pp. 6–7.
[35] *ibid.*, p. 24.
[36] See Michael Sandel, "The Procedural Republic and the Unencumbered Self," *Political Theory*, vol. 12 (1984), p. 93.
[37] Bellah, *Habits*, p. 4.
[38] *ibid.*, p. 290.

All this leads one to ask, finally: To what extent has individualism undermined association in America? And what kinds of political and economic reforms are called for?

Bellah notes that America remains the most religious of Western nations. According to a recent Gallup poll, 57 percent of Americans say that religion can answer "all or most of today's problems," 55 percent say religion is "very important" in their lives, and another 30 percent say "fairly important."[39] Seven in ten Americans are church members.[40] These figures have remained constant over the last five years, while materialistic yuppiedom has come into its own.[41] The continuing vitality of religion in America suggests not only that many people value association, but also that many would not regard the ends of life as arbitrary in the ways Bellah has suggested.

Volunteerism was at least as prevalent in 1986 as at any time in the previous decade: 36 percent reported being *currently* engaged in private charitable activity, up from 27 percent in 1977.[42] Indeed, volunteerism rose disproportionately among 18–29 year olds (again, yuppies). And Bellah himself found evidence that tolerant cosmopolitan yuppiedom can be combined with civic activism and responsibility.[43]

Americans are still participators: significantly more Americans belong to associations and are active in them than citizens of other industrial countries.[44] There have, undoubtedly, been changes over the longer run: participation seems to decline with urbanization, but to increase with education and socioeconomic status.[45] In their classic study of participation in America, Verba and Nie argue that while the personal proclivity to participate is increasing (with education and status) the opportunities for effective participation may be declining somewhat (with urbanization).[46] The issue of participation is worth addressing, but the evidence does not suggest that an associative ethos has been destroyed or that we face an impending crisis.

If, at the personal level, people nowadays feel somewhat more uncertain about their ultimate goals and values and about the stability of their personal relationships, perhaps this has something to do with the apparent lessening of social pressures to marry, the more widespread acceptance

---

[39] *The Gallup Report*, #259, April 1987, p. 10.
[40] *ibid.*, p. 35.
[41] *ibid.*, p. 13. "Yuppies," young, upwardly mobile professionals, are usually regarded as the vanguard of materialism and self-centeredness.
[42] *The Gallup Report*, #248, May 1986, p. 14.
[43] See the discussion of Mary Taylor at *Habits*, pp. 192–5.
[44] See Verba and Nie, *Participation*, chapter 11, Tables 1 and 9.
[45] *ibid.*, p. 20 and chapter 13 generally.
[46] *ibid.*, p. 264.

of divorce, and the far greater range of options open to women.

Economic progress has also encouraged mobility, and rendered communities and extended family ties less stable. And so, Bellah comes back, over and over, to the complaint that the "commercial dynamism at the heart of the ideal of personal success . . . undermines community involvement. . . . The rules of the competitive market, not the practices of the town meeting or the fellowship of the church, are the real arbiters of living."[47] But it is not merely avarice, or the desire for gain, that "estranges" one from community and "the public household" (as Bellah puts it).[48] The trade-offs between remaining in a familiar community setting and moving on for some new challenge raise hard and genuine problems (as any academic ought to appreciate). The interviews reported in *Habits* suggest, in fact, that people are often thrilled by the prospect of a promotion, a new job, and a new environment: "moving on" is often stimulated by a search for new challenges and a desire to avoid becoming "bored" and "stale."[49] It is wrong, then, to write off the attractions of change and mobility as the products of mere grasping ambition, as Bellah often seems to do.

People seem well aware of the genuine and difficult trade-offs between new career challenges and settled commitments. "Practically everyone we talked to would agree," say the authors of *Habits*,

> that two of the most basic components of a good life are success in one's work and the joy that comes in serving one's community. And they would also tend to agree that the two are so closely intertwined that a person cannot usually have one without having the other.[50]

And so it seems, on Bellah's own testimony, that Americans are fairly self-conscious about the choices they are making, that people continue to value family, participation, and association while making hard choices among these and competing goods that really are to some degree incompatible. Bellah presents no real evidence to show that America has experienced a critical, or even significant, decline in group participation.

Why does the theme of impending crisis recur so frequently in *Habits* when the stories Bellah relates seem hardly to support a fear of immediate social collapse? The crisis theme has more to do with Bellah's desired prescriptions than with the actual state of individualism in America.

While the conception of freedom of many Americans is resistant to

---

[47] Bellah, *Habits*, p. 251.
[48] *ibid.*, p. 197.
[49] *ibid.*
[50] *ibid.*, p. 196.

"overt forms of political oppression," it also "leaves them with a stubborn fear of acknowledging structures of power and interdependence in a technologically complex society dominated by giant corporations and an increasingly powerful state."[51] In the face of "predatory capitalists," and the "untrammeled pursuit of wealth without regard to social justice," the "old moral order" that governed small-town America has proved ineffective. The "crucial change" in American life has been the shift from economic and social relationships that were "visible and . . . morally interpreted as parts of a larger common life – to a society vastly more interrelated and integrated economically, technically, and functionally."[52]

Lamentably for Bellah, Americans continue to look at the problems of corporate giants like Chrysler in terms of the presence or absence of "small-town" virtues: "To maintain their moral balance, town fathers have to pretend they live in a kind of community that no longer exists."[53] They ignore their "dependence on a complicated national and international political economy."[54]

For Bellah the American way represents not an assertion of a set of guiding values, but the inability of the "language of individualism" to "make sense of human interaction."[55] In order to "minimize 'cognitive dissonance,' many individuals tend not to deal with embedded inequalities of power, privilege, and esteem in a culture of self-proclaimed moral equality."[56] Those who see threats to the "viability" of middle-class American vlaues from "poor people who have never learned any self-restraint" are simply falling back on "highly personal and moralistic rhetoric with no clue to the understanding of large-scale structures and institutions."[57]

So hegemonic is the American ethos of individualism that even those progressive souls in the Campaign for Economic Democracy are really moved by a "conception of community as a voluntary gathering of autonomous indivduals [which] is not radically different from the views of the others" interviewed by the Bellah team. So, in a sense, Americans may share too many values, they may be too homogeneous in their expectations about behavior and their beliefs about virtue:

---

[51] ibid., p. 25.
[52] ibid., p. 43.
[53] ibid., p. 175.
[54] ibid., p. 176. For an excellent argument about the prohibitive costs involved in trying to compensate people for a variety of forms of bad luck, see Richard A. Epstein's contribution to this volume.
[55] ibid., p. 204.
[56] ibid.
[57] ibid., p. 205.

> Americans, it would seem, feel most comfortable in thinking about politics in terms of a consensual community of autonomous individuals, and it is to such a conception that they turn for the cure of their present ills. . . . [S]uch a society is really constituted only of autonomous middle-class individuals.[58]

Americans, apparently, share a rather thick set of expectations about personal independence and responsibility, and they tend to be judgmental when people fail to measure up. If groups persist in poverty that "must be someone's fault . . . perhaps because their culture is defective, and they lack a 'work ethic.'"[59]

But just when Americans might seem, from a communitarian perspective, to be getting it right, behaving like a "substantive" cultural community, with expectations and standards of conduct and united by more than "relativistic tolerance," Bellah simply scoffs. Americans have "difficulty coming to terms with genuine cultural or social differences . . . [and] even more difficulty coming to terms with large impersonal organizations and institutions."[60]

Americans, unlike sociologists and economists, cannot see the "invisible complexity" of society, little less make "moral sense of significant cultural, social, and economic differences between groups."[61] In the "moral vacuum" of their ignorance, Americans tend to "translate group claims and interests into the language of individual rights."[62] But this will not do, because there are "individuals and groups or categories of individuals" who "insist" that "they are owed or entitled to certain benefits, assistance, or preference as a matter of right" and "such claims are not readily accepted as matters of justice. . . . They begin to be treated instead simply as competing wants. . . . [and are] interpreted in terms of power."[63]

So Americans continue to lodge their confidence in market competition, and to respect personal effort. The criteria of inclusion in America's political community include, apparently, economic self-support and responsibility: classical liberal, bourgeois virtues that make people resistant

---

[58] *ibid.*, p. 206. See Louis Hartz's discussion, *The Liberal Tradition in America* (New York: Harcourt Brace Jovanovich, 1955), esp. ch. 8.

[59] *ibid.*

[60] *ibid.*, p. 207.

[61] *ibid.*

[62] *ibid.*

[63] *ibid.* The "moral" egalitarianism of Bellah and his cohorts turns out, after all, to be a rather thin patina glossing a thoroughly intellectual elitism (economists and sociologists understand the complexity "invisible" to most Americans). Bellah is, finally, derisive about middle-class American values (the work ethic, suspicion of politcs, and insistence on independence). Middle-class attitudes are systematically reduced to a failure "to come to terms" with reality.

to democratizing and socializing the economy. Americans are unwilling to "accept" cultural groups that they consider lazy or irresponsible, and they insist on a distinction between rights and welfare entitlements.

Do Americans go too far in emphasizing economic independence and personal responsibility? That proposition is arguable, but largely beyond the scope of this paper. It should be emphasized, however, that the popular attitudes and economic conditions that Bellah considers most troubling seem hardly new. The attitudes resemble Weber's "protestant ethic."[64] The conditions (economic complexity and invisible interdependence, uncertainty, risk, and inequality) are not recent features of capitalism; they are the characteristics of the commercial order that Adam Smith described in the *Wealth of Nations*.[65] Apart from asserting what now seems patently false (that we have reached the limits of economic growth, a "zero-sum" society in which liberal capitalism can no longer sustain itself),[66] Bellah and company, as I have noted, really present no evidence to show that these attitudes and conditions have taken a new, self-destructive turn. And so, the quest for transformation that underlies *Habits* has less to do with contemporary conditions than with the nature of liberal capitalism as such.

The ultimate political ambition of Bellah and company is to "transform" a society that they find deeply flawed.

> What has failed at every level – from the society of nations to the national society to the local community to the family – is integration.... We have put our own good, as individuals, as groups, as a nation, ahead of the common good.[67]

All that Bellah can hope for is:

> A conception of society as a whole composed of widely different, but independent, groups might generate a language of the common good that could adjudicate between conflicting wants and interests, thus taking the pressure off the overstrained logic of individual rights. But such a conception would require coming to terms with the invisible complexity that Americans prefer to avoid.[68]

Since our moral turpitude springs, in great part, from our free market individualism, redemption must lie in "economic democracy and social

---

[64] Max Weber, *The Protestant Ethic and the Spirit of Capitalism*, trans. Talcott Parsons (New York: Scribner's 1930).

[65] See especially Book 1.

[66] Bellah, *Habits*, pp. 185–189.

[67] *ibid.*, p. 285.

[68] *ibid.*

responsibility."[69] We must "give up our dream of private success for a genuinely integrated societal community."[70] Without this "transformation," Bellah warns, "there may be very little future to think about at all."[71]

To revitalize our "social ecology," Bellah proposes to increase taxes and raise welfare benefits, thus reversing "Reaganomics." The aim would be to alter the relationship between work and reward, substituting vocationalism for careerism: "If the extrinsic rewards and punishments associated with work were reduced, it would be possible to make vocational choices more in terms of intrinsic satisfactions."[72] Nobler motives and deeper satisfactions are, it seems, suppressed by capitalist avarice and cupidity: "The social wealth that automation brings, if not siphoned off into the hands of a few, can be used to pay for work that is intrinsically valuable, in the form of a renewal of crafts . . . and in the improvement of social services."[73] It would take a very deep social transformation indeed to get corporate lawyers and longshoremen to transfer their energies and aspirations to "crafts" (pot throwing? basket weaving?) and social work.

Bellah wishes to avoid the "soft despotism" that Tocqueville feared lurks behind an increasingly powerful regulatory/welfare state.[74] Because he opposes further centralization and bureaucratization, he must hope for a moral transformation of the polity broadly: a revival of "civic virtue" centered on a "substantive" conception of the common good and on a new awareness of our intricate economic "connectedness and interdependence."[75] This new politics will involve not so much the altruistic subordination of personal concerns to a larger good as the identification of one's interest with a polity committed to common deliberation and dialogue:

---

[69] *ibid.*, p. 287.

[70] *ibid.*, p. 286.

[71] *ibid.*

[72] *ibid.*, p. 288. Bellah's critique of market relations seems more than a little indebted to Marx, especially the discussions of money as the universal "pimp" of mankind, and of commodity fetishism, in the *Economic and Philosophical Manuscripts*, and *Capital*, vol. 1, respectively; *The Marx-Engels Reader*, 2nd ed., ed. Robert C. Tucker, (New York: Norton, 1978), pp. 101–105, 319–329. Besides tax increases, Bellah proposes that government promote this moral transformation via economic democracy, measures establishing the "social responsibility" of corporations, and a "revitalized party system"; see *Habits*, p. 287. He offers few details. Would revitalizing the party system, for example, require reversing the "democratic" reforms of the early 1970s?

[73] *ibid.*, p. 288.

[74] See Tocqueville's famous discussion in *Democracy in America*, trans. G. Lawrence, ed. J.P. Mayer (Garden City: Anchor, 1986), pp. 690–695.

[75] Bellah, *Habits*, p. 256, 289. Sandel, I might add, also suggests moving against capitalism to shore up community by allowing states to enact plant closing laws "to protect their communities from the disruptive effects of capital mobility and sudden industrial change." See Michael Sandel, "Morality and the Liberal Ideal," *The New Republic*, May 7, 1984, pp. 15–17.

> Politics . . . is a forum within which the politics of community, the politics of interest, and the politics of the nation can be put into a new context of wider possibilities for accomodation and innovation. This view of politics depends upon a notion of community and citizenship importantly different from the utilitarian individualist view. It seeks to persuade us that the individual self finds its fulfilment in relations with others in society organized through public dialogue.[76]

There would seem to be more than little wishful thinking built into Bellah's proposals. He wants a more substantial sense of national purpose, but not one imposed from Washington.[77] Bellah wants people to work for pleasure rather than pay – raising income taxes, he hopes, will lead people to embrace intrinsically "meaningful" work, not make them lazy and listless. But do we have any good reason to really expect the emergence of a more substantial sense of the common good? And have socialist countries been successful in dissociating work and reward? Bellah presents no hard evidence to suggest that his high hopes are anything more than that.

Bellah's frequent recurrence to the abyss theme suggests a desperate need to frighten people into accepting his bitter medicine, and perhaps a hope that moral renewal will emerge from a sense of crisis:

> In the late twentieth century, we see that our poverty is as absolute as that of the poorest nations. We have attempted to deny the human condition in our quest for power after power. It would be well for us to rejoin the human race, to accept our essential poverty as a gift, and to share our material wealth with those in need.[78]

Must we, one must wonder, pin our hopes on Bellah's exasperated pleas for a radical transcendence of pluralism and self-interest?

On Bellah's account, many Americans adhere to the paradigm of associationism that is compatible with the acceptance of economic self-interest and the value of self-support. Bellah disparages these attitudes and practices, but the phenomena he describes are open to a happier interpretation than the one he presents.

II. CAPITALISM AND COMMUNITY

Bellah finds evidence that government welfare may displace the efforts of private association and, so, the impetus toward voluntary public involvement. Jim Reichart, another *Habits* interviewee

---

[76] Bellah, *Habits*, p. 218.
[77] As in the bumper-sticker: "Think Globally – Act Locally."
[78] Bellah, *Habits*, p. 296.

muses that his loss of commitment is "probably caused by too much government. The government's like a domineering mother. It takes away all the people's incentive and tries to do everything for them. You know what it's like for children who have been dominated all their lives by a strong, powerful mother. They become damn near vegetable cases. It's the same with the government."[79]

One reason why government programs may discourage Americans from participating is not hard to find. Americans, according to Bellah, value success based on personal effort: "It is only insofar as they can claim that they have succeeded *through their own efforts* that they can feel they have deserved that achievement."[80] And earned success is not all they value; they also value voluntary service because it is voluntary:

> truly to deserve this joy, one has to make a personal, voluntary effort to "get involved." But one of the greatest sources of unhappiness for most Americans is the sense of being involuntarily involved – "trapped" – in constraining social relationships. Those with whom we talked tend to think of themselves as deserving joy only if they make such a commitment beyond having to do so.[81]

The thread that unifies the emphasis on earned achievement and voluntary service is free, responsible action, and the satisfaction derived from individual effort.

Americans understand the good life as a balance between these two types of free action: "without some individually deserved success, an individual would have little voluntarily to contribute to his choosen community."[82] And "practically all of those we talked with are convinced, at least in theory, that a selfish seeker after purely individual success could not live a good, happy, joyful life."[83]

The authors of *Habits*, aside from their concern with greater equality, have two main objections to the vision of voluntary community implicit on liberal capitalism. First, liberalism implies that "community is a voluntary association of neighbors who personally know one another and freely express concern for one another, an essentially private, rather than public, form of association."[84] This objection is crucial, for it is the main reason why Bellah also rejects the "Welfare Liberalism" of Democrats like Ted

---

[79] *ibid.*, p. 197.
[80] *ibid.*, p. 198, emphasis in original.
[81] *ibid.*
[82] *ibid.*, p. 199.
[83] *ibid.*
[84] *ibid.*, p. 263.

Kennedy: "the Welfare Liberal vision articulated by Kennedy shares with Neocapitalism a fundamental assumption about the relationship between public and private life. . . . [It] offers only what Neocapitalists such as Reagan offer: 'compassion,' the subjective feeling of sympathy of one private individual for another."[85]

This objection seems to rest, in part, on an extremely narrow conception of what counts as a *public* association. It is wrong to identify an emphasis on voluntarism with the elevation of merely personal or private concerns. The Red Cross, the National Audubon Society, the Salvation Army, and the Moral Majority are just as much constituted by "public" concerns as NASA or the Commodity Futures Trading Commission or the local sanitation department. We certainly have no reason to think that voluntary associations are inherently incapable of forming "constitutive" features of a person's identity: certainly religious commitments often do so. For purposes of passing judgment about the "communal" character of people's involvements, one must consider the purposes, motives, and membership criteria of voluntary associations before simply writing them off as "private."

Bellah also objects that proponents of voluntary community are unwilling to grasp and take hold of the large-scale economic forces shaping their lives.

> [W]hen they think of the kind of generosity that might redeem the individualistic pursuit of economic success, they often imagine voluntary involvements in local, small-scale activities such as a family, club, or idealized community in which individual initiatives interrelate to improve the life of all. They have difficulty relating this ideal image to the large-scale forces shaping their lives.[86]

This unwillingness to extend political control over the economy is consistent with the American preference for voluntarism, but this makes it "difficult to address the problems confronting us as a whole."[87] The preference for voluntarism is coupled with an antipolitical bias: "For a good number of those we talked to, politics connotes something morally unsavory, as though voluntary involvement were commendable up to the

---

[85] *ibid.*, p. 265. And so, between Neocapitalists and Welfare Liberals, the debate "is over procedures to achieve fairness for each, not about the substantive meaning of justice for all." In Hegelian terms, Neocapitalists and Welfare Liberals stand for different versions of *moralitat*, or civil society, while Bellah pursues a vision of *sittlichkeit*, a substantive ethical community; see *Hegel's Philosophy of Right*, trans. T.M. Knox (Oxford: Oxford University Press, 1967), third part.

[86] Bellah, *Habits*, p. 199.

[87] *ibid.*, p. 250.

point at which it enters the realm of office holding, campaigning, and organized negotiating."[88]

But Americans are not against politics per se, or at least not equally against all politics. They appreciate and support, according to Bellah, a politics of local deliberation and moral consensus, and are suspicious of interest-group politics, the politics of "adversarial struggles, alliance building, and interest bargaining."[89] Americans, on moral grounds, prefer the market whose "legitimacy rests in large part on the belief that it rewards individuals impartially on the basis of fair competition."[90]

Besides local consensus politics and interest group bargaining, there is a politics of "national order and purpose," sustained by "patriotism" and a "revered Constitution."[91] For Bellah this positive politics of the nation "is a notion that bypasses the reality of utilitarian interest bargaining by appealing for legitimacy to . . . the vision of consensual, neighborly community."[92]

This ideal for liberal/capitalist community has room for a limited conception of politics. Foreign policy making often transcends narrow interests. Domestic issues like civil rights involve matters of principle that also transcend interest bargaining.[93] People sometimes pursue a national good, most evidently during wartime, but also at other times, as during the Civil Rights movement.[94]

Bellah associates this alternative vision of community with Ronald Reagan. Reagan certainly represents a bridge with the past, a "community of memory" of the sort that *Habits* espouses.[95] His political credo encourages the economic energy that Tocqueville saw as the animating feature of democracy in America.[96] But he links this energy with traditional

[88] *ibid.*, p. 199. And see Robert Lane, "Market Justice and Political Justice," *American Political Science Review*, vol. 80, no. 2 (June 1986), pp. 383–402.

[89] Bellah, *Habits*, p. 201.

[90] *ibid.*, p. 200. Robert Lane also reports that Americans view the market as more "fair and wise" than political processes; see Lane, "Market Justice," p. 385.

[91] Bellah, *Habits*, pp. 201–202.

[92] *ibid.*, p. 202.

[93] Bellah notes, at page 252 of *Habits*, that the civil rights movement drew on "strength and vitality still latent in the sense of the public good Americans have inherited." Well it did, until it turned into claims for affirmative action and special privileges which a majority of Americans oppose.

[94] "But social movements quickly lose their moral edge if they are conceived as falling into special pleading, as when the Civil Rights movement was transformed into 'Black Power.' Then we are back in the only semilegitimate realm of the politics of interest." See Bellah, *Habits*, pp. 202–203.

[95] *ibid.*, p. 263.

[96] In the relative prosperity of the last several years, people's satisfaction with their own lives and the state of the union has, according to some measures at least, been quite high. *The Gallup Report* #246, March 1986, informs us that, when asked whether they are satisfied or dissatisfied "with the way things are going in the United States at this time," the ratio of

groups like the family. "Work and family are the center of our lives, the foundation of our dignity as a free people."[97] And Reagan links economic self-support with a call for voluntarism: "It's time to reject the notion that advocating government programs is a form of personal charity. Generosity is a reflection of what one does with his or her resources – and not what he or she advocates the government do with everyone's money."[98] ·

If we leave aside Bellah's poorly substantiated claims that liberal capitalism in American is self-destructing, we might turn from his transformative program and consider other ways of invigorating opportunities for association and participation within a liberal-capitalist framework. If voluntary association is important for promoting a self-reliant, energetic citizenry, then we should be willing to accept some inefficiency in the delivery of some public benefits for the sake of providing opportunities for the exercise of the capacity for spontaneous association.

Since state and local governments provide more numerous, varied, and accessible opportunities for participation than the federal government, a concern with the popular capacity for self-government provides a reason to favor concentrating political activity at the lowest level of government possible. Perhaps we should resist, for example, the progressive federalization of education, a traditional preserve of state and local governments, and a great source of local concern and involvement.

Of course, one might worry that a "new federalism" could become a front for the old states-rights opposition to the Bill of Rights. One way to help insure that individuals will continue to be able to appeal to the federal government for protection of their basic constitutional rights would be to avoid linking federalism with judicial restraint. Judges actively committed to the enforcement of individual rights might themselves reconsider the constitutional limitations on the powers of Congress.

Article 1, Section 8 of the Constitution enumerates Congress's powers, but that enumeration has become all but a dead letter. These enumerated powers speak to the legitimacy of national policies regarding commerce and national security broadly understood. Section 8 concludes with an "elastic clause": Congress may "make all laws necessary and proper for carrying into execution the foregoing powers. . . . " But the very fact that powers are enumerated and means sometimes specified implies that some things not enumerated must be beyond Congress's power. Article 1 provides judges with a critical perspective for examining the legitimacy of further federal

---

responses was 66–30% in March of 1986, as compared with 12–84% in August of 1979. These figures vary considerably from one month to another, and the latter figure is a real low point, but the change has been substantial and is closely related to people's financial outlook.

[97] Bellah, *Habits*, p. 263.
[98] *ibid.*, p. 263.

encroachments on the political responsibilities of states and localities.[99]

Voluntarism speaks to the need for a citizenry capable of energetic, spontaneous action. Federalism speaks to the value of opportunities to participate in self-government.[100] And liberal constitutionalism provides a vision of the good of our political whole: it attempts to preserve the overarching norms of mutual respect for basic liberal rights that makes ours a union of liberal communities. The principles of liberal constitutionalism are, of course, more abstract than the principles of communities united around particular religious, ethnic, or local visions. But liberal constitutionalism has helped promote an open, diverse, tolerant, and prosperous national community.

Is liberal constitutionalism a mere legal framework, incapable of constituting a polity united by a shared identity? The uncommon patriotism of Americans, focused on our constitutional heritage, suggests that an ongoing historical struggle for the establishment and extension of liberal values can create and support a shared and robust identity, one that leaves room for certain norms of universal respect and critical reflection on more particular attachments.[101]

We should, in any case, be leery of attachments which displace critical reflection by constituting one's identity too fully or deeply. Liberal constitutionalism embraces a kind of integration, but not one that seeks to overcome all divisions and tensions within individual lives or society as a whole. We live in a diverse society, situated in a world composed of a dizzying array of cultural and religious communities. We need, in our political arrangements with one another and with other societies, to cultivate not an exclusive attachment to our own ways, but a reflective willingness to pay others their due. Liberal justice, established through our constitutional structures, emphasizes the importance of a reflective respect for legitimate diversity. But one whose character is too "thickly" constituted by more narrowly partisan commitments may lose precisely the ability to distance the self from one's "own kind," and with it the ability to respect those who are different.

All of this suggests (albeit quite sketchily) a certain division of political responsibilities, and a three-pronged program to promote liberal virtues, citizenship, and community: greater emphasis on voluntarism to promote citizen initiative, federalism to beef up the possibilities for local diversity

---

[99] I deal with these issues at somewhat greater length in *The New Right v. The Constitution*, 2nd ed. (Washington, DC: Cato Institute, 1987); much more needs to be said.

[100] Once liberals recognize that the preservation of our constitutional arrangements depends on a certain active quality of citizenship, they should take more seriously the principle of "subsidiarity," discussed in John Finnis, *Natural Law and Natural Rights*, (Oxford: Oxford University Press, 1980), p. 146 and passim.

[101] These themes are discussed at much greater length in my *Liberal Virtues*.

and participation, and a national politics of rights enforcement (and certain limited common ends like national security) to protect the liberal right to choose.

III. A TOCQUEVILLEAN PERSPECTIVE

Bellah depicts himself as embracing and extending the project of Tocqueville's *Democracy in America*. But does *Habits* preserve the central features of Tocqueville's analysis of democratic capitalism? I would suggest not: in two crucial respects, *Democracy in America* lends support to the model of voluntary community that I have advanced as an alternative to Bellah's egalitarian/communitarian vision.

First, Tocqueville understood that liberal rights in a free market order provide Americans with a vision of the political whole that is uniquely "graspable" by average people, because it is not far removed from their interests. Second, Tocqueville's discussion suggests that a liberal vision of economic independence and voluntary community helps sustain self-government by speaking not only to our interests, but also to our pride: it speaks to our pride by cultivating self-esteem based on individual responsibility, earned achievement, and voluntary action.[102]

Tocqueville was not an uncritical friend of democratic capitalism, but he certainly perceived the particular virtues of a liberal form of democracy. Free enterprise disperses power and sets property in motion.[103] It animates the ambition of every man by holding out the prospect of economic betterment. Tocqueville argued that the last thing democracies need to worry about is the old fear of being consumed by the heat of demagogic passion or anarchy. The danger, rather, is the loosening of individual attachments to those decentralized institutions and associations that support individuality by bolstering personal self-confidence in the face of mass opinion and a centralizing, paternalistic state. "Breathless cupidity" might, indeed, consume the mind of democratic man, were it not for the existence of a complex variety of mechanisms that check, constrain, temper, and broaden the pursuit of self-interest in America: local self-government, voluntary associations, religion, respect for rights, law, and education, the federal Constitution, and family life. All of these support liberal democracy by warding off its worst tendency: personal isolation and anxiety leading to the passive acquiescence to a "soft despotism."

Associations mediate men's relations with, and strengthen them in the

---

[102] As Harvey C. Mansfield, Jr.'s, recent excellent discussion of American conservatism suggests, Bellah is not alone in failing to take adequate account of the interplay of interests and pride that helps sustain liberal constitutionalism; see "Pride versus Interest in American Conservatism Today," *Government and Opposition*, vol. 22, no. 2 (Spring 1987), pp. 194–205.

[103] Tocqueville, *Democracy*, p. 52.

face of, "public opinion": that form of majority tyranny that "leaves the body alone and goes straight for the soul."[104] Association relieves the nervous anxiety that forms beneath the restless animation and uncertainty of vast, ever-changing market societies. People need, on Tocqueville's account, the stable moorings of religious belief, a "caring" sphere of family life, and a variety of ties to intermediate groups to sustain their confidence in their own ability to manage and direct their individuality – an individuality that, for Tocqueville, is far more fragile than that found in Mill's classic defense of liberty.[105]

Associative supports for individuality help nurture the capacity for, and confidence in, self-government, broadly understood as governing one's own life and participating in the management of politics. Trust in one's capacity for self-government is necessary to sustain liberty because, without self-trust, anxiety-ridden individuals will be all too willing to choose equality in a safe and secure slavery, handing power over to a paternalistic state that promises to manage their interests better than they can themselves. By failing actively to exercise their capacity for "self-government," Tocqueville suggests, people will lose confidence in that capacity and will cease to insist on their right to freedom.

But the collapse of self-government is as much a triumph of integration as the failure of it. Tocqueville's good form of democracy is characterized by something more ethically substantial than "integration" or "community"; it is characterized by liberty. Not, to be sure, mere "negative" liberty, but liberty as the realized, exercised, self-confident capacity for self-direction and self-government, exercised through economic activity, politics, and associations. The confident sense of one's capacity for self-government sustains the demand for actual political liberty and independence.

The virtues prompted by liberal capitalism, then, help sustain liberal self-government by addressing man's interests, and gently turning these outward toward the good of larger wholes. People take an interest in property rights partly because they have some property; they take an interest in local government because everyone has an interest in the mundane concerns of local governments, such as roads and schools. Tocqueville seeks to contain and shape economic self-interest in a variety

---

[104] *ibid.*, p. 255.
[105] The contrasts between Mill and Tocqueville (on religion, for example) are striking. The confidence, so striking in Mill, in an inner core of individuality needing only to be liberated and stimulated by diversity in order to flourish is lacking in Tocqueville. Compare Tocqueville's discussion in *Democracy*, pp. 429–436 with John Stuart Mill, *On Liberty* (New York: Norton, 1975), pp. 27–38 and 46–50. And for an interesting similarity with Tocqueville, see Adam Smith's discussion of religious sects in *An Inquiry into the Nature and Causes of the Wealth of Nations*, ed. R.H. Campbell, A.S. Skinner, and W.B. Todd (Oxford: Oxford University Press, 1979), vol. 2, pp. 794–796.

of ways; he does not seek to deny "self interest rightly understood."[106] And so, "In the United States there is hardly any talk of the beauty of virtue. But they maintain that virtue is useful and prove it every day."[107]

Indeed, far from disparaging the profit motive, Tocqueville praises the character of the entrepreneur as holding out a model of virtue and honor appropriate to democratic ages:

> The American will describe as noble and estimable ambition which our medieval ancestors would have called base cupidity. He would consider as blind and barbarous frenzy that ardor for conquest and warlike spirit which led the latter every day into new battles. In the United States fortunes are easily lost and gained again. The country is limitless and full of inexhaustible resources. . . . Boldness in industrial undertakings is the chief cause of their rapid progress, power, and greatness. . . . Such a people is bound to look with favor on boldness in industry and honor it. . . . The Americans, who have turned rash speculation into a sort of virtue, can in no case stigmatise those who are rash.[108]

Indeed, the associative zeal of Americans, as Tocqueville portrays it, is an extension of the same brash power, the same "spirit of liberty," that animates the entrepreneur. In both cases people are motivated by tangible, "local" benefits, whether profits in the one case, or good schools and good roads in the other.[109] "He trusts fearlessly in his own powers, which seem to him sufficient for everything." When such a man conceives an idea for public improvement, "It does not come into his head to appeal to public authority for its help. He publishes his plan, offers to carry it out, summons other individuals to aid his efforts, and personally struggles against all obstacles."[110] Here, then, Tocqueville speaks not only to the interests, but also the pride that energetic, enterprising men take in the active exercise of their powers: pride, Tocqueville says, is the "vice" that most needs to be nurtured in democratic peoples.[111] If Tocqueville is right, it makes sense not to separate economic energy and voluntary effort on behalf of shared goods, but to promote them together, recognizing that they combine to promote an ideal of virtue accessible to a free democratic nation.

It is, of course, absolutely crucial to Tocqueville's whole scheme that the individual become active in conditions of real opportunity, where "the idea

---

[106] Tocqueville, *Democracy*, p. 526.
[107] *ibid.*, p. 525.
[108] *ibid.*, p. 622.
[109] *ibid.*, p. 92.
[110] *ibid.*, p. 95.
[111] *ibid.*, p. 632.

of progress comes naturally into each man's mind," and where "the desire to rise swells in every heart at once."[112] And the crucial background condition of this attitude is faith in the attainability of advancement through personal effort: "Nowhere does he see any limit placed by nature to human endeavor; in his eyes something which does not exist is just something that has not been tried yet." The active liberal citizen, as Tocqueville depicts him, could not flourish in the zero-sum society, since to sustain his energy he needs actually to see the results of his efforts, and that means he needs a growing economy replete with opportunity.

In its preoccupation with distributive justice, with the "fair sharing" of "social wealth," and its anxiety in the face of change with no promise of growth, the zero-sum society would seem much more conducive to the "debased taste for equality, which leads the weak to want to drag the strong down to their level."[113]

Indeed, the political ambitions of *Habits* could not animate and sustain the sort of energy that Tocqueville discusses. Tocqueville's citizens are animated by plans for local roads, schools, church projects; their "ambition is both eager and constant, but in general it does not look very high. For the most part life is eagerly spent in coveting small prizes within reach."[114] Local activism gives men a tangible sense of accomplishment. But how many people could feel they are successfully participating in shaping large issues of economic justice and social planning? In transforming a national "social ecology"? The remoteness of the large "structural" economic issues that worry Bellah and his colleagues argues against their ability to engage personal ambition. And were ambitions engaged, the diversity of groups in our society, each with its own vision of an ideal order, will help ensure that the energies of most will be frustrated.

Tocqueville, finally, gives a central place to voluntarism. It is especially valuable, says Tocqueville, for people to act voluntarily to promote public projects because relying on government discourages direct popular attention to, and responsibility for, their own affairs.[115] And so, anticipating Brian Palmer, Tocqueville warns that government action will "crowd out" private initiative: "The more government takes the place of associations, the more will individuals lose the idea of forming associations and need the government to come to their help. This is a vicious circle of cause and effect."[116]

Voluntary association does not, for Tocqueville, serve our interests more

[112] *ibid.*, p. 629.
[113] *ibid.*, p. 57.
[114] *ibid.*, p. 629.
[115] *ibid.*, p. 514–517.
[116] *ibid.*, p. 515; and see pp. 681–683.

effectively than government action. Centralized administration could achieve many common purposes more efficiently than private activity. The case for voluntarism speaks not to our interests (not, at least, to a "cowardly love of immediate pleasures") but to our pride as free, independent persons, doing things for ourselves.[117] Again, only in exercising our capacity for free action with others do we retain confidence in our capacity for freedom.

Self-trust is undermined when the government does things for people that they might do for themselves: "It would resemble parental authority if, fatherlike, it tried to prepare its charges for a man's life, but on the contrary, it only tries to keep them in perpetual childhood."[118] Whether government produces some genuine "public good" or not is irrelevant: Tocqueville's point is that the pride of free men is undermined by being provided for, by being made happy rather than securing their own happiness: "it daily makes the exercise of free choice less useful and rarer, restricts the activity of free will within a narrower compass, and little by little robs each citizen of the proper use of his own faculites."[119] An active central government may promote people's interests, but in doing so too readily it will undermine their pride, their self-confident independence, their insistence on liberty, thus promoting the "soft despotism" Tocqueville feared.

Tocqueville's insights were fashioned over 150 years ago: applying his ideas to contemporary America is, obviously, not unproblematic. The economy has changed drastically since Tocqueville's day: the labor force has shifted away from agriculture and small towns to urban manufacturing and now toward a service economy. Families are no longer the same sources of stability they once were.

Tocqueville did foresee certain changes, such as the weakening of religion. In response he stressed that rights were all the more important: if, he said, "you do not succeed in linking the idea of rights to personal interest, which provides the only stable point in the human heart, what other means will be left to you to govern the world, if not fear?"[120] It must be admitted, as well, that Tocqueville feared that the rise of great industries would create a permanent and deep inequality. Like Adam Smith, he feared that workers incessantly performing monotonous tasks would become degraded and intellectually enervated: "he no longer belongs to himself, but to his choosen calling. . . . As the principle of the division of labor is ever more completely applied, the worker becomes

---

[117] *ibid.*, p. 645.
[118] *ibid.*, p. 692.
[119] *ibid.*, p. 692.
[120] *ibid.*, p. 239.

weaker, more limited, and more dependent."[121] The worker loses, in short, his capacity for self-government.[122]

Liberty, then, is threatened by the loss of the confident capacity for self-government: the feeling of impotence before large forces that makes people feel incapable of running their own affairs.[123] It is precisely excessive attention to personal interests that makes people too anxious and weak, and too attentive to their immediate comforts, to sustain free self-government.

For Tocqueville the survival of liberty depends upon the possession of a sufficient measure of the right kind of virtue: virtue as the insistence on one's equal rights as a chooser. This virtue is not of a very "high" sort: it is not a saintly submission of self and interests to the divine, or the heroic identification of one's interests with the glory of the polity. It is self-interest elevated and shaped by the attachment to freedom and its active exercise. All of the supports for liberty that Tocqueville praises (local self-government, free association, law and courts) are designed to retain that measure of virtue that free democratic peoples are capable of. And that measure is "love of independence"[124] and liberty:

> I am firmly convinced that one cannot found an aristocracy anew in this world, but I think that associations of plain citizens can compose very rich, influential, and powerful bodies, in other words, aristocratic bodies.[125]

I do not mean to argue, in any case, that Tocqueville's analysis and prescriptions should be applied wholesale to the United States. But if Tocqueville's depiction of the psychological condition of citizens of a liberal capitalist polity remains important (as I believe it does), then economic freedom needs to be supplemented with opportunities for voluntary association and local participation. The liberal virtues compatible with, and not far removed from, the energies unleashed by economic liberty, find their expression in the American ethos of voluntary community that was advanced above as an alternative to Bellah.

CONCLUSION

The suggestions advanced in this article, while far from complete or conclusive, speak largely against Bellah's positive program for the

---

[121] *ibid.*, p. 556. And see Adam Smith's discussion in *Wealth of Nations*, pp. 782, 787–788.
[122] On the other hand, Tocqueville defended the Bank of the United States, and argued that opposition to its power was motivated by the levelling equality he feared; *Democracy*, pp. 178, 388–389.
[123] *ibid.*, p. 642.
[124] *ibid.*, p. 667.
[125] *ibid.*, p. 697.

reformation of our economic system and political culture.[126] This is not to say, however, that Bellah's concern with the social supports and cultural setting of liberal individuality is frivolous. In their preoccupation with arguments about rights and liberty, liberals too often neglect the forms of virtue and citizenship necessary to maintain liberal democracy. If Tocqueville's depiction of the human condition in liberal capitalist societies is still cogent, then the readiness to associate spontaneously to accomplish common projects and the willingness to participate in the practices of self-government are among the virtues that liberal polities depend upon.

Liberal constitutionalism presupposes and exercises capacities for reflective self-government that embody a genuine form of virtue. Taking pride in the active exercise of one's capacity for self-government (broadly understood as running one's own life and taking a hand in politics) is the higher form of life that democratic citizens are capable of. Liberals have a hard time discussing "high" and "low" forms of life of character.[127] The levelled understanding of personality deployed by most liberals finds its alternative in Tocqueville.

Liberal theorists are often equally unwilling to make use of the idea of pride. But without the idea of pride it would be hard to appreciate the stubborn insistence on choice and independence that Bellah and his colleagues found in America, and that Tocqueville emphasized 150 years ago. Contemporary studies confirm that participation in the market and small primary groups are the principal sources of self-esteem for Americans.[128] If Tocqueville was right, then it is crucial to displace the idea of interests as the sole support for liberty: liberty may not be in our "interests"; it may be the hard road, the road that requires effort, discipline, and self-control, a road that is sometime the less efficient means to achieving satisfaction, the road that requires the acceptance of a certain amount of risk, uncertainty, and material inequality.

Liberals who take Tocqueville seriously should be concerned about

[126] I am all too conscious that much more needs to be said about the variety of ways one might attempt to support the popular capacity for self-government. Joshua Cohen, for example, provides some very powerful arguments for a bevy of measures I would want to resist; see his "The Economic Basis of Deliberative Democracy," *Social Philosophy and Policy*, vol. 6, no. 2 (Spring 1988).

[127] Precursors of certain variants of today's liberal thought, such as Hobbes and Bentham, heaped scorn and cynicism on the idea that qualitative discriminations could be made about the value of different ways of life. The hegemony of these ideas is also transmitted through the influence of economics: *homo economicus* has interests only, and his motto is *de gustibus non est disputandum*. Bentham's famous maxims are illustrative: "pushpin is as good as poetry," and "better a pig satisfied than Socrates dissatisfied." See his *The Principles of Morals and Legislation* (New York: Hafner, 1948); and Thomas Hobbes, *Leviathan* (Harmondsworth: Penguin, 1981).

[128] See Lane, "Market Justice," p. 385, and "Government and Self-Esteem," *Political Theory*, vol. 10 (1982), pp. 5–31.

people's connections with larger wholes that sustain their allegiance while supporting their individuality, their liberty, and their capacity for self-government. It is not enough to hold out a vision of selfless social harmony that is incapable of attracting the energetic support of people as we know them. But neither is it enough to preserve people's economic freedom if they lose, as a consequence, the strength to insist on liberty. Contemporary defenders of democratic virtue (like Bellah) need to think more about interests; both they and liberal skeptics need to think more about pride and virtue.

The strongest defense of liberalism and the free market must be complex. It would stress liberalism's unique ability to combine interests, freedom, pride, and virtue – a kind of virtue that is not especially noble, but that is attainable and conducive to peace and prosperity. That is how I have interpreted Tocqueville's claim: liberal virtue equals the proud exercise of the capacity for self-government in public and private life. By refusing to take this claim seriously, defenders of capitalism may surrender their most effective weapons against communitarian and republican critics of liberalism.

Political Science, Harvard University

CAPITALISM AND THE DEMOCRATIC ECONOMY*

BY GARY A. DYMSKI AND JOHN E. ELLIOTT

Mainstream economics evaluates capitalism primarily from the perspective of efficiency. Social philosophy typically applies other or additional normative criteria, such as equality, democracy, and community. This essay examines the implications of these contrasting sets of criteria in the evaluation of capitalism. Its first two sections consider the criteria themselves, assuming that a trade-off exists between them. The last three sections question whether such a trade-off necessarily occurs, and explore the claim that improvements in nonefficiency dimensions of capitalist society may enhance, rather than conflict with, efficiency.

I. THE PRIMACY OF EFFICIENCY

The emergence of the mainstream tradition in economics in the late eighteenth century, and its subsequent systematization as a discipline, coincided with both the emergence of market capitalism as the dominant form of economic organization and the rise of democracy as a type of political system. Market capitalism can be defined as an economic system characterized by the free disposal of labor, private ownership and inheritance rights in property, and reliance on market processes to determine prices and allocate resources. Unless otherwise defined in context, the term democracy refers herein to a system of active participation in the political process by citizens whose preferences are given equal weight in decision making, implemented through a procedure of majority rule.[1] This presupposes universal adult suffrage and protection of the civil liberties and rights of individuals and minorities from arbitrary and capricious action by the majority as well as by political leaders.[2] Given this rough coincidence in the historical emergence of capitalist economy and democratic politics, the dominant intellectual rationale for capitalism has

* The authors would like to acknowledge the insightful comments of Peter Gordon, Timur Kuran, Sam Bowles, and members of the USC Economic Development Seminar on the ideas presented in this paper. Remaining errors are our own.

[1] Robert A. Dahl and Charles E. Lindblom, *Politics, Economics, and Welfare* (New York: Harper and Row, 1953), pp. 41ff.

[2] C.B. Macpherson, *The Life and Times of Liberal Democracy* (New York: Oxford, 1977); John E. Elliott and Joanna V. Scott, "Theories of Liberal Capitalist Democracy: Alternative Perspectives," *International Journal of Social Economics*, vol. 14 (1987), pp. 52–87.

encompassed arguments both for its economic superiority and for its compatibility with democracy.

The Defense of Capitalism. The economic superiority of capitalism has characteristically been established using some variant of "efficiency" as an evaluative criterion. Efficiency can be defined as that deployment of all available resources in production whose output provides maximum consumer satisfaction.[3] Several components of this definition are sometimes distinguished. One of these is full employment of each available resource, for example, labor. Another is attainment of maximum output per unit of fully employed resources.[4] The attainment of maximum output from fully deployed resources through adroit resource combinations and the achievement of maximum consumer satisfaction through optimum composition of output is often termed "allocative efficiency." Lastly, the increase in maximum desired output of fully deployed resources over time, notably through innovations and technological progress, is usually called "dynamic efficiency." The terms "economic efficiency" and "efficiency" are used generically herein to refer to any one or combination of the above, depending on the context.

Classical economists such as Adam Smith centered on dynamic efficiency, arguing that the division of labor and capital accumulation enhance productivity and growth. Mainstream economists since the late nineteenth century have emphasized the static efficiency associated with resource allocation based on individual choice coordinated through markets. Other economists have offered their own variants of efficiency. Hayek has emphasized economies in the acquisition and use of information, especially under conditions of changing tastes and technologies.[5] Schumpeter has focused on dramatic qualitative changes or innovations (for example, new products or methods of production).[6] Even

---

[3] Sen has observed that it is not sufficient to defend capitalism using a more restrictive conception of efficiency, such as the efficiency of the market mechanism per se, for "the specification of the market mechanism is essentially an incomplete specification of a social arrangement." Amartya Sen, "The Moral Standing of the Market," *Social Philosophy & Policy*, vol. 2 (1985), pp. 1–19. The quotation is found on page 18.

[4] This component of efficiency includes both "allocative" and, for want of a better expression, "X" efficiency dimensions. The former refers to efficiencies associated with the allocation and combination of resources within and between enterprises (for example, that the ratio of marginal costs for any pair of commodities is equal for any pair of enterprises). The latter refers to maximizing output per unit of input through management and labor effort, organization of work, worker morale and spirit, etc.; see Harvey Leibenstein, "Allocative vs. 'X Efficiency'," *American Economic Review*, vol. 56 (1966). Through either "X" efficiency or this dimension of "allocative" efficiency, output of any one product, given inputs and technology, may rise without reducing the output of any other product.

[5] Friedrich A. Hayek, "The Use of Knowledge in Society," in *Individualism and Economic Order* (Chicago: University of Chicago, 1948).

[6] Joseph E. Schumpeter, *The Theory of Economic Development* (Cambridge: Harvard University, 1934).

Keynes's immanent critique of mainstream economics uses an efficiency criterion – that is, whether a given set of economic policies will lead to the full (and hence efficient) employment of labor. So some notion of efficiency has been central to the defense (or, in the case of Keynes, critique) of capitalism as an economic system.

Economists' emphasis on the efficiency criterion has been reinforced by their proclivity to consider evaluative criteria separately. This has the effect of compartmentalizing efficiency from other desiderata.[7] For example, given the distribution of wealth, it is claimed, one may examine measures to increase valued production. Although limited in scope, such analysis is defended as significant largely because it can be carried out without making the interpersonal welfare comparisons which arise in assessing the social desirability of changes in distribution. This need not tie evaluations of capitalism to the status quo and should not prevent pursuit of egalitarian principles if desired.[8]

In practice, however, severing efficiency from nonefficiency criteria has relegated the latter to a position of lesser normative significance. In contemporary welfare economics, efficiency is postulated as a minimum, and in effect primary, welfare criterion. Only after attaining a position of maximum efficiency is *that* position, in turn, secondarily subject to redistributions of wealth or income to achieve justice.[9] The corollary following from this distinction is that capitalism is perceived to excel at that which is mainstream economics' primary criterion for human well-being, that is, efficiency. Any deficiencies associated with capitalism – poverty, inequality, insecurity, unemployment (other than its associated loss of output), and so forth – lie in secondary domains; at least, such problems are perceived to be better accommodated once economic efficiency has been achieved.[10] Conversely, it is common for Western economists, in

---

[7] Note that allocative efficiency and justice are not identical concepts. Allocative efficiency refers to a state wherein resources are fully deployed to produce a set of goods which provide maximum satisfaction to societal members, given those members' endowments of wealth, their preferences for various output goods, and the income earned on resources (including labor) committed by societal members to production. The question of whether the wealth and resource endowments which societal members "own" is "just" may be separately considered, even though it is beyond the scope of allocative efficiency considerations.

[8] Hla Myint, *Theories of Welfare Economics* (New York: Augustus M. Kelley, 1965), pp. 103–104.

[9] Leonid Hurwicz, "Conditions for Economic Efficiency of Centralized and Decentralized Structures," G. Grossman, ed., *Value and Plan* (Berkeley: University of California, 1960).

[10] The following provides a clear and representative statement of the priority of efficiency and the view that nonefficiency claims, such as justice, can be better met after and within the framework of maximum efficiency:

"To some people, it may appear irrelevant to demand maximum efficiency when the objective is to achieve a 'just' distribution of income or wealth in society. On closer inspection, this is a doubtful argument, perhaps most readily seen once we observe that in general the

assessing Soviet and other existing socialist societies, to concentrate on such societies' economic inefficiencies, rather than on such areas of relative strength as full employment, lower inequality, and workers' welfare benefits.[11]

The Compatibility of Capitalism and Democracy. Accepting the primacy of efficiency transforms the question of the compatibility of capitalism and democracy into the problem of whether "too much democracy" threatens capitalism and property interests. Both mainstream[12] and radical[13] economists have argued that it may.

Nonetheless, the predominant argument, from Jeremy Bentham and James Mill to Joseph Schumpeter[14] and Charles Lindblom,[15] has been that capitalism and democracy are at least roughly consistent. Indeed, theorists such as Milton Friedman[16] and Peter Berger[17] have gone further, making the claim that market capitalism is a necessary, if not sufficient, condition for Western-style political democracy.[18] Prima facie, because capitalist and democratic processes rely on contradictory principles for apportioning influence, it would seem difficult to affirm either position. In principle at least, democracy grants members equal weight, while capitalism weights influence by wealth. Wealthy people both cast more "dollar ballots" than poor ones in market purchases and exercise an influence on political decisions disproportionate to their numbers.[19] And, indeed, the demonstra-

higher the level of efficiency the more there will be to transfer to those it is desired to favour, given the amount that is to be taken away from others." [Peter Bohm, *Social Efficiency: A Concise Introduction to Welfare Economics* (New York: Wiley, 1973), p. 73]

[11] Branko Horvat, *The Political Economy of Socialism* (Armonk, NY: Sharpe, 1982).

[12] James M. Buchanan, *The Limits of Liberty: Between Anarchy and Leviathan* (Chicago: University of Chicago, 1975).

[13] Richard Edwards, *Contested Terrain: The Transformation of the Workplace in the Twentieth Century* (New York: Basic Books, 1979).

[14] Joseph A. Schumpeter, *Capitalism, Socialism, and Democracy* (New York: Harper and Row, 1950).

[15] Charles E. Lindblom, *Politics and Markets* (New York: Harper and Row, 1977).

[16] Milton Friedman, *Capitalism and Freedom* (Chicago: University of Chicago, 1962).

[17] Peter L. Berger, *The Capitalist Revolution* (New York: Basic Books, 1986).

[18] The phrase "not sufficient" recognizes that many capitalist societies are illiberal and undemocratic. Macpherson aptly observes that historical correlation does not in itself demonstrate causation, and that the empirical data is consistent *both* with the interpretation that liberal political society was conducive to the development of capitalism *and* with the converse argument. See John E. Elliott and John Cownie, *Competing Philosophies in American Political Economics* (Santa Monica: Goodyear, 1975). Whatever one's conclusion on this debate, it is clear that democracy is at best a secondary and supplementary normative criterion in the mainstream tradition.

[19] For incisive recent analyses of the disproportionate influence of the wealthy in U.S. electoral processes and government policy decisions, see Thomas B. Edsall, *The New Politics of Inequality* (New York: W.W. Norton, 1984); Thomas Ferguson and Joel Rogers, *Right Turn: The Decline of the Democrats and the Future of American Politics* (New York: Hill and Wang, 1986); William Greider, *Secrets of the Temple: How the Federal Reserve Runs the Country* (New York: Simon and Schuster, 1987).

tion of compatibility has been accomplished by restricting the domain of comparison: democracy is defined as a "political" matter, pertaining to the "public sector" of capitalist society. Although a public sector is required to adjudicate capitalist property relations and rectify its problematic accompaniments to capitalism (such as "externalities" and gross distributional injustices), it need not intrude on market capitalism's basic institutions and processes.

This argument rests on the distinction between a "public" realm, where democratic norms apply, and a "nonpublic" realm, where they do not. There is a dual justification for excluding democratic norms from the "nonpublic" realms of production, exchange, and consumption (in the broadest sense). The first draws on the methodological individualism informing the mainstream conception of society. The individual is prior to society, and is assumed to be "rational" – that is, goal-oriented and purposeful in adjusting means in the pursuit of ends. Hence, social optima in realms where social coordination is "automatic" or "spontaneous" are achieved through atomistic behavior. This applies to consumption and, under the "invisible hand" theorem, to exchange, which is perceived to be coordinated by "impersonal" demand and supply relationships. Production, of course, normally requires social interaction which, under capitalism, on its face is both self-conscious and hierarchically organized. Here, a second justification applies. Given consumer preferences, resources, and technology, and given the assumptions that rational behavior is "greedy" (that is, occurs under conditions of "nonsatiation"), that the "invisible hand" acts as a "natural selection" mechanism, and that technology underlies production, then efficiency considerations make democracy economically superfluous for production. Resource and output levels and compositions determined by pure "efficiency" criteria leave no room (or need) for discretionary judgments by democratic procedures. Intra-enterprise decisions thus only appear to be autocratic. Under competitive conditions, business "leaders" motivated by the criterion of profitability (which here coincides with efficiency) are impelled to make the decisions they do. A "democratic" organization of industry, under competition and subject to efficiency criteria, would be impelled to make the same decisions concerning resource employment, resource combinations, and output levels and compositions. Alternative decisions would not be economically viable.

This line of thought explains why efficiency is so central to the mainstream paradigm. Because efficiency can be derived from mainstream axioms, it is a "pure" concept independent of nonefficiency considerations. As such, it can be used to show how optimal economic behavior is rooted in what Sargent has termed the "deeper aspects of the model" – that is, preferences and technology.[20]

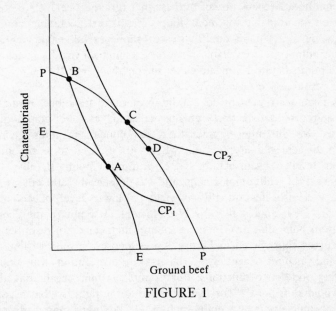

FIGURE 1

A Neoclassical Efficiency Parable. In neoclassical economics, the demonstration of the economic superiority of capitalism is typically accomplished via the concept of Pareto optimality: specifically, given "invisible hand" market processes and rational individuals, preferences and technology insure the achievement of a point which is efficient and which has the property that no agent's position can be improved without a deterioration in at least one other agent's position. Graphical analysis can readily be used in this exposition.

Consider Figure 1, wherein the maximum potential for producing an illustrative set of commodities is shown by curve PP. PP's concavity is due to the (assumed) increasing cost of moving resources from the production

[20] In a discussion of James Tobin's financial theory, Sargent writes that:

 . . . in this line of model [that is, in neoclassical equilibrium models of the financial sector], the parameters of cross substitutabilities of asset demands remain important, but are not themselves among the free parameters of a model, instead being dependent on deeper aspects of the model such as agents' locations in time and space and their preferences, production possibilities, the probability laws governing the random variables in the model, the structure of legal restrictions on intermediaries, and monetary and fiscal policy, in the sense of laws of motion for the components of government indebtedness. It is the parameters of this list of objects which are the free parameters of the model . . . [Thomas Sargent, "Beyond Supply and Demand Curves in Macroeconomics," *Staff Report 77*, (Research Department: Federal Reserve Bank of Minnesota, February 1982), p. 6].

of one commodity (chateaubriand) to another (ground beef); PP's position depends on the available volume of inputs (resources), including labor, and on technology. Any point on PP thus presupposes full employment and maximum output given available resources. Points above PP are unattainable, and points below it indicate either unemployment or the failure to use available resources "efficiently."

The CP curves represent commodity preference functions. Along each curve, aggregate satisfaction remains constant as one commodity is substituted for the other. Under these conditions, maximum economic efficiency is achieved at point C, where PP is tangent to the highest attainable level of satisfaction, CP2. Although point B, like C, is characterized by full employment and "economically efficient" use of resources – it also lies on PP – it yields a lower level of commodity satisfaction, CP1, and is allocatively inefficient. At point A, the economy suffers from both allocative inefficiency and inefficiency in resource use.

The curves constructed in Figure 1 presuppose a given distribution of wealth and income. Typically, a change in distribution will alter the commodity preference functions. For example, a more egalitarian distribution would shift the CP curves downward to the right, so that maximum efficiency would occur at a point such as D. The poor, now eating more ground beef, are better off; the rich, enjoying less chateaubriand, are worse off. By contrast, in moving from points A or B to point C, efficiency can be enhanced in such a way that one or more individual's positions improve without adverse effects on other individuals' positions.

In Figure 2, curve UU – referred to as either a "utility locus" or "contract curve" – traces out the implications for utility of wealth and income redistributions in a two-person economy. Each point along UU embodies maximum efficiency in that the position of one is enhanced only at the expense of the other. The "social welfare" (SW1, SW2 ...) curves depict social evaluations (for example, by political leaders or social philosophers) of the relative desirability of different utility pairs for the two individuals. Total social welfare is constant along each SW curve, and increases with higher-numbered SW curves. Under these assumptions, points B, C, and D are all "Pareto-optimal," in that each is economically efficient; but ascending levels of social welfare are associated with each point, up to a maximum at D. Point A is "Pareto-inferior" to points B, C, and D; it lies below the utility locus UU and thus is not economically efficient.

II.   A CRITIQUE OF THE PRIMACY OF EFFICIENCY

Despite this considerable intellectual legacy, the superiority of capitalism as an economic system cannot be sustained using the efficiency criterion.

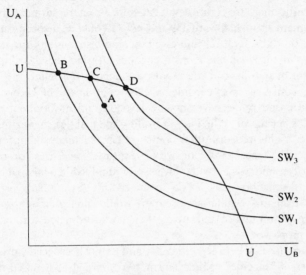

FIGURE 2

First, efficiency is not a sufficient criterion. In the above neoclassical parable, more efficiency is not invariably preferable to less. Point A in Figure 2, for example, encompasses a higher level of social welfare than is found at point B, despite the greater efficiency at B. In general, the set of economically efficient points does not welfare-dominate all economically inefficient points. So other normative criteria cannot be brought in as merely secondary criteria.

Second, and more fundamentally, the efficiency criterion is necessarily interdependent with other evaluative criteria. It is impossible to establish a social outcome using one evaluative criterion which is immune to evaluation using another. Any given set of preferences, like those embodied in the CP curves in Figure 1, presuppose particular distributions of income, wealth, and power; hence, judging a particular pattern of efficiency to be socially desirable implies approval for these underlying distributions as well. Suppose there is a norm of "justice" based on the extent of equality in income distribution. Then any change in either the norm of efficiency or of justice will affect both – neither can be independently altered. Reducing unemployment, for example, significantly raises the income of the unemployed, hence reducing inequality in income distribution; and because purchasing power is differently distributed, effective preferences are also changed; this, in turn, changes the location of allocative efficiency. In Figure 1, a reduction in unemployment may result in a movement from A toward D, and not C (since C's specification rests on a given set of preferences and given income distribution); the movement toward D, in turn, simultaneously changes the income distribution, the composition of output, and the point of allocative efficiency.

For the converse case, consider a classic argument of Henry Simons. Simons proposed progressive income taxation and government transfers, *inter alia*, as means of reducing "prevailing inequalities in wealth, income and power." This redistribution could be carried out with no effects on efficiency; only "charlatans," he wrote, confuse "measures for regulating relative prices and wages with devices for diminishing inequality."[21] But Simons's distinction fails. The changes in (expressed) preferences stemming from his egalitarian program would alter relative prices, thus yielding new positions of allocative efficiency coordinated through market exchange processes.

The sharp division between efficiency and equity is especially problematic in instances of "specific" egalitarianism.[22] We have already noted that votes are apportioned equally in most liberal democracies, while wealth is unequally distributed. Presumably, there are many rich people who would value an additional vote more highly than a marginal unit of money ($100?), and many poor people with the opposite preference ordering. That market exchange of votes for money is illegal, despite the prospective enhancement of allocative efficiency achievable thereby, may attest to the widespread egalitarian sentiment for specific patterns of resource allocations themselves. A modified version of this principle applies to rationing of necessities in times of scarcity. In such circumstances, allocative efficiency rules in a market setting imply large price increases, which may drive many of the poor from the market. Redistributions of wealth and income to resolve this problem might have to be very large, and thus politically impractical. Especially if the scarcity is perceived to be temporary (as with gasoline rationing in the 1970s), temporary rationing (for example, by queuing) "may be a better alternative, even if it does distort the allocative efficiency of the economy. . . ."[23]

Because evaluative criteria are interdependent, positing both the primacy of one criterion, efficiency, and its compatibility with other criteria involves logical contradiction. Consider the mainstream argument for the compatibility of democracy and capitalism. Suppose capitalism is justified as good

---

[21] Henry Simons, *Economic Policy for a Free Society* (Chicago: University Press, 1948).
[22] James Tobin, "On Limiting the Domain of Inequality," E.S. Phelps, ed., *Economic Justice* (Baltimore: Penguin, 1973).
[23] J. de V. Graff, *Theoretical Welfare Economics* (New York: Cambridge University, 1967).

because it is efficient. This immediately raises the question of whether the use of the efficiency criterion undercuts the achievement of a democratic society. A contradiction between the two principles could arise if a firm, say, would make different allocations when run autocratically by a rational manager than when run democratically by its workers; for them efficiency would require ignoring workers' votes. No contradiction arises if it can be shown that areas in which two criteria might imply differ allocations are beyond the competence of one. Specifically, the mainstream argument denies that democracy is relevant in production; it posits that technology and resource prices dictate an optimal method of organizing production, so democratic decision making in this realm would be at best redundant. But on what basis is it determined that the organization of production is a purely technical matter? On the basis that, due to greed, all producers seek out efficient methods; those who do not will disappear due to the discipline imposed by the "invisible hand"; firms observed in the marketplace are not democratic; hence democratic criteria are irrelevant in the achievement of productive efficiency.[24] But this argument for banishing democracy from production is circular – efficiency is both the test of market survival and the criterion for evaluating system performance. Efficiency cannot be used to justify the primacy of efficiency as an evaluative criterion; for if it is, then market processes become both means and ends. This attempt to recruit technology in the defense of a fundamentally social form of organization fails on logical grounds.

A third objection to the efficiency paradigm is that efficiency cannot be postulated as a "pure" and primary criterion without making socially implausible or abhorrent assumptions. Consider what is required to separate the notion of economic efficiency from nonefficiency considerations. A simple engineering rule selecting that use of inputs which yields maximum output may be sensible (leaving aside externalities such as pollution) for nonhuman inputs. In the above parable, labor is merely one among many readily-quantifiable "resources" available for "use" in production. But "labor" does not consist merely of some quantum of manual or mental energy. There are several reasons for this. First, human interaction is irreducible to the sum of its atomistic parts. Second, because laborers are not dead, the timing of market processes is such that labor cannot be prespecified; the worker learns both from others and from engaging in production processes, *after* the sale. Third, the quality of labor and the

---

[24] In their analysis of capitalism and democracy, Bowles and Gintis have termed this separation an "isomorphism of sites and practices" [Samuel Bowles and Herbert Gintis, *Democracy and Capitalism* (New York: Basic Books, 1986), p. 100]. See also Bowles, "The Production Process in a Competitive Economy: Walrasian, Neo-Hobbesian, and Marxian Models," *American Economic Review*, vol. 75 (1985), pp. 16–36.

decision to maintain an employment relation depends on factors irrelevant for nonhuman inputs.[25]

Labor is performed within the constraints imposed by a capitalist organization of production, by human beings whose ongoing processes of struggle, negotiation, conflict, and cooperation – with one another and with owners and managers – define what labor is, how much and how intensely labor is actually applied in production, and how it will be compensated. Thus, determination of what is economically "efficient" is a social – not merely technical – matter. We see again the impact which conceptualizing production as technological – as a "thing" – and labor as independent of social context has on mainstream theory. Insofar as people engage in production, a portion of their existence is sold to an employer. As workers, people are themselves things, to be manipulated and controlled like other inputs. Hence, people who sell their capacity to work often have left to themselves only their role as consumers, as recipients and enjoyers of things. But if the distinctive quality of human beings is understood, for example, as the creation, development, and exercise of capacities and talents in cooperative association, the traditional efficiency paradigm breaks down, because the efficiency category changes its human and social content.[26]

Postulating efficiency as a "pure" criterion leads to another conclusion which is absurd in experience. If efficiency and nonefficiency criteria were in fact distinct, it would be a matter of indifference whether the inefficiency associated with an unemployment rate of 10 percent resulted from an across-the-board reduction of 10 percent in working hours for the entire labor force, or from a one hundred percent reduction in employment for 10 percent of the labor force. But the latter alternative is radically inferior to the former in terms of insecurity of income,[27] "terror [in] the private life of the unemployed,"[28] and the social dislocation associated with family dissolution, crime and incarceration, alcoholism and drug abuse, suicide, and so forth.

A final objection is that the efficiency paradigm abstracts from institutional structure and from the imperfections beleaguering any existing economy. Of course, textbook expositions show how, in a perfectly-competitive general equilibrium, perfectly flexible prices guarantee the achievement of efficiency in an idealized market capitalist utopia. In practice, imperfections abound – monopoly, resource immobilities, uncertainty, indivisibilities,

---

[25] See, for example, Albert O. Hirschman, *Exit, Voice, Loyalty* (Cambridge: Harvard University, 1970).
[26] Macpherson, *Life and Times.*
[27] John K. Galbraith, *The Affluent Society* (Boston: Houghton Mifflin, 1957).
[28] Schumpeter, *Economic Development*, p. 70.

coordination failures, and so on; hence, "it is probable that a society will find itself well within the [production possibility] frontier. Sub-optimal situations will usually be the only *feasible* ones."[29]

For example, the production possibility curve PP shown in Figure 1 assumes the maximal exploitation of resources; the tangency C assumes tastes are completely expressed in market transactions. The "efficiency locus" EE, by contrast, portrays illustrative production possibilities actually attainable in a feasible capitalist economy. As a further example of how institutional structure is ignored, in Figure 2 it is assumed that the distribution of wealth and income can be adjusted, by lump-sum taxes and transfers, in such a way that efficiency is unaffected. Any such scheme, however, would most likely be economically (as well as politically) unfeasible.[30] Tension between feasibility and optimality pervades the real choices only hinted at by this parable, casting fundamental doubt on the efficacy of evaluating capitalism based on a pure efficiency criterion.

III.   THE PRIMACY OF LIBERTY AND THE DEMOCRATIC ECONOMY

Whereas the efficiency paradigm has been dominant in mainstream economics, dissenting intellectual traditions and political movements have either interpreted efficiency more broadly than the mainstream tradition, or viewed it as just one of a set of normative criteria. While far from homogeneous, these traditions have emphasized democracy, equality, and community to a far greater degree than the mainstream. We consider here the writings of Marx, Tawney, and Rawls.

In Marx's critique of capitalism, inefficiencies – notably crises, depressions, unemployment, waste of human and natural resources, economic concentration and monopoly – are duly criticized as contradictory elements in capitalist industrialization. But these inefficiencies are offset by capitalism's technological progressivity. In any event, Marx primarily excoriates capitalism not so much for its inefficiency as for its dehumanizing alienation and exploitation.[31] Marx envisions enhanced efficiency in the future, but focuses primarily on the emancipation of labor, the supersession of alienation and exploitation, and the creation of democratic processes of cooperative association and self-governance.[32]

---

[29] Graff, *Welfare Economics*, p. 67.

[30] Paul A. Samuelson, *Foundations of Economic Analysis* (Cambridge: Harvard, 1947).

[31] John E. Elliott, "Continuity and Change in the Evolution of Marx's Theory of Alienation: From the Manuscripts through the Grundrisse to Capital," *History of Political Economy*, vol. 11 (1979), pp. 317–362. See also Elliott, "Marx's Category and Typology of Exploitation," mimeo, Los Angeles: University of Southern California, 1988.

[32] John E. Elliott, "Karl Marx, Founding Father of Workers' Self-Governance?" *Economics and Industrial Democracy* (August 1987).

What is important for our purposes is that Marx viewed production not as a "natural" process, but as a site of human exploitation: he rejected the designation of production as immune to evaluation by nonefficiency norms.

But if, following Marx, the primacy of efficiency in organizing production is rejected, what principle can take its place? Richard Tawney responded to this question directly. Unlike mainstream theorists, for whom the efficiency criterion offers a means of evaluating capitalism on the morally neutral ground of rational optimization, for Tawney the central issue in the critique of capitalism is "moral and political, even more than economic. It is a question, not only of the failures of the existing order, but of its standards of success."[33]

In Tawney's ethical theory of capitalism, liberty is the preeminent political value, and institutions enabling people to become "the best of which they are capable are the supreme political good." Liberty is then superior to equality, in event of conflict. But when liberty is extended from polity to economy, so that all are equally protected against abuses of power, and power is used for the "general advantage," "a large measure of equality, so far from inimical to liberty, is essential to it."[34]

According to Tawney, liberty and equality are also complementary to community, where community is understood as the incorporation of individuals in rich human associations pursuant to solidarity and social cohesion. Community is fostered by abolishing social and economic privileges, making health and education, *inter alia*, generally available, and through superseding industrial autocracy by democratic systems of workers' self-governance. Indeed, for genuine democracy, democratic principles must be extended beyond the political realm into such matters as education, the distribution of wealth, and the governance of enterprise.[35]

In this dual insistence on the inseparability of social and economic relations[36] and on the right of "self-direction," the outlines of an alternative principle for economic organization can be discerned. The introduction of worker ownership and direction on the basis of democratic participation – what we might term the democratic economy – can, in Tawney's analysis, bring about liberty in the economic sphere (hence opening the possibility of liberty in all of society).[37]

---

[33] Richard H. Tawney, *The Radical Tradition*, ed. Rita Hinden (London: Allen and Unwin, 1964), pp. 139–140.

[34] Richard H. Tawney, *Equality* (New York: Harcourt Brace, 1931), pp. 221–226.

[35] *ibid.*, pp. 131, 148. See also Tawney, *The Radical Tradition*, p. 121.

[36] Tawney's view and our own clearly clashes with Walzer's argument that an evaluative assessment of society can examine the various social domains separately; see Michael Walzer, *Spheres of Justice* (New York: Basic Books, 1983).

[37] Tawney believed that democratizing economic life would increase economic efficiency (see Section IV below), and viewed increases in efficiency consistent with liberty – and hence

An application of John Rawls's theory of justice to the evaluation of capitalism also suggests the replacement of the efficiency paradigm with different evaluative norms.[38] Rawls's first principle of justice – that each person has an equal right to the most extensive system of basic liberties consistent with a similar system of liberty for all – gives first priority, as in Tawney's argument, to liberty. Improving economic conditions both reduce obstacles to the exercise of equal liberties and render further economic amenities of declining marginal importance; hence, liberty will not be exchanged for enhanced economic well-being, "at least not once a certain level of wealth has been attained."[39]

Rawls's second or "difference principle" pertains to equality and fraternity: inequalities should be arranged so as to most benefit the least advantaged members of society. Differences in wealth and income are justified only if the situation of all improves, and if offices and positions associated with inequalities are open to all under conditions of fair equality of opportunity. Consequently, justice is "prior to efficiency," in that reform of the structure of an unjust society is warranted even if efficiency suffers thereby. Conversely, increasing efficiency is not permissible if it introduces inequalities yielding economic improvements for some and disadvantages for others.

In sum, whereas the primacy of efficiency criterion advocates the highest level of justice consistent with maximum efficiency, both Tawney and Rawls espouse the highest level of efficiency consonant with stated principles of justice. Both authors' critique of the primacy of efficiency rests on an alternative evaluative norm, liberty, which must be redefined for their purposes. In their arguments, the domain of liberty is social relations, its content the ability to pursue self-realization; in the efficiency paradigm, the domain of liberty is demarcated by property relations, its content the freedom to dispose of what one owns.[40] These contrasting definitions, in

---

with equality, community, and democracy – as desirable. But efficiency considerations must always yield to these more basic values, when they conflict. Efficiency is not an acceptable "substitute for liberty" as an evaluative norm. Nor, over a wide range, is efficiency superior to justice, for what is at stake is not whether capitalism "is efficient, but whether it is just. If industry could be so organized that the mass of workers would feel that the social order was just, a decrease in efficiency would be cheap at the price." Indeed, the deposition of England's ruling "economic oligarchy" is worth a "generation of disorder and inefficiency . . . "[Tawney, *R.H. Tawney's Commonplace Book*, ed. J.M. Winter and D.M. Joslin (Cambridge: Cambridge University, 1972)]

[38] For an analysis interpreting Rawls in this way, see Jeffrey Reiman, "The Labor Theory of the Difference Principle," *Philosophy & Public Affairs*, vol. 12 (1983), pp. 133–159.

[39] John Rawls, *A Theory of Justice* (Cambridge: Harvard University, 1971), pp. 542, 543.

[40] The following sources provide alternative recent discussions of relationships among liberty, equality, and democracy: Sidney Verba and Gary Orren, "The Meaning of Equality in America," *Political Science Quarterly*, vol. 100 (1985), pp. 369–388; Philip Green, "Equality Since Rawls: Objective Philosophers, Subjective Citizens, and Rational Choice," *Journal of*

turn, reveal these authors' dissent from the variant of individualism underlying the efficiency paradigm: in their writings, the individualism of human beings is defined not prior to society, but jointly with their social identity as members of communities and social totalities.

IV. THE EFFICIENCY-EQUITY TRADE-OFF AND THE DEMOCRATIC ECONOMY

The compatibility of capitalism and democracy in the mainstream argument is premised on the restriction of nonefficiency norms to noneconomic realms. To the extent that the latter norms invade the economic sphere and interfere with the working of the efficiency criterion, efficiency will suffer. This conclusion is aptly illustrated by the writing of Arthur Okun. Okun states that equality in the distribution of income "would be my *ethical* preference" [emphasized in original]. This preference is derived from an extension of the argument for equal political and civil rights: income equality would reinforce the moral worth and respect of citizens and the "equivalent value of membership in society for all." However, he argues that income equality would impose substantial costs on society, because it would forgo the opportunity to use material rewards as incentives to production. In short, a trade-off exists between economic equality and economic efficiency. It is sensible, therefore, to accept some inequality in practice to insure efficiency.[41]

Okun's equality/efficiency trade-off has long passed into the realm of common economic wisdom. But why *does* more equity in income yield less efficiency? Okun himself argues that competitive markets pay workers and investors the "value of their contributions to output."[42] Among these contributions, he singles out acquired assets, natural abilities, and effort. So, although the game is fair, market processes generate winners and losers.

Okun's argument has a dual basis. In part, it rests on the marginal productivity theory of distribution, wherein there exists an objective basis for assessing the individual contribution to output of each resource used in production. So any production process can be divided into a sum of divisible constituent elements. In addition, Okun relies on the invisible

---

Politics, vol. 47 (1985), pp. 972–997; Jan Narveson, "Equality vs. Liberty: Advantage, Liberty," *Social Philosophy & Policy*, vol. 2, no. 1 (Autumn 1984), 33–60; Bowles and Gintis, *Democracy*, p. 4ff.

[41] Arthur M. Okun, *Equality and Efficiency: The Big Tradeoff* (Washington: Brookings, 1975), pp. 48–49. The very notion of an equality/efficiency trade-off suggests that *in*equality is required for efficiency. But this assumes that incentives are important only to motivate those at the upper end of the income scale; that is, entrepreneurial and managerial activities alone must be stimulated, not those undertaken in production processes by lower-paid workers. Here again is the fundamental neoclassical assumption that production is technical.

[42] *ibid.*, p. 41.

hand to insure that ideal and actual rewards to factors of production correspond.

But the premises of Okun's argument become untenable once one admits that production is not solely a technological process; for activity in structured social contexts cannot be completely mediated by an objective invisible hand. This point has been repeatedly emphasized in discussions of the firm.

Consider Coase's insights on the nature of the firm. In Coase's classic article, firms exist because the market mechanism is costly: the boundary of the firm is determined by transactions costs. Within the firm, "the direction of resources is dependent on an entrepreneur."[43] But then these intrafirm resources do not have fixed unit prices, and the marginal productivity theory cannot be reliably used to cost them out: firm production processes are "indivisible."[44]

More recently, the literature on efficiency wages has explored the fact that a firm hiring a worker faces a principal/agent problem: the firm's outcome depends on the agent's effort, but the firm lacks perfect information about that effort.[45] Even if implicit contracts can be written that bridge the gap between firm offer and employee performance, such contracts will be, in Rosen's terms, *bilateral*; the firm will not make *unilateral* employment offers on the basis of given labor-market demand curves.[46] But then economic efficiency results from negotiation; it is not pregiven – the invisible hand theorem is defended by sacrificing marginal productivity pricing. If contracts guaranteeing worker behavior cannot be written, then there is an indivisible social dimension to behavior in production. The amount of work actually done may be determined by custom, power, loyalty, or other factors.[47]

Improving the Terms of the Trade-off. But if the sphere of production is

[43] Ronald Coase, "The Nature of the Firm," *Economica*, New Series vol. IV (1937), pp. 386–405. The quotation is on p. 397.

[44] Aoki has also argued that Coase's theory of the firm requires a conception of behavioral coordination beyond that which the market can supply. Grubb finds empirical support for the notion that there are indivisible aspects of contributions to production. Masahiko Aoki, *The Co-operative Game Theory of the Firm* (New York: Oxford University, 1984). David Grubb, "Ability and Power over Production in the Distribution of Earnings," *Review of Economics and Statistics*, vol. 67 (1985), pp. 188–194.

[45] See George Akerlof and Janet Yellen, *Efficiency Wage Models of the Labor Market* (Cambridge: Cambridge University, 1986).

[46] Sherwin Rosen, "Implicit Contracts: A Survey," *Journal of Economic Literature*, vol. 23 (1985), pp. 1144–1175. Stiglitz also argues that models incorporating private information repeal the law of supply and demand; see Joseph Stiglitz, "The Causes and Consequences of the Dependence of Quality on Price," *Journal of Economic Literature*, vol. 25 (1987), pp. 1–48.

[47] See, respectively: George Akerlof, "Labor Contracts as Partial Gift Exchange," *Quarterly Journal of Economics*, vol. 97 (1982), pp. 543–569; Bowles and Gintis, *Democracy*; Hirschman, *Exit*.

in part constituted by social interaction, the application of evaluative norms besides efficiency may improve labor productivity. This argument can be made on two grounds. Consider first the case of "gift" exchange in production. Akerlof suggests that workers are motivated to exceed work quotas when the firm pays gift wages – that is, wages above market-clearing levels.[48] In effect, workers are greedy, and the firm plays to their greed. It is quite possible that in some cases the payment of gift wages implies a redistribution of total income within the firm along more egalitarian lines. In such a case, more equality yields more efficiency.[49]

A second argument proceeds by interpreting equality as pertaining to the distribution of decision-making authority within firms, not merely to income. In this perspective, workers place themselves under the authority of firm owners or managers, but – because of the principal/agent problem – the actual content of the production process is not spelled out in the labor contract. Employers, especially in large-scale operations, impose hierarchical organization over production to control and direct workers. Workers shirk labor not so much because of inherent disposition, but to resist domination. Therefore, they must be monitored as well as bribed into laboring. The efficacy of the command process within firms thus depends on the extent and intensity of managerial supervision of work effort, the likelihood that workers will be fired in the event of noncompliance with management directives, and the cost to workers of losing their jobs (which, in turn, depends on macroeconomic conditions).[50]

These two arguments yield different conclusions. If Akerlof is right, there is no need to punitively monitor workers – only to pay them off. A paternalistic but shrewd employer could elicit a tacit exchange embodying greater work effort simply by paying a "gift" of higher wages. But if writers such as Bowles and Gintis are correct, the antagonism between capital and labor attributable to hierarchy and domination suggests that the establishment of more democratic modes of industrial organization can reduce conflict over power relations in production. The reorganization of work along less hierarchical lines and participation by workers in investment decisions may have dramatic behavioral effects: "economic democracy, by providing an alternative to unaccountable hierarchical authority in

[48] Akerlof, "Labor Contracts."

[49] The gift analogy might be further extended. Suppose workers evaluate social interaction using a justice criterion wherein kindness should be shown to the weak. If the firm's manager performs an act which shows consciousness of this criterion – for example, by granting extra-contractual benefits to a fellow worker stricken by an unusual emergency – then workers might increase their output in exchange.

[50] Bowles, "Production Process"; and Bowles and Gintis, *Democracy*. The presence of surveillance methods in production suggests that Akerlof's depiction on the "sociology" of production is incomplete.

investment and production, can promote loyalty, commitment, and accountability on the part of workers and those who control investment resources."[51] So increasing equality in the sense of access to workplace decision making can improve efficiency; stated differently, for any given expenditure on wages and surveillance, an increase in workplace democracy can improve productivity, *ceteris paribus*.

This argument is reinforced by the distinctions between allocative, dynamic, and "X" efficiency. It has sometimes been contended that, because of their tendency to maximize net income per worker instead of profit, worker-managed enterprises may exhibit a lower degree of allocative efficiency than their capitalist counterparts.[52] Supporters of industrial democracy generally deny this claim,[53] and debate continues on this matter.[54] But even if this claim of traditional capitalist superiority on grounds of allocative efficiency is correct, gains in "X" efficiency and dynamic efficiency net of costs of changing factory conditions under worker management – by reducing labor-management strife, eliminating strikes, enhancing worker morale and team spirit, and promoting a greater sense of justice and community – may more than offset any loss in allocative efficiency.[55]

Recent analyses postulating complementarity between nonefficiency and efficiency evaluative criteria are reminiscent of earlier arguments, especially those made by dissenting schools of thought. The most famous such argument, perhaps, belongs to Adam Smith, who observed that higher wages, by permitting improvements in nutrition and health care, could well increase the quality of productivity of labor. Another familiar example pertains to the experiences of Robert Owen at his experimental factory in New Lanark. There, Owen demonstrated that (at least under auspicious conditions) higher wages, shorter hours, better working conditions, and better health, education, and recreational opportunities can be accompanied by significant improvements in labor productivity and enterprise profitability.

[51] Bowles and Gintis, *Democracy*, p. 211.

[52] Benjamin Ward, *The Socialist Economy: A Study of Organizational Alternatives* (New York: Random House, 1967).

[53] Bronko Horvat, "On the Theory of the Labor-managed Firm," B. Horvat, M. Markovic, and R. Supek, eds., *Self-Governing Socialism, Vol. II* (White Plains: International Arts and Sciences Press, 1975), pp. 229–240; David E. Sisk, "The Cooperative Model vs. Cooperative Organization," *Journal of Economic Issues*, vol. 6 (1982), pp. 211–220.

[54] James E. Meade, *Alternative Systems of Business Organization and Workers' Remuneration* (Winchester: Allen and Unwin, 1986).

[55] Jaroslav Vanek, "Toward a Just, Efficient, and Fully Democratic Society," D. Jones and J. Svejnar, eds., *Advances in the Economic Analysis of Participatory and Labor Managed Firms, Vol. 2* (Greenwich: JAI Press, 1987); Vanek, "Decentralization under Workers' Management: A Theoretical Appraisal," J. Vanek, ed., *Self-Management: Economic Liberation of Man* (Baltimore: Penguin, 1975).

In a more extensive analysis, Karl Marx contended that if production (both within enterprises and throughout the economy at large) were under the democratic coordination and control of the "associated laborers," the greater spirit of community and cooperation thus created would both stimulate creativity and inventiveness and provide a collective framework for facilitating reductions in working hours. This, in turn, could elicit a dialectical process of progressive improvements in productivity and technology. Expanded leisure, presupposing democratization and expansion of educational opportunities, would increase the productive powers of labor. Rising labor productivity would then permit additional reductions in working hours, which could again foster expansions and improvements in education and science, *etc.*, in a dynamic and progressive chain. Thus, democracy, community, and liberty (in the sense both of participation in democratic decision-making processes and opportunities for cultivation of capacities and talents in leisure time), rather than reducing efficiency, could raise it.[56]

To take a final example, Tawney claimed that efficiency is fostered by "cohesion and solidarity" and a "strong sense of common interests." A vigorous program of communal provision of health, education, and other fundamental components of civilized living, in addition to enhancing equality of opportunity, contributes to the sense of community, and thereby increases efficiency. According to Tawney, industrial autocracy drives a wedge between workers' responsibilities and powers, thereby damaging efficiency. Democratic arrangements for industrial administration and governance would unite power and responsibility, thereby stimulating efficiency. The first task is to establish, for each enterprise and industry, a "constitution securing its member an effective voice in its governance" through a comprehensive system of coparticipation and democratic representation.[57]

---

[56] Karl Marx, *Grundrisse* (New York: Random House, 1973), pp. 709, 712.

[57] Tawney, *Radical Tradition*, p. 103; Tawney, *Equality*, pp. 131, 135. The following sources provide empirical assessment (generally favorable) of efficiency and other performance criteria under workers' self-management: Derek Jones and Jan Svegnar, eds. *Participatory and Self-Managed Firms: Evaluating Economic Performance* (Lexington: Lexington, 1982); Hem Jain, ed., *Worker Participation: Success and Problems* (New York: Praeger, 1980); Stephen Sachs, *Self-Management and Efficiency: Large Corporations in Yugoslavia* (London: George Allen and Unwin, 1983); David Schweickart, *Capitalism or Worker Control? An Ethical and Economic Appraisal* (New York: Praeger, 1980); Henk Thomas and Chris Logan, *Mondragon: An Economic Analysis* (Winchester: George Allen and Unwin, 1982).

[58] The second question is not identical to that asked in Section I. There, the question was whether a capitalist economic sector governed by the primacy of efficiency is consistent with democratic politics. In this section, the question is whether capitalism is compatible with a society in which democratic principles have been diffused throughout both the polity *and* the economy.

V. THE COMPATIBILITY OF CAPITALISM AND
THE DEMOCRATIC ECONOMY

Thus far, we have argued that economic behavior – especially in production – in a democratic society cannot be evaluated consistently or fully using only the criterion of efficiency. Indeed, once the primacy of efficiency (and the image of production as a technical process) is rejected, the possibility is created that interjecting nonefficiency criteria into production will increase efficiency. This argument leads to three fundamental questions. First, if a more democratic economy can increase efficiency, why shouldn't it emerge spontaneously through capitalist market processes? Second, can democratization be thoroughly or consistently achieved throughout economy and society?[58] Third, can capitalist economy be democratic (or, at least, can the extent of economic democratization substantially increase within a capitalist integument)? These questions are addressed in turn.

Impediments to the Spontaneous Emergence of Democratic Economy. We noted earlier that, according to neoclassical theory, intra-enterprise democracy is superfluous under capitalism, because efficiency considerations impel the same decisions regardless of politico-economic structure. As a corollary, "if democratic decision making were efficient, it would thus be chosen by market forces alone."[59] Insofar as it is not so chosen, it is presumably less efficient than its alternative(s).

The case for top-down hierarchy and authoritarian systems of governance in industry "is the case for autocratic government all the world over. It is efficient; it saves trouble; responsibility is placed in few hands; there is no nonsense about consulting committees."[60] In addition, mainstream expositors contend that inequality in decision making power – as well as in wealth and income – is dictated by the benefits for efficiency of economic leadership which, by some combination of nature and nurture (including division of labor between managerial and nonmanagerial workers), is concentrated in the hands of a small minority of the population.[61]

---

[59] Bowles and Gintis, *Democracy*, p. 80.

[60] Tawney, *Commonplace Book*, p. 26.

[61] Joseph Schumpeter, to take a prominent example, believed that "entrepreneurs" constitute a "special type of person," engaged in a "special type of conduct" (innovation) and guided by special kinds of motives (the "will to conquer," to "found a private kingdom," and to create). Such conduct "is accessible in very unequal measure and to relatively few people." The special character of entrepreneurial leadership creates a "boundary beyond which the majority of people do not function promptly by themselves and require help from a minority." Moreover, entrepreneurs must overcome opposition to innovations by groups threatened by them as well as win over consumers to new products. Schumpeter, *The Theory of Economic*

Exponents of economic and industrial democracy are typically unimpressed by elitist defenses of autocratic decision modes. They believe that purely genetic differences have been exaggerated, that education and training can often compensate for former nongenetic differences, and that the potentialities for efficacious democratic coparticipation in decision making are substantial. The major obstacles, then, to establishing a robust program of economic democratization – that is, a vigorously progressive tax structure, significantly expanded public programs for health, education, and job training and employment, a strong commitment to full employment, and widespread emergence of worker cooperatives and comanagement schemes in industry – are social and institutional impediments.

Impediments to economic and industrial democratization have a dual character. On the one hand, those whose relative wealth, income, and power are most vulnerable to reduction through expanded democracy – loosely the capitalist, corporate, propertied rich – must at least acquiesce to substantial socio-institutional change. On the other, the major prospective beneficiaries – workers and the lower two-thirds of the wealth and income distribution generally – must develop the unity, discipline, organization, and countervailing power to overturn old decision modes and institutions in favor of new ones.

Hence, the obstacles to economic democratization are considerable. In general, it is not necessarily true that a "stable economic structure does a better job at promoting productivity than any other alternative" and that a particular economic system or stage thereof will vacate in favor of a rival when it is no longer economically optimal.[62]

A central impediment is the inability of worker-directed firms to obtain credit, due to their lack of collateral and to the differing goals of workers and owners of financial capital. Moreover, substantial

---

Development, pp. 83n, 87, 93. If this view is correct, democratic participation, majority rule, and reductions in wealth and income inequalities would be discordant with robust innovation.

"Natural" inequality in industrial authority and decision making power is sometimes justified also by reference to alternative preference orderings. Suppose, for example, that the economic world is divided into (a large number of) "risk averters" and (a small number of) "risk takers." We shouldn't be surprised if the former become sellers of labor power, contenting themselves with a smaller but relatively more stable and secure contractual income, and the latter become capitalist employers, accepting the risks of more volatile, but on the whole higher, residual incomes.

[62] Richard W. Miller, *Analyzing Marx: Morality, Power, and History* (Princeton: Princeton, 1984), p. 209. It is quite possible, Miller states, that an economy dominated by peasants and artisans would have been just as efficient or more so than the feudal economic structure in late medieval Europe. But "sustained unity and collective discipline over large geographic areas would have been required to break the bonds that the overlords forged from the surpluses they controlled." Moreover, landowning families were able to sustain elements of wealth, power, and privilege long into the capitalist era even though feudal economic structures were manifestly inferior to capitalist ones.

difficulties [are] presented by the workers' lack of marketing networks, by the inexperience with democratic decision making fostered by a lifetime of work in hierarchical economic organizations, and even by the structure of a technology whose development has been attuned to gaining acceptance within a centralized and autocratic pyramid of economic power.[63]

The Creation of a Consistent Democratic Economy. Is it plausible that economic democracy could be implemented in such a manner that an economy would be consistently democratic at both the local (plant, enterprise, community) and societal levels? Critics raise several problems. For example, suppose worker cooperatives and/or comanagement arrangements were established in a significant number of enterprises in an advanced capitalist setting. Such industrial reform presumably would enhance democracy in decision making and reduce inequalities in power, wealth, and income within those enterprises. By itself, however, such reform would not suffice to ensure democracy and equality throughout industry as a whole. Indeed, the efficiency-wage and dual labor market literatures posit differences in wages and benefits, employment, and job security between a "core" or "primary" sector and a "periphery" or "secondary sector." Because it is precisely enterprises with a disproportionate number of "primary-sector" jobs that could most readily accommodate greater industrial democratization, reduction of inequality within such enterprises could be accompanied by greater relative inequality between primary and secondary sector workers. In addition, if a "got mine" mentality (or willingness to collaborate with employers) characterizes social action by primary workers, the spread of industrial democracy to the secondary sector might be thwarted.

An allied problem stems from the existence of multiple arenas of participatory action. Suppose economic democracy were implemented at the enterprise level throughout an economy, but that, thereafter, a small percentage of workers had relatively high incomes and a large percentage had relatively low incomes. Is it plausible to expect the now relatively well-off workers (or the majority of them in each enterprise) to be sufficiently sympathetic with their poorer brethren to support political actions designed to reduce inequalities in labor income among regions, industries, and enterprises? If not, industrial democracy and economic equality may conflict, as illustrated by large interregional income and unemployment differences in Yugoslavia.

It seems unlikely, in any event, that appeal to any abstract principle can

---

[63] Bowles and Gintis, *Democracy*, p. 86.

yield a definitive conclusion about the internal cohesion of programs for economic democratization. Tension between enterprise-level and society-wide democracy is probably inevitable, as is indicated in Tawney's classic exposition. Workers are properly the "centre of industrial authority," Tawney states, but only "subject to such limitations upon their sovereignty as may be imposed in the interest of the community as a whole." That the "industrial sovereignty" of workers within an enterprise or industry is appropriately subject to the "larger sovereignty of the community" is an "inevitable contradiction."[64] Several elements of complementarity, however, help to soften this "contradiction." First, economic democracy requires unity, solidarity, and widespread support. This, in turn, is fostered by a more, rather than less, comprehensive program of democratization, with benefits extending significantly beyond the "labor aristocracy" in the primary sector. Next, a vigorous full employment program tends both to reduce income inequality and to enhance the bargaining capacities for industrial democracy in primary sector enterprises. Moreover, if reduction of industrial autocracy does increase efficiency, then benefits from higher productivity in the enterprises which pioneer with democratic decision processes will tend to be shared, to some extent, throughout society.

Implications of Democratic Economy for Capitalism. Earlier, we characterized capitalism as embodying free disposal of labor, market processes in allocation and pricing, and private ownership and inheritance rights in property. On the face of it, the first two are consonant with a democratic economy, including a substantial transfer of intra-enterprise industrial authority to workers. What about property relations? Traditionally, the notion of private ownership has included usufruct, beneficiary, and disposal rights. Usufruct rights within capitalist enterprises, in turn, have classically presumed a capital-labor relationship exhibiting the authority and directorial control of capitalist employers or their managerial agents over the use of labor power. The precise impact of significant transfers of usufruct rights to workers in intra-enterprise decisions thus depends on the extent of "separation of ownership and management." In owner-managed enterprises, conflicts over usufruct authority could be large, and worker owned cooperatives would be a major alternative to directly challenging owner authority within capitalist enterprises. In principle, within management-controlled enterprises, it should be possible to substantially expand workers' authority or usufruct rights relative to management while retraining customary beneficiary and disposal rights for capitalists.

Democratic economy may also conflict with beneficiary and/or disposal rights. A key element in industrial democracy would be a transfer to

---

[64] Tawney, *The Radical Tradition*, pp. 103, 109.

workers by owners of at least a portion of their interest in and direction of the enterprise's net income. Such transfers may be nonvoluntary or voluntary. Nonvoluntary transfers, in fact, are an ongoing feature of capitalist economies. Regulation of externalities associated with production of particular commodities mitigates the right of disposal based on ownership. Consequently, some yardstick must be developed to indicate when the scale of perceived social need is sufficiently great to warrant public relation or empowerment of worker control over benefits or property disposition.

Might owners of firms *voluntarily* give up a portion of their dividends and their right of free disposal to their workers in exchange, say, for enhanced productivity (and hence net income)? The proposition is problematic, in large part because such contracts typically would be asymmetric – the capitalist must surrender her portion of the quid pro quo before receiving the payoff. A bargain of this type, then, is only remotely possible, as when firm performance has deteriorated beyond some threshold of acceptable return on net income. So "lemon" firms normally constitute the pool of candidates for voluntary surrender of capitalists' carte blanche rights. Even with "lemon" firms, however, experience has shown that this bargain is rarely struck: for one thing, many "lemons" are components of conglomerate firms, so that underproductive assets are interwoven into an overall scheme (as in the case of USX); for another, capitalists may be far more inclined to sell out altogether than, in effect, to bargain away their ability to walk away from firms whose ability to generate returns has become questionable.

Economic democracy traditionally connotes processes for democratic decision making in industry and society at large, not merely within enterprises. What is critical here is not ownership *per se*, but rather disposal over capital assets. One of capitalism's fundamental property rights has been capitalists' freedom to change the form and location of investment. A "socialization of investment," not only in Keynes's sense of a substantial supplementation of private by public expenditures as an integral part of a full employment program, but in the broader sense of infusion of more democratic and egalitarian aspirations into the structure of investment may well raise a greater challenge for substenance of capitalist property relations than extension of intra-enterprise worker participatory democracy.[65]

An empirical assessment of the compatibility of alternative arrangements and institutions of economic democracy with capitalist economy is beyond

[65] Michael Harrington, *Socialism* (New York: Saturday Review of Literature, 1972); Martin Carnoy and Derek Shearer, *Economic Democracy: The Challenge of the 1980s* (Armonk, New York: M.E. Sharpe, 1980); Shearer Carnoy and Russell Rumberger, *A New Social Contract: The Economy and Government after Reagan* (New York: Harper and Row, 1983).

the scope of this essay. It is worth noting, however, that societies widely regarded as capitalist have differed greatly in the extent of their egalitarian and democratizing programs (the United States and Sweden provide an often-cited contrast). In addition, capitalism has shown remarkable resiliency in adapting to new challenges and pressures. Establishment of a genuinely democratic economy within a (modified) capitalist framework is, no doubt, problematic and faces numerous practical difficulties. But it is not at all clear that significantly enhanced economic democracy, combining both nonefficiency and efficiency criteria, can be ruled out of hand in principle in a capitalist environment.

Economics, University of Southern California

SOME ETHICAL IMPLICATIONS FOR CAPITALISM OF THE SOCIALIST CALCULATION DEBATE

By Israel M. Kirzner

The debate that raged in the interwar period between the Austrian economists (who argued the thesis that under socialism it would not be possible to engage in rational economic calculation) and socialist economists (who rejected that thesis) was, narrowly conceived, a debate in positive economics. What was being discussed was certainly not the morality of capitalism or of socialism. Nor, strictly speaking, was the debate even about society's economic well-being under socialism; it concerned the ability of central planners to make decisions that take appropriate account of relevant resource scarcities, in the light of consumer preference rankings. To be sure, the extraordinary interest which surrounded the debate and the passions that lurked barely below its surface testified to the powerful *implications* of the debate for crucial issues in welfare economics. The Austrians were not merely exploring the economies of socialism; they were in effect demonstrating that, as an economic system attempting to serve the needs of its citizens, socialism must inevitably fail. But, even if the debate is interpreted in its broadest terms, as a debate in welfare economics, it represented a sharp break with traditional polemics relating to the socialism-capitalism issue. Traditionally the arguments for or against capitalism had, until 1920, been deeply involved in ethical questions. Mises's 1920 challenge to socialism, in contrast, was explicit in making no attempt to address any claims concerning the alleged moral superiority of socialism. He simply argued that, as an economic system, socialism was inherently incapable of fulfilling the objectives of its proponents; central planners are unable to plan centrally. For Mises this issue seemed paramount. "Everything brought forward in favour of Socialism during the last hundred years, in thousands of writings and speeches, all the blood which has been spilt by the supporters of Socialism, cannot make Socialism workable."[1] This challenge lifted the debate from being an emotional one concerning the alleged injustices arising out of a system that allows selfish capitalists to indulge their greed, to a scientific level that could, at least in

---

[1] L. Mises, *Socialism, An Economic and Sociological Analysis*, trans. J. Kahane from 2nd German edition [1932], (London: Jonathan Cape, 1936), p. 135.

principle, permit dispassionate analysis of the economics of socialism. Whatever one's ethical preferences as between socialism and capitalism might be, Mises was asserting, it must be pointed out that socialism necessarily fails to satisfy the criteria for a rational economic system.

In this paper it will be argued that, properly understood, the Austrian position in the socialist calculation debate did – in spite of everything in the preceding paragraph – hold important implications for the ethical appraisal of capitalism. Neither Mises nor Hayek appear to have been aware of these ethical implications (although we cannot rule out the possibility that, perhaps subconsciously, these implications played a role in undergirding their defense of capitalism as an economic system). My argument thus maintains that the debate not only broke new ground in the scientific analysis of socialism; it was at the same time capable of enriching the moral appraisal of capitalism. This potential for enriching moral discourse was a potential that depended strictly on the scientific content of the debate. What the Austrian side of the debate contained, we shall see, was the possibility of a new way of understanding, not merely socialism, but also the operation of the capitalist system. In arguing the inability of central planners to achieve what the decentralized market is able to achieve, Mises and Hayek were, in effect, teaching us revolutionary lessons in positive economics about the capitalist system. These lessons do not depend on, and may be studied independently of, any ethical judgments concerning capitalism. But my contention will be that once these lessons have been adequately learned, once we understand capitalism as Mises and Hayek came to understand it, it is difficult to avoid recognizing the possible implications these lessons hold for an ethical assessment of capitalism. Paradoxically, therefore, it turns out that Mises's attempt to lift discussion concerning capitalism and socialism to the level of dispassionate science carried with it implications for a "feedback" capable, in turn, of enriching the nonscientific moral judgment of capitalism. I should perhaps add that this kind of ethical byproduct of science is not at all atypical of economics. Most moral judgments concerning economic systems are rooted, explicitly or implicitly, in some specific understanding of how these systems respectively operate. It is entirely to be expected, therefore, that a revolutionary lesson in the way capitalism works should carry with it correspondingly revolutionary implications for the moral appraisal of it.

I.   THE SOCIALIST CALCULATION DEBATE: AN ABRIDGED HISTORY

The history of the debate I provide in this section is deliberately abridged. The abridgement is motivated not merely by the obvious objective of remaining within reasonable space constraints,[2] but also, quite frankly, in order to highlight those features of the history that illustrate my thesis. The justification for this selective history is the judgment that what are important, both for the general history of economic ideas and for the history of the debate itself, are indeed those segments of the debate to which I will be drawing attention.

Before 1920 the questions of how and whether socialism could work as an economic system were rarely taken up. Where these questions were raised (as by Gossen, Pareto, and Pierson[3]) the discussion failed to be taken account of either by economists in general or by socialist theoreticians. In 1920 Mises threw out his challenge to socialists by asserting flatly that "in the socialist community economic calculation would be impossible."[4] Mises's reasoning focused on the role played in the market economy by the prices of factors of production. It is these prices which "furnish a basis for reckoning. Where there is no market there is no price system, and where there is no price system there can be no economic calculation."[5] Because socialism is, by definition, the system in which all factors of production are owned by the state ("Society"), it follows that there can be no market for factors. "Exchange relations in productive goods can only be established on the basis of private property in the means of production. If the Coal Syndicate delivers coal to the Iron Syndicate a price can be fixed only if both syndicates own the means of production in the industry. But that would not be Socialism."[6]

Mises's article was reproduced virtually verbatim in his 1922 *Die Gemeinwirtschaft*. Although that book was a full-length treatment of socialism (its English translation is described in its subtitle as "An Economic and Sociological Analysis," and runs to more than five hundred pages), Mises himself describes "the doctrine of the impossibility of economic calculation in a socialist community" as constituting the "gist" of the book. The book's publication was followed by a large volume of socialist responses. As Mises noted in the second edition of the book, "socialists of all kinds have poured out attempts to refute my arguments and to invent a system of economic calculation for Socialism."[7] During the 1920s these writings attempting to refute Mises' thesis were mainly

---

[2] Two excellent book length histories (both sympathetic to the Austrian side of the debate) are: T.J.B. Hoff, *Economic Calculation in the Socialist Society*, trans. from Norwegian edition (1938), (London: W. Hodge, 1949); D. Lavoie, *Rivalry and Central Planning, The Socialist Calculation Debate Reconsidered* (Cambridge: Cambridge University Press, 1985).

[3] For detailed references, see Hoff, *Economic Calculation*, p. 1; L. Mises, *Socialism*, p. 135.

[4] Mises, *Socialism*, p. 131.

[5] *ibid.*

[6] *ibid.*, p. 132.

[7] *ibid.*, p. 135.

German and Italian.[8] But the literature of the 1930s most heavily involved English language writers. This latter literature had its beginning, perhaps, in Fred M. Taylor's presidential address to the American Economic Association in December 1928, "The Guidance of Production in a Socialist State."[9] Taylor envisaged a central authority fixing (nonmarket) prices for productive factors and altering these prices through a system of trial and error. Taylor's suggestion for solving the socialist calculation problem was taken up in considerably greater detail by Oskar Lange in a 1936 article which came to be recognized as the definitive socialist position (at least at the theoretical level) in response to Mises. At about the same time A.P. Lerner was writing along similar lines.[10] It was also about this time that F.A. Hayek edited a collection of classic papers addressing the calculation problem (including not only a translation of Mises's original 1920 paper, but also several papers that preceded Mises). Hayek introduced the collection with an essay on "The Nature and History of the Problem," and concluded the volume with an essay on "The Present State of the Debate."[11] In these two papers Hayek lucidly restated the Misesian argument and presented the major socialist response to that argument, together with his own critical assessment of them. Although Hayek was not able to deal fully with Lange's argument (which had not yet appeared in print),[12] nonetheless his papers constituted an influential and powerful updating of the Mises position. Mises's side of the debate came to be known as the Mises-Hayek position.

It seems, therefore, historically valid to perceive the debate as crystallizing into a confrontation between the Mises-Hayek position on the one hand, and the Lange-Lerner suggested solution on the other hand. In the postwar literature on comparative economic systems it was this confrontation that was highlighted, and (as already noted) it was the Lange-Lerner position that came to be cited in that literature as providing the satisfactory socialist response to the Mises-Hayek arguments. For this

[8] See Hoff, *Economic Calculation*, p. 131 footnote, and entire chapter 11.

[9] F.M. Taylor, *American Economic Review*, vol. 19, no. 1 (March 1929), reprinted in B.J. Lippincott, ed., *On the Economic Theory of Socialism* (University of Minnesota Press, 1938; reprinted by McGraw-Hill, 1964).

[10] O. Lange, "On the Economic Theory of Socialism," *Review of Economic Studies*, vol. iv, numbers 1,2 (October 1936 and February 1937), reprinted in Lippincott, *Economic Theory*, (subsequent page referencs will be to the Lippincott edition). A.P. Lerner, "Economic Theory and Socialist Economy," *Review of Economic Studies*, vol. ii (1934); and "A Note on Socialist Economics," *Review of Economic Studies*, vol. iv (1936); see also, A.P. Lerner, *The Economics of Control* (New York: MacMillan, 1944).

[11] Both papers were reprinted in F.A. Hayek, *Individualism and Economic Order* (London: Routledge and Kegan Paul, 1949).

[12] Hayek did address Lange's solution (together with those of several others) in "Socialist Calculation III: The Competitive 'Solution'," in *Individualism and Economic Order*, chapter six (original paper first published in *Economica*, vol. vii, no. 26, May 1940).

literature the Taylor-Lange-Lerner trial and error approach using nonmarket prices constituted the decisive refutation of Mises's original assertion denying the economic workability of central planning.[13] Mises and Hayek, it should be emphasized, never conceded that Lange's argument addressed their concerns.[14]

Looking back on this confrontation from the perspective of a half century of subsequent development in economic thought, it appears illuminating to interpret the confrontation as one involving two quite inconsistent alternative paradigms. Professor Lavoie has provided the definitive interpretation of the debate along those lines.[15] The Lange-Lerner approach proceeded strictly along the lines of neoclassical equilibrium theory; the Mises-Hayek position sees it as an entrepreneurial-competitive discovery process. A good deal of the complete (and somewhat mystifying) failure of the two sides of the debate to reach any sort of mutual understanding seems to stem from the circumstance that they were unwittingly working within entirely different theoretical frameworks. It is this that explains how, for the Austrians, the suggestions of Lange and Lerner failed even to begin to address the calculation problem which they had identified as existing in the centrally planned economy. It is this that explains how, nonetheless, Lange and Lerner (and a host of postwar writers) genuinely believed that the trial-and-error proposal had decisively refuted the Austrian claims regarding the unworkability of central planning.

This writer has elsewhere[16] developed an interpretation of the calculation debate that sees the Austrians as having been forced, during the course of the debate, towards a far greater degree of self-awareness than they had possessed at the outset of the debate. Much of the confusion in the debate appears, as I have noted, to stem from the circumstance that the Austrians were initially unaware of any fundamental difference that separated their understanding of the theory of the market from that of other schools of economic thought.

In 1931, before Lange and Lerner, Mises could write the following: "Within modern subjectivist economics it has become customary to distinguish several schools. We usually speak of the Austrian and the Anglo-American Schools and the School of Lausanne. . . . [The fact is] that these three schools of thought differ only in their mode of expressing the same fundamental idea and that they are divided more by their

---

[13] See Lavoie, *Rivalry*, p. 13, for a list of postwar writers who took this position.
[14] See Hayek, "Socialist Calculation III"; see also L. Mises, *Human Action* (New Haven: Yale University Press, 1949), pp. 700–706.
[15] See D. Lavoie, *Rivalry*.
[16] See I.M. Kirzner, "The Economic Calculation Debate: Lessons for Austrians," *The Review of Austrian Economics*, vol. 2 (1987).

terminology and by peculiarities of presentation than by the substance of their teaching."[17]

It was the confrontation with the response of critics such as Taylor and Lange which taught the Austrians how profoundly their theory of the market differed from that of the neoclassical orthodoxy. Only ten years after writing about the insignificance of the differences between the Austrian School and the other schools of economic theory, at the end of a decade in which the Lange-Lerner position was articulated, Mises was writing very emphatically about the fundamental character of these differences. "What distinguishes the Austrian School ... is precisely the fact that it created a theory of economic action and not of economic equilibrium or nonaction.... The Austrian School endeavors to explain prices that are really paid in the market, and not just prices that would be paid under certain, never realizable conditions. It rejects the mathematical method ... because it does not emphasize a detailed description of a state of hypothetical static equilibrium."[18] In subsequent sections of this paper I will briefly outline the lessons in self-awareness which the Austrians learned, and take note of the characteristic understanding of the market economy which the Austrian position came explicitly to embody. But I must first set out the Lange-Lerner position in some detail.

II. THE LANGE-LERNER APPROACH

Oskar Lange proposes that the centrally planned economy should operate on a trial and error procedure essentially similar to the procedure he believes to characterize the competitive market economy. In developing this proposal (which he considers as no more than an elaboration of the Fred M. Taylor plan) Lange reveals with great clarity exactly how he understands the operation of a competitive market economy. Central to this understanding is the assumption that each decision by consumers, producers, and resource owners is made "only on the basis of a *given* set of prices. ... The prices are regarded by the individuals as constants independent of their behavior."[19] This assumption is central, in particular, to the trial and error procedure which Lange attributes to the market. "The solution by trial and error is based on what may be called the *parametric function of prices*, i.e., on the fact that, although prices are a

---

[17] L. Mises, *Epistemological Problems of Economics*, trans. G. Reisman, (New York: Van Nostrand, 1960), p. 214. The passage appears in a paper whose original German version was published in 1931.

[18] L. von Mises, *Notes and Recollections* (South Holland, IL: Libertarian Press, 1978), p. 36. See Foreword (by Margit von Mises) pp. viii-ix, for the information that the book was completed in 1942.

[19] Lange, "Theory of Socialism."

resultant of the behavior of all individuals on the market, each individual separately regards the actual market prices as given data to which he has to adjust himself."[20] At the outset a set of random prices is assumed given to each market participant; each participant makes his buying and selling decisions on the basis of these given prices. If the demand for a commodity exceeds its supply, competition of buyers will cause its price to rise; if the opposite is the case, competition of sellers will cause it to fall. Thus a new set of given prices is generated, and the process is repeated. "And so the process goes on until the objective equilibrium condition is satisfied (i.e. that demand for each commodity is equal to its supply) and equilibrium finally reached."[21]

It is this picture of the market that underlies Lange's views concerning the workability of socialism. Careful consideration of this picture reveals its key features. It is a picture thoroughly characteristic of standard neoclassical textbook price theory. As already noted, Lange's picture concentrates, of course, on market equilibrium, but this is so to a degree perhaps not immediately apparent. As Hayek showed many years ago,[22] to assume the perfectly competitive conditions (that underlie Lange's "parametric" treatment of prices) is already to assume a degree of knowledge on the part of market participants which it is the function of real market processes to generate. In particular, the parametric treatment of price really requires us to renounce any ambition to understand, say, *how* competition by buyers causes price to rise when demand exceeds supply (since we have been told to assume that at each instant each buyer believes that price is not subject to his own actions).[23] In Hayek's phrase the standard neoclassical treatment of competitive price "*assumes* the situation to exist which a true explanation ought to account for as the effect of the competitive process."[24]

I shall argue in the following sections that it is here that the nub of the disagreement exists. For the Austrians, Mises and Hayek, the essence of the market is perceived precisely in that "true explanation" which is absent from Lange's narrowly neoclassical understanding of the market. This essential element in the market process, it turns out, is simply not able to be duplicated under socialism. Indeed, nothing in Lange's proposal offers any suggestion or assertion as to how it might be so duplicated, since

---

[20] *ibid.*, p. 70; italics in original.
[21] *ibid.*, p. 71.
[22] F.A. Hayek, "The Meaning of Competition," in *Individualism and Economic Order*, chapter v.
[23] On this see I.M. Kirzner, *Competition and Entrepreneurship* (Chicago: University of Chicago Press, 1973), pp. 42, 91ff.
[24] F.A. Hayek, *Individualism and Economic Order*, p. 94.

Lange utterly failed to recognize this element at all. Given an Austrian understanding of market processes, Lange's proposal must appear well-nigh incomprehensible. It purported to show how socialism could simulate the competitive market, but failed entirely to address the problem of simulating the market's most essential element. But my goal in this paper is not to explicate the misunderstandings in the debate. It is to draw out the ethical implications of the Austrian position. My procedure will be to show how this Austrian position was itself crystallized through the course of the debate. Thereafter I will attempt to demonstrate the ethical implications of this position.

III. THE CRYSTALLIZATION OF THE AUSTRIAN POSITION

We may distinguish several elements in the developing self-awareness on the part of the Austrians. These are: (a) the role assigned to market prices; (b) welfare aspects of the market process; and (c) the interpretation of the competitive market process. I take these up briefly in order.

(a) A superficial student of Mises's original statements (of 1920 and 1922) on the calculation problem might be excused for concluding that Mises's understanding of the role of market prices in achieving social efficiency did not differ substantially from Lange's emphasis on the parametric character of prices. For Mises in 1920 and 1922, market prices provide an adequate basis for calculation because they confront each market participant with social valuations which *already* reflect the activities and preferences of all other market participants.[25] But after the debate had run its course we find Mises altogether explicit in setting forth a quite different understanding of the nature and role of market prices. In particular he emphasized that prices are not in any sense *given* to entrepreneurs but are the results of their own activity *as individual agents*. "The entrepreneurs, eager to earn profits, appear as bidders at an auction, as it were. . . . Their offers are limited on the one hand by their anticipation of future prices of the products and on the other hand by the necessity to snatch the factors of production away from the hands of other entrepreneurs competing with them. . . . The essential fact is that it is the competition of profit-seeking entrepreneurs that does not tolerate the preservation of *false* prices of the factors of production."[26] We thus see that it was during the period of the calculation debate that Mises came to articulate with clarity his treatment of prices as expressing the outcome of entrepreneurial actions, rather than as parameters to which entrepreneurs adjust. We shall see that this treatment has significant implications.

---

[25] Mises, *Socialism*, p. 115.
[26] Mises, *Human Action*, pp. 332–335; italics in original.

(b) For neoclassical economics, the normative criterion that came to be applied to a society in assessing the effectiveness of its economic system was that of the efficient allocation of society's resources among the competing available uses for them. It is now well recognized that this criterion was an *extension* of Lionel Robbins's concept of the activity of individual economizing. In other words, neoclassical normative economics treats the entire economy exactly as the economizing individual treats his own little economic world, viz., as if all relevant data for decision making are, in principle, already known or readily ascertainable. As we shall see, this approach to judging the effectiveness of an economic system is thoroughly alien to the Austrian view. Yet the Austrians themselves had not always understood this. As late as 1935 Hayek defined "the economic problem" as being the "distribution of available resources between different uses," and he declared that this is "no less a problem of society than for the individual."[27] Hayek was clearly entirely satisfied to extend Robbins's notion of economizing to the level of society-wide "choices." He was apparently quite unaware of the extraordinary assumptions concerning the availability of information that would have to be made in order to sustain this extension. Yet, only two years later, we find Hayek asserting that the "central question of all social sciences [is]: How can the combination of fragments of knowledge existing in different minds bring about results which, if they were to be brought about deliberately, would require a knowledge on the part of the directing mind which no single person can possess?"[28] And by 1940 we find Hayek applying this very insight to criticize the socialist position in the calculation debate. The "main merit of real competition [is] that through it use is made of knowledge divided between many persons which, if it were to be used in a centrally directed economy, would all have to enter the single plan."[29] And, ten years after his extension of the Robbinsian notion of economizing to society as a whole, we find Hayek, in effect, completely repudiating his earlier statement of the economic problem facing society. "The economic problem of society is thus not merely a problem of how to allocate 'given' resources – if 'given' is taken to mean given to a single mind which deliberately solves the problem set by these 'data.' It is rather a problem of how to secure the best use of resources known to any of the members of society, for ends whose relative importance only these individuals know. Or, to put it briefly, it is a problem of the utilization of knowledge which is not given to anyone in its totality."[30]

---

[27] Hayek, *Individualism and Economic Order*, p. 121.
[28] *ibid.*, p. 54.
[29] *ibid.*, p. 202.
[30] *ibid.*, pp. 77f.

It seems inescapable that it was Hayek's experience during the latter 1930s (during which he was confronted by the Lange-Lerner suggestion for economic calculation under socialism) that sensitized him to the dubious meaning that can be attached to the idea of the efficient allocation of social resources. It was out of this debate, it seems evident, that there emerged Hayek's now celebrated insights concerning the dispersed knowledge that challenges societal "efficiency." And it was in following up these calculation-debate-generated insights that modern Austrians have explored the possibility of developing a new approach to normative economics based on the concept of *coordination*.[31]

(c) Perhaps the best known element in the modern Austrian understanding of markets is that which sees the market as a "discovery procedure,"[32] an on-going process of spontaneous and induced change. It was Mises who in his 1940 *Nationalökonomie* (revised and translated as *Human Action* in 1949) emphasized with unsurpassed clarity how important it is to see the market as an entrepreneurial process rather than as a state of equilibrium affairs. And by 1940 Hayek was pointing out that some of the socialists following the Lange-Lerner proposal were guilty of "excessive preoccupation with problems of the pure theory of stationary equilibrium" and failed to understand how real-world markets are likely to have the advantage in regard to the rapidity of "adjustment to the daily changing conditions in different places and different industries."[33] Yet it must be acknowledged that in his earliest statements on the socialist calculation issues, Mises reads as if the central feature in his appreciation for markets is their continual ability to generate near-equilibrium prices and near-equilibrium patterns of resource allocation. Under "the economic system of private ownership of the means of production," Mises claimed, "all goods of a higher order receive a position in the scale of calculations in accordance with the immediate state of social conditions of production and of social need."[34] Once again, we must conclude, it was the experience of the socialist calculation debate that sharpened Austrian self-awareness. At the outset Austrians genuinely believed that the overlap between their own theory of markets and that of the other schools of economic thought was so

[31] See Gerald P. O'Driscoll, Jr., *Economics as a Coordination Problem: The Contribution of Friedrich A. Hayek* (Kansas City: Sheed, Andrews and McMeel, 1977; I.M. Kirzner, *Competition and Entrepreneurship*, chapter 6 ("Competition, Welfare, and Coordination").

[32] See F.A. Hayek, "Competition as a Discovery Procedure" (first delivered as a lecture in 1968), in *New Studies in Philosophy, Politics, Economics and the History of Ideas* (Chicago: University of Chicago Press, 1978).

[33] Hayek, *Individualism and Economic Order*, p. 188.

[34] L. Mises, "Economic Calculation in the Socialist Commonwealth," trans. S. Adler from the 1920 German article, F.A. Hayek, ed. *Collectivist Economic Planning: Critical Studies on the Possibilities of Socialism* (London: Routledge and Sons, 1935), p. 107.

overwhelming as to subordinate the differences between them. It was the calculation debate that demonstrated that, quite the contrary, these differences ran so deep as to generate radically divergent understandings of how markets work.[35]

IV. THE AUSTRIAN PERSPECTIVE ON THE CALCULATION DEBATE

It will be useful to sum up what we have learned. The Austrian position in the debate depends, we now appreciate, on a very special theoretical understanding of market. Markets work, on the Austrian view, because they are characterized by continual processes of entrepreneurial discovery. These processes are set in motion by the maladjustments that are, at each moment, caused by imperfect information, itself simply the manifestation of Hayek's dispersed knowledge. What drives the market process is the entrepreneur's eagerness to discover pockets of pure profit. In seeking to grasp these profits, entrepreneurs are not merely discovering opportunities for gain for themselves; they are at the same time discovering the nuggets of information possession of which can eliminate the above-mentioned maladjustments. The crucial role in the creation of these profit opportunities (and their discovery) is played by market prices. These prices, themselves the expression of entrepreneurial bids and offers, reflect on the one hand the degree of discovery already achieved by the market process, and on the other hand the extent to which full coordination has not yet been achieved. Price movements are simply expressions of entrepreneurial discovery, of steps being taken in the coordinating process of the market.

From this perspective on the market it is clear how centrally planned economies are, by definition, precluded from simulating any of the essential functions of the market process. The basic driving element in the market process, entrepreneurial eagerness for pure profit, is *necessarily* excluded from the socialist economy. There is nothing that can quite replace it. Lange's opinion that the socialist economy can simulate the achievement of market equilibrium overlooks the critical assumption needed to make equilibrium theory relevant at all – the assumption that entrepreneurial discovery processes can be relied upon to proceed swiftly and "noiselessly." The net effect of taking this assumption entirely for

---

[35] We interpret these changes in the Austrian articulation of their position as increasing self-awareness of the implications of the Mengerian paradigm, rather than as any substantive modification in Austrian theory, for reasons that need not detain us here. For discussion of these issues, see D. Lavoie, *Rivalry and Central Planning*, p. 26; and I.M. Kirzner, "The Economic Calculation Debate: Lessons for Austrians"; see also I.M. Kirzner, "Ludwig von Mises and Friedrich von Hayek: The Modern Extension of Austrian Subjectivism," N. Leser, ed., *Die Wiener Schule der Nationalökonomie* (Vienna: Böhlau, 1986).

granted is to assume away that imperfection of knowledge, that dispersal of information, which is the very root of the economic problem.

We are now in a position to assess the ethical implications which I believe to be entailed by this Austrian view of the market process, a view which, as we have seen, emerged from the socialist calculation debate.

V. THE DISCOVERY VIEW VERSUS THE ALLOCATION VIEW

Throughout the history of socialism it is the question of distributive justice that has at all times been the most central issue. It is this issue that has fired enthusiasms, lifted hearts, inspired revolutions. Whatever Marx's own views on this issue may have been,[36] it cannot be doubted that socialists the world over have been and still remain convinced that the capitalist market economy represents an immoral system of exploitation and economic injustice. I shall argue that the Austrian side of the calculation debate implied a response to these ethical criticisms of capitalism – a response that has not yet been explicitly articulated. This implied response differs sharply, I shall claim, from the standard neoclassical responses.

Neoclassical-type defenses of market justice have depended heavily on two (often only implicit) premises: (a) the premise that *initial* resource endowments can be taken as justly held in the first place, and (b) the premise that market-generated incomes can be taken as approximating their equilibrium levels. It is upon these implicit premises, for example, that J.B. Clark's celebrated defense of the economic justice of capitalism was constructed.[37] Clark argued, on the basis of the marginal productivity theory of resource price, that each resource owner tends, in the capitalist economy, to receive the value of the productive contribution he has permitted to be made with his resources. Since the laborer receives the full value of the productive contribution that his sweat and effort have generated, the capitalist cannot be accused of robbing him of any slice of the final product. What the capitalist himself receives is no more than the value contributed by the capital resources which *he* has committed to production. Since the validity of the capitalist's ownership of his capital resources is being taken for granted in this defense, it follows that all incomes are justly received. But it is clear that this convenient conclusion for capitalism rests, in effect, on faith that in the capitalist economy incomes reflect substantially perfect mutual information on the part of all

[36] On this see A. Wood, "The Marxian Critique of Justice," *Philosophy & Public Affairs*, vol. 2 (Spring 1972), and W. Baumol, "Marx and the Iron Law of Wages," *American Economic Review*, vol. 73, no. 2 (May 1983), p. 306.

[37] See J.B. Clark, *The Distribution of Wealth: A Theory of Wages, Interest and Profits* (New York, 1908), esp. chapter 1; see also M. Friedman, *Capitalism and Freedom* (Chicago: University of Chicago Press, 1962), chapter x.

market participants. And, indeed, Clark makes no attempt to justify the grasping of pure entrepreneurial profit (other than to treat it as somehow less significant because it is a strictly temporary share that is being rapidly eroded, at each instant, by the forces of competition). Once again, it seems, the possibility of incomes resulting from the existence of serious market error is virtually ignored.

It should be noted that this equilibrium view of the market that underlies neoclassical defenses of capitalist justice itself implied a very definite view of the distribution problem. Not only does equilibrium imply perfect mutual awareness on the part of market participants, it carries with it a perspective on the aggregate economy that permits it to be treated analogously to the economic situation confronting the individual. Since, in principle, all information existing in the economy is able to be centralized (since we assume *everyone* to know how to command every piece of information existing anywhere), it is quite natural to treat the economic problem facing society as essentially a problem of the efficient allocation of known resources among competing known uses. (I have noted earlier in this paper how it was the calculation debate that moved Hayek to renounce this view of the economic problem and to focus on the problems raised by genuinely dispersed information – i.e., information so dispersed as to defy centralization, even in principle.) But this way of perceiving society's economic problem as an allocation problem implies, in turn, that the problem of distribution is *a problem of sharing out a given pie*. This given pie was not, it is true, seen by the neoclassicals as given societal *output*; but it was seen in the form of given arrays of "society's" resources which are to be shared out – with full awareness that the sharing out of resource services implies the sharing out of the corresponding pie-to-be-produced.

It is this view of distribution, as a case of sharing out a given pie, that is emphatically ruled out by the Austrian side of the calculation debate. Let us remember that it was precisely the equilibrium view of the market (which we have seen to underlie the neoclassical defense of the capitalist ethic) which informed the socialist side of the calculation debate as represented by Lange.

From the developed Austrian perspective on the debate, the fundamental brute fact of dispersed knowledge transforms not only our understanding of markets, how they work, and how they address society's economic problem. Awareness of the fact of dispersed knowledge transforms, in addition, our perception of the problem of distribution. What is distributed in markets is not a known, given pie – neither a pie of produced national output, nor a pie of given societal resources. What is to be distributed is *an aggregate which must be discovered* in the course of the very market processes through which it is "distributed." In fact, the circumstance that aggregate output (and aggregate available resources, too) must be discovered in the course of the market process renders the entire notion of "distribution" highly dubious. Not only must the aggregate volume of societal resources, and certainly the aggregate volume of societal output, be discovered; in fact, from the Austrian perspective, each and every income receipt is, to a degree, a discovered income. This is perhaps most easily seen in the case of the winning of pure profit, but it is also the case to a greater or lesser degree for each unit of resource income received. Let us consider the nature of pure profit.

Pure profit is the surplus remaining in the hands of a vendor of a good after he has deducted *all* the costs assumed in order to be able to make the good available to the buyer. In the case of simple arbitrage, where an entrepreneur is able to buy an item in a market where price is low, and, without incurring any cost of transportation, to sell the same item simultaneously in a second market where the price is high, pure profit is the difference between these two prices. In the case of entrepreneurial production, pure profit is what is left out of total revenue to the entrepreneur-producer after deducting *all* the costs of production (including all interest charges, transportation and delivery costs, and the like) needed to achieve delivery of the product to its buyer.

In the equilibrium world of standard neoclassical economics, with full knowledge assumed on the part of all participants, analysis proceeds as if pure profits never do occur. The possibility of more than one price existing at a given time for an item is not considered. The profits that are discussed in the theory of the producing firm are not pure profits at all, but rather quasi-rents earned on the firm's fixed capital assets. (Thus a producer may be using his factory, built in the past and thus calling for no new current cost sacrifices, using two million dollars worth of current inputs to produce three million dollars worth of product. But the million dollars of "profit" so won is not true profit; since the productive capacity of the factory is known to everyone, the producer could have leased his factory to other producers for up to a million dollars, which they would be prepared to pay, since the factory enables them to generate this net revenue. So our producer, in calculating his total costs of production, would have to include this sacrifice of a million dollars of lease-revenue foregone, leaving no pure profit at all.)

But for the Austrian view pure profit is not only possible, it is central to the understanding of market processes. Pure profit emerges, in this view, because genuinely dispersed information is a fact of life. An entrepreneur may indeed be able to buy an item for two dollars and sell it for three. A producer may indeed be able to produce an item for two million (*including* the cost of foregone lease-revenue at current market prices for the lease of his factory) and sell for three million. All this is possible because of genuinely dispersed information, i.e., information so dispersed that market participants are unaware of the nature and the very existence of the information which they lack. It is only this circumstance which makes possible the existence of two prices – and thus a pure profit opportunity – in the same market for essentially the same item. (The bundle of resources which are capable of producing a given product is treated, in this context, as essentially the same item as that product.) Absent genuinely dispersed information, no pure profit opportunities can be imagined to exist. Any apparent price differentials cannot qualify as profit opportunities since, absent genuinely dispersed information, such differentials must be treated as necessary to cover the cost of obtaining needed (and known-to-be-needed) information (or of otherwise transferring the purchased item to its point of high-priced sale). Without genuinely dispersed information no "unexplained," "unnecessary" price differentials can be imagined. True pure profit opportunities, evidenced by genuine price differentials, are not *necessary*, in the sense of being *needed* to permit the item purchased at the low price to be sold at the higher price. True profit opportunities are the result of sheer ignorance. Their exploitation is a matter of the *discovery that replaces sheer ignorance by full awareness*. It is to be emphasized that discovery is quite distinct from deliberate search. Deliberate search is engaged in when one has already known that there is something worth being searched for. If one has already known that there is something worthy to be searched for, the reason for its not having already been found must lie in the perceived cost of the search. Pure discovery occurs when one notices the existence of something that could, in principle, have been costlessly grasped earlier. The reason for its not having already been grasped lies, therefore, not in any cost of finding it, but in earlier sheer ignorance concerning its existence. To grasp pure profit is to notice the presence of two market prices *for the same* item. Pure profit is won through discovery.

Once we have grasped the nature and origin of pure discovery, we can perceive how discovery may occur not only in the context of pure profit opportunities, but also in regard to all market transactions. Pure profit occurs only in the absence of equilibrium, and it is not difficult to see how each market transaction in disequilibrium shares significant elements in common with the grasping of pure profit. We must distinguish sharply between (i) the transactions undertaken in a world of perfect relevant information (such as under equilibrium conditions) and (ii) those undertaken in the real world of open-ended possibilities for ignorance (and thus for discovery). The first are undertaken by simply exercising one's preferences between given, fully known entities (even if these entities are "fully known" only in the sense that one knows the precise statistical odds governing the payoffs to be expected from them). There is no room for surprise in these transactions. The second kind of transactions, on the other hand, are undertaken in contexts in which the ever-present possibility of surprise is of the essence. If the first kind of transaction results in an improvement in one's situation, this improvement must be described as having been deliberately grasped. This improvement was clearly visible to all; grasping it did not involve any creative leap, any entrepreneurial daring. But if the second kind of transaction, that taken under disequilibrium conditions, results in an improvement in one's situation, one sees this improvement as having been *discovered*. Through the fog of conflicting possibilities and potential surprises, one has "seen" the prospect for gain. This gain has been "discovered" in a sense very similar to that in which we have seen pure profit to be the result of pure discovery.

Not only are the individual transactions (including especially the market transactions which yield income receipts) characterized by discovery. The aggregate outcome of these countless acts of discovery under disequilibrium conditions must also be seen as a discovered outcome. The market process, carried on by definition under disequilibrium conditions, is a process of discovery. The incomes generated by this disequilibrium process are discovered incomes. We must now contemplate the possible ethical significance of this important insight.

VI. OBSERVATIONS ON THE FINDERS-KEEPERS ETHIC

A person is hiking on a mountain trail, on land owned by no one; he notices a beautiful mountain flower, picks it, and brings it home with him. There are probably few who would question the hiker's right to have done this. Moreover, if another person grabs the flower from the hiker's lapel on his way home, there are probably few who would not agree that that person is robbing the rightful owner of his flower. Let us examine the ethical premises that underlie these views concerning the property rights of our mountain hiker in this beautiful flower. What is it that confers upon him the ownership rights in this flower? Granted that the flower was ownerless when he noticed it, what transformed it into becoming his private property? I will submit that the ethical grounds for the view that the hiker is the owner of the flower are those usually described as the finders-keepers principle. I wish to maintain that this finders-keepers principle is of considerable ethical significance. In seeking to persuade the reader of this importance I do not need to persuade him of its definitive validity. My purpose is thus not to advance this principle itself; it is to draw attention to its profound relevance for an understanding of widespread attitudes towards the ethics of private property. I wish, that is, to point out what appears to be the underlying moral intuition that nourishes the fairly widespread view that this beautiful flower (and all other objects similarly discovered in an ownerless state) properly belongs to its discoverer.

This finders-keepers ethic confers ownership of the flower upon its discoverer not because his claim antedates any other possible subsequent claims,[38] but because finding and taking the flower is seen as giving him a unique moral claim over it that possesses greater weight, on the scales of justice, than any other possible claim can possess. This unique moral claim appears to arise from the circumstance that the undiscovered flower, blooming unseen was, in a certain sense, a nonexistent flower. It existed for no human mind, so that, regardless of philosophical profundities, its physical existence was economically and socially irrelevant. The discoverer of the flower, appreciating its beauty and worth, is in effect *creating* this flower, as it were *ex nihilo*; it is his perception of the flower that brings it within the scope of human interest. Its subsequent existence as a valued object, the pleasure it is able to give to human beings, is to be attributed to the discoverer's perceptive alertness. He originated the flower; he created it; the finders-keepers principle declares that the flower is therefore his own. This *seems* to be the moral intuition that underlies the finders-keepers ethic.

VII.   THE FINDERS-KEEPERS ETHIC AND THE DISCOVERY VIEW

If the widespread (implicit) acceptance of this finders-keepers principle is acknowledged, it seems difficult to avoid recognizing the profound ethical implications of the Austrian side of the calculation debate which I have identified in this paper. That side of the debate sees the market process, we saw, as a process of discovery in the context of open-ended scope for ignorance. Each unit of income received, we saw, was, at least in some degree, discovered income. In particular, the important species of capitalist income, pure profit, was won only as a result of pure entrepreneurial discovery. Aggregate national output comes into existence through countless mini-processes of productive discovery. Implied in these mini-processes of discovery are in turn the countless elements of resource incomes which are discovered wages; the employer discovered a way of putting the laborer's hands to worthwhile productive use; the laborer discovered an employer capable of putting his (the laborer's) hands to worthwhile productive use. To the extent that a resource owner (such as a laborer) is acting – in a world pervaded by ignorance – to secure the highest-paid use for his resource, his discovery of the employer does mean that he, the resource owner, has in a sense acted "entrepreneurially"; in a sense, he has *created* the opportunity to secure that high income. Had he

---

[38] See Robert Sugden, *The Economics of Rights, Cooperation and Welfare* (Oxford: Basil Blackwell, 1986), p. 88, for a view of the finders-keepers rule that appears to differ from that developed here.

not seen, "created," this opportunity, he would be putting his resource to work at a less rewarding task; the higher-valued contribution to production of which this particular unit of resource is capable might never have been noticed. In a world of disequilibrium, all market participants are to a certain extent intent on noticing better opportunities for themselves; to the extent that this generates discoveries that might otherwise have been missed, this transforms their incomes from being mere quid-pro-quo payments in exchange for productive services into being genuine creations. What I grasp when I discover an income opportunity in the market place is an opportunity that others have not yet perceived. It is, therefore, exactly as if I have grasped a discovered mountain flower that has been ownerless (because no one had perceived it up until now). The same finders-keepers ethic that declares the mountain flower to belong rightfully to its discoverer, surely declares these discovered incomes won by resource owners in the market to be rightfully theirs.

These ethical implications of the Austrian side of the calculation debate have both a positive and a negative side. The negative class of implications are those that challenge the standard perspectives on the ethics of distribution. Those perspectives start, we have already noticed, from the notion of a given pie to be distributed. It is not easily appreciated how heavily standard views on distributional ethics depend on this premise of a given entity that must somehow be shared out among an array of claimants. As soon as we perceive how unrealistic such a starting point is, we are instantly liberated from the ethical baggage which that starting point entails.

The positive class of implications of the Austrian side of the calculation debates are those which I have associated with the finders-keepers ethic. As soon as we appreciate the nature of the market as an ongoing process of mutual discovery, we are in a position to recognize the possible applicability of this ethic to a wide range of seemingly surprising cases.

Mises and Hayek never did realize these ethical implications that follow from their position in the calculation debate. But, again, Mises and Hayek were themselves less than completely appreciative of the fundamentally different understanding of the market which their position reflected. Just as one byproduct of the calculation debate was the more careful articulation of this fundamentally different understanding, it is possible that yet another byproduct – one still to be carefully articulated – is the crystallization of a novel approach to capitalist morality. It is towards such a crystallization that this paper wishes to point.

Economics, New York University

THE DYNAMIC OF CAPITALIST GROWTH

BY ANTONY FLEW

It has often been remarked that the most eloquent tribute ever paid to the incomparable effectiveness of capitalist social arrangements as means for achieving economic growth was that of the *Communist Manifesto*. Yet it is rather rare to notice that neither Marx nor Engels, either there or elsewhere, either asks or attempts to give an answer to a question which, to anyone proposing to revolutionize these arrangements, ought to have appeared crucial: namely, "What was the secret, and how shall we ensure that, under our proposed alternative arrangements, that secret is not lost?"

I

The never too often repeated tribute in the *Manifesto* reads:

> The bourgeoisie, during its rule of scarce one hundred years, has created more massive and more colossal productive forces than have all preceding generations together. Subjection of Nature's forces to man, machinery, application of chemistry to industry and agriculture, steam-navigation, railways, electric telegraphs, clearing of whole continents for cultivation, canalisation of rivers, whole populations conjured out of the ground – what earlier century had even a presentiment that such productive forces slumbered in the lap of social labour?[1]

"But how was it done," we ought to ask, "what was and is the secret of this fabulous, unprecedented, undeniable and undenied triumph?" To this the first response – a surprising response from such a hostile source – is that it was all perfectly peaceful and non-violent:

> The bourgeoisie, by the rapid improvement of all instruments of production, by the immensely facilitated means of communication, draws all, even the most barbarian, nations into civilisation. The cheap prices of its commodities are the heavy artillery with which it batters down all Chinese walls, with which it forces the

---

[1] Karl Marx, "The Communist Manifesto," David McLellan, ed., *Karl Marx: Selected Writings* (Oxford: Oxford University Press, 1977), p. 225. (Hereinafter cited parenthetically in the text as *CM* followed by a page number.)

barbarians' intensely obstinate hatred of foreigners to capitulate. It compels all nations, on pain of extinction, to adopt the bourgeois mode of production. . . . In one word, it creates a world after its own image. (*CM*, p. 225)

So far, so good; indeed, rather too good to be perfectly true history. But we still have to press the question: "Why did they want, and how did they become able, to do all this?" For that, in Communist eyes, most frightful Hydra, "the bourgeoisie," is in fact no science fiction monster, no "strange creature from another world, with powers which pass our understanding." It is instead a class or collection of ordinary, finite, flesh and blood humans, a class or collection consisting of nothing but individuals of our own familiar species. Apparently members of this assemblage have a peculiar and characteristic need, and it was in the course of satisfying this need that "the bourgeoisie" found itself creating "a world after its own image." Thus the *Manifesto* asserts: "The need of a constantly expanding market for its products chases the bourgeoisie over the whole surface of the globe. It must nestle everywhere, settle everywhere, establish connexions everywhere."

But, again, why? The nearest we get to an answer in that document simply pushes the question one stage further back. This interim response is that these producers need to find an ever wider market for their products because they will keep producing ever more of the wretched things. Presumably this is because they are, with an equally stubborn constancy, forever increasing the efficiency of their methods of production. For, we are told:

> The bourgeoisie cannot exist without constantly revolutionising the instruments of production, and thereby the relations of production, and with them the whole relations of society. . . . Constant revolutionising of production, uninterrupted disturbance of all social conditions, everlasting uncertainty and agitation distinguish the bourgeois epoch from all earlier ones. (*CM*, p. 224)

This "constant revolutionizing of production" is, of course, what Schumpeter was later to characterize as a "gale of creative destruction."[2] About this gale two things must be said at once. The first, obvious and less important, is that we still require some explanation of why constantly to revolutionize "the instruments of production" is supposed to present itself to every individual bourgeois as a compelling need. The second, more important and – once the first point has been put – almost equally obvious,

---

[2] J. Schumpeter, *Capitalism, Socialism and Democracy* (London: Allen and Unwin, 1963), Ch. 7.

is that it does not. For there are in fact plenty of firms, not protected by monopoly privileges, which nevertheless continue to stay in business for long periods without even trying to effect any revolutions in their methods of production. (Can anyone, for instance, point to any reference in the Marx-Engels correspondence to any such revolution effected in the Manchester mill of that mini-multinational, Ermen and Engels, during all the long years of the managerial involvement of Friedrich Engels?) Much the same can be true even of entire industries.

The importance of that second point is to remind us that all innovation presupposes new ideas and fresh initiatives. In industrial production, for instance, someone has to think of what would in fact be a better, more efficient way of doing whatever it may be. Or, more fundamentally, some-one has to invent a new product to be produced or a fresh service which might be provided. After that someone – perhaps, yet not necessarily, someone else but very necessarily someone who is in, or can get into, a position to realize that creative idea – someone has to become both persuaded that it is a winner and persuaded actually to put it into effect.

Yet even where you do have people both trying to invent such ideas and people able and eager to implement them if and when they become available, there neither is nor can be any guarantee that potential winners will be, first, thought of, then recognized to be such, and, finally, adopted. This very fact, that the occurrence, recognition, and realization of successful human creativity is not guaranteed – neither by God nor by History nor by anything else – constitutes just one more good reason why those who want economic growth should seek and favor social arrangements ensuring that those with the power to take maximally wealth-creating productive initiatives have the greatest possible personal incentives to do so.

Marx and Engels seem to have been among the first to describe as capitalist what Adam Smith knew only as "the natural system of perfect liberty and justice" or "the obvious and simple system of natural liberty."[3] One main part of the reason why neither Marx nor Engels ever formulated, nor appear even to have seen, this crucial reason for the productive success of competitive capitalism is that – like Lenin[4] – their purpose of pinning the label was not so much to understand as to destroy an opponent. There might have been more truth in the first claim made by Engels at the graveside, that Marx was the Darwin of the social sciences, had not his

---

[3] A. Smith, *An Inquiry into the Nature and Causes of the Wealth of Nations*, ed. R.H. Campbell and A.S. Skinner (Oxford: Clarendon, 1976), IV (vii) 3 and IV (ix).

[4] Lenin was fond of quoting G.V. Plekhanov: "First, let's stick the convict's badge on him, and after that we can examine his case." See R. Conquest, *Lenin* (London: Collins Fontana, 1972), p. 40.

second claim been altogether too correct: that always and "above all Marx remained a revolutionist." For the fact is that, again and again, in all his published writings, scientific truth is sacrificed to revolutionary rhetoric.[5]

Why, for example, is the central concept in *Capital* itself that of value, which is defined in terms of whatever is from time to time and from place to place the (socially necessary) labor time required to produced that value, rather than that of price, presumably defined similarly as a function of relative scarcity and effective demand? The inadequate answer – and the insufficient excuse for all the excruciating elaboration of consequent complexities – can only be, surely, that this tortuous and tortured exercise is necessary if the suposedly infamous thing, capitalism, is to be exposed as essentially, irreformably, and viciously exploitative?[6] Certainly a truly Weberian *wertfreiheit* in economic science can permit no place for any notion of value which is not a function of price. (Thus the just price of anything, and hence presumably its real value, was for the late Scholastics its actual price in an ideally normal, competitive market.[7])

Another and more fundamental source of Marxist reluctance to recognize the importance of incentives to creativity and to innovation lies in

---

[5] Consider just two vital examples, both examined thoroughly in B.D. Wolfe, *Marxism: One Hundred Years in the Life of a Doctrine* (New York: Dial, 1955): first, the gulf between the inspirational legend of the Paris Commune as presented by Marx in his address to the International on *The Civil War in France*, and the historical truths as honestly recognized only in his private papers (Part III, pp. 103–47); and, second, the fact that even before publishing Volume I of *Capital*, Marx knew that the notorious immiseration thesis – so essential to sustain the treasured revolutionary morals of the whole work – was false (Part III, pp. 322–3).

For example, in the published account of the Commune we read of the egalitarian mandate: " . . . all functionaries to do their jobs at workingmen's wages." Yet even at the time of writing "this man of scholarship" knew perfectly well that " . . . the 6000 franc annual wage the Commune deputies voted themselves and set as a maximum for state officials was nearly twelve times the amount being paid to the National Guard who were defending Paris" (Wolfe, *Marxism*, p. 141). As for the falsification of the immiseration thesis, the data were – in the interests, of course, of the revolution – simply suppressed. True to form, Marx made no relevant corrections in later revisions of *Capital*.

For a less admiring assessment of the scientific pretensions of Marx, as compared with Darwin, see A.G.N. Flew, *Darwinian Evolution* (London: Granada Paladin, 1984), III/3, pp. 92–112. Sir Karl Popper, *The Open Society and its Enemies* (London: Routledge and Kegan Paul, fifth edition, 1956), even after reading Leopold Schwartzschild, *The Red Prussian* [1948] (London: Pickwick, New Edition 1986), still gives far too much credit to the fundamental scientific good faith of Marx.

[6] One testing exercise for Marxist casuists would be to explain how, in operating a wholly automated factory, surplus value is to be profitably extracted by *not* buying any labor power at all. A reading of the most relevant Chapter XV, "Machinery and Modern Industry" (in Volume I, Part IV, "Production of Relative Surplus-value"), suggests that, controversially, their best bet would be to divert discussion to the more urgent and practical problem of what alternative employment, if any, might be found for workers displaced by automation.

[7] See R. Roover, "The Concept of the Just Price," *The Journal of Economic History*, vol. XVIII (1958); and compare Alejandro A. Chafusen, *Christians for Freedom: Late-Scholastic Economics* (San Francisco: Ignatius, 1986).

the commitment to materialist metaphysics. The materialist conception of history which was, notoriously, reached by standing Hegel on his head (or, rather, by putting him for the first time on his feet) required Marx and Engels to insist that – this side of the Revolution, at any rate – ideas occur or arise and are adopted when and only when the development of the material conditions of production makes their occurrence and adoption timely.

II

For anyone to whom no such revelatory guarantee has been vouchsafed, the central question is who – what man or assembly of men as Hobbes would have had it – makes the decisions to invest, or to reinvest, or to disinvest. Once this question is answered science requires us to go on to ask under what constraints, and subject to which incentives and disincentives, these key people make their decisions. The third alternative of reinvestment is introduced to cover the case in which, perhaps because its market has collapsed or perhaps because its competition has become too formidable, an enterprise can no longer carry on producing what previously it was producing; but the decision is not to shut down, dismiss the staff, and sell off the plant for what it will fetch, but instead to employ (much) the same equipment and (much) the same workforce to produce something else which will – it is hoped – sell better. When the market for widgets has collapsed, maybe there is still a future in gizmos.

The making of decisions to invest or to reinvest or to disinvest constitutes the role of the enterpriser. This is a different role from that of the manager, although it is one which may at different times be played by the same one man (or assembly of men) who (or which) plays the role of manager. I write "enterpriser" rather than "entrepreneur" because it is long overtime for the language of the people which made the first Industrial Revolution to employ a native word for members of the set which led it. By Cantor's Axiom for Sets the sole, essential feature of a set is that its members have at least one common characteristic, any kind of characteristic.

We should not, perhaps, be surprised to find Marx unwilling to make room in *Capital* for a discussion of the role of the enterpriser. For he would have been bound to regard any halfway sympathetic treatment – at least of a capitalist enterpriser – as a treacherous defense of the class enemy. Indeed, and presumably for similar reasons, he showed almost as little understanding of the function of management. He would like to make out that "the labour of supervision and management" consists only in the supervision of labor. But one unexplained reference to "the wages of management both for the commercial and industrial manager" suggests some awareness that sometimes something further might be involved.[8] This awareness could have been stimulated by remarks in letters from Engels. For instance: "Since I have become the boss, everything has become much worse because of the responsibility" (April 27, 1867).

The capitalist answer to the question which we have been contending to be crucial is that decisions to invest, to reinvest, or to disinvest are far too important to be entrusted to anyone save those who have the greatest possible individual interest in getting them right – in making them, that is, in such ways that they will turn out to have been maximally wealth-creating, and/or minimally wealth-destroying. In particular they must, therefore, be made either by the immediate owners of the capital to be employed, or misemployed, or else by the directly and immediately and individually responsible agents of those owners. Precisely this is the argument which Smith is putting in a never too often quoted but much too frequently misunderstood and misrepresented passage from that first, and greatest, and maybe only masterpiece of development economics, *An Inquiry into the Nature and Causes of the Wealth of Nations*:

> But it is only for the sake of profit that any man employs a capital in the support of industry. . . . As every individual, therefore, endeavours as much as he can . . . to employ his capital . . . that its produce may be of the greatest value; every individual necessarily labours to render the annual revenue of the society as great as he can. He generally, indeed, neither intends to promote the public interest, nor knows how much he is promoting it. . . . By directing . . . industry in such a manner as its produce may be of the greatest value, he intends only his own gain, and he is in this, as in many other cases, led by an invisible hand to promote an end which was no part of his intentions. Nor is it always the worse for the society that it was no part of it. By pursuing his own interest he frequently promotes that of the society more effectually than when he really intends to promote it.[9]

I myself first met this material now all of forty years ago, as an undergraduate in the University of Oxford. It was cited in a popular series of lectures given by G.D.H. Cole, then Chichele Professor of Political and Social Theory. Like most of us in his audience then, Cole could see

---

[8] K. Marx, *Capital* [1867], ed. F. Engels, trans. S. Moore and E. Aveling (Moscow: FLPH, 1961), Vol. III, Ch. XXIII, pp. 376–82.

Wolfe (*Marxism*, p. 113n) is incorrect in asserting that the phrase in the note to Vol. I, Ch. XV, p. 371 – "machinery has greatly increased the number of well-to-do idlers" – is *Capital*'s sole reference to managers. For that phrase does not in fact refer particularly to redundant managers; and there is the discussion mentioned immediately above.

[9] Smith, *Inquiry*, IV (ii).

nothing more here than the occasion for a swift passing sneer. This was, after all, merely a piece of apologetics for those obviously outmoded and altogether indefensible arrangements called by Cole laissez-faire capitalism. To such principled secularists as Cole himself, this particular defense was made the more repugnant by what we quite wrongly interpreted as the suggestion that these ongoings are benevolently guided by the Invisible Hand of an All-wise Providence.

Certainly Cole and the rest of us were right to see in this passage some defense of pluralistic and competitive capitalism. For it does indeed offer, for that and against monopoly socialist alternatives, an argument far more powerful than anything which Cole was able to recognize or, I will now add, to meet. But where we were utterly wrong was in suspecting Smith of making some sort of anti-scientific appeal to supernatural intervention. On the contrary: this text is a landmark in the history of the growth of the social sciences. For – almost a century before Darwin – Smith was uncovering a mechanism by which something strongly suggesting design could come about without any actual, conscious design; or, rather, without any intention directed towards that particular, ultimate outcome.

Smith and others are – even by people paid to know and to teach better – still frequently sneered at for allegedly cherishing a paradigmatically superstitious belief, the belief that, if only governments would let matters alone, then Providence can be relied upon to ensure that "all manner of things will be well." Even Carl Menger, founder of the Austrian tradition in economic theory, notwithstanding that he was himself advocating exactly what Smith actually maintained, seems totally to have failed to grasp that this was indeed Smith's message also:

> What Adam Smith and even those of his followers who have most successfully developed political economy can actually be charged with is ... their defective understanding of the *unintentionally created social institutions* and their significance for economy. It is the opinion appearing chiefly in their writings that the institutions of economy are always the *intended* product of the common will of society as such, results of expressed agreement of members of society or of positive legislation. ... The result is that the broad realm of unintentionally created social structures remains closed to their theoretical comprehension.[10]

Menger scarcely could have been more diametrically wrong. For, as Friedrich Hayek – the leading living representative of that same Austrian

[10] Carl Menger, *Problems of Economics and Sociology* [1883] (Chicago: Illinois University Press, 1960), p. 93, emphasis added.

tradition – has been at pains to teach us, the truth is that Smith was one of the Scottish founding fathers of social science, men of the Edinburgh Enlightenment concerned above all to show that and how the fundamental social institutions, and not the economic only, arose as unintended consequences of intended human action.[11]

To appreciate this is to realize how mistaken it is to construe Smith's invisible hand as an instrument of supernatural direction. To do this is as preposterous as to interpret Darwin's natural selection as being really supernatural selection. For Smith's invisible hand is no more a hand directed by a rational owner than Darwin's natural selection is selection by supernatural intelligence. It was precisely and only by uncovering the mechanisms operative in the two cases that they both made supernatural intervention superfluous as an explanation. Adam Smith's invisible hand is not a hand, any more than Darwin's natural selection is selection. Or – to put the point in a somewhat more forced and technical way – "invisible" and "natural" are in these two cases just as much alienans adjectives[12] as are "positive" and "people's" in the expressions "positive freedom" and "people's democracy."

Again, it is wrong to accuse Smith, as he so often is accused, of assuming or asserting that the results of the operations of all such unplanned and unintended social mechanisms are always, if only in the long run, Providentially happy. Indeed, the paradoxical truth would instead appear to be that the charge of making unwarranted Providential assumptions rests rather against the atheists, Marx and Engels, than against the theist, Smith.[13]

The most elegant refutation of this particular accusation against Smith is to be found in his treatment of the division of labor. Certainly, he writes, this "is not originally the effect of any human wisdom, which foresees and intends the general opulence to which it gives occasion. It is the necessary though very slow and gradual consequence of a certain propensity in human nature which has in view no such extensive utility: the propensity to truck, barter, and exchange one thing with another."[14] But Smith then goes on to describe and lament the dehumanizing consequences of extreme

---

[11] F.A. Hayek, *Studies in Philosophy, Politics and Economics* (London: Routledge and Kegan Paul, 1967).

[12] "Alienans adjective" is a medieval, Scholastic technicality. Whereas, for example, the ordinary adjectival expression "red book" is used to imply that something is both red and a book, such alienans adjectives as "imaginary," "fictitious," or "non-existent" are not similarly employed in order to pick out a subset for some more extensive set: imaginary books, unlike red books, are not species of the genus books!

[13] For supporting argument see my "Prophecy or Philosophy? Historicism or History?" R. Duncan and C. Wilson, eds., *Marx Refuted* (Bath, England: Ashgrove, 1987), p. 68–88.

[14] Smith, *Inquiry*, I (ii).

developments in this occasion of opulence. It is these purple passages which Marx himself quotes in *Capital* to support his own polemic on this count;[15] but neither there nor anywhere else does Marx even attempt to show how and why socialism can be relied on to make an end either of the division of labor or of the evils perceived to be consequent upon it.

III

Having disposed of misconceptions about what Smith's contention was, we can now see that he had excellent, down to earth, altogether this-worldly reasons for concluding that, if the object of the exercise is – as the title of his book indicates that for him it was – to maximize GNP, then the enterpriser role is best filled by the immediate owners of the capital either already at risk or about to be put at risk. For, necessarily, they have obvious, direct, and exactly proportionate, personal interests in achieving the most satisfactory combination of maximum security of and maximum return on the capital employed. Of course there is no guarantee that all such persons will get all their decisions right. Even those who usually turn out to have spotted winners will sometimes pick losers. It is indeed precisely because things are so difficult, and so apt to come unstuck, that anyone concerned to increase the wealth of nations has such an excellent reason for wanting to have the crucial decisions made, the crucial initiatives taken, always and only by directly and appropriately interested parties.

Also, where and insofar as people are – as Smith nicely has it – "investing their own capitals," the unsuccessful will, to the extent that they have made bad investments, necessarily be deprived of opportunities to make further costly mistakes, while the successful will by a parallel necessity be enabled to proceed to further and, we may hope, greater successes. Smith himself seems never to have emphasized or even seized this corollary point about feedback, although it must be of the last importance in any consideration of alternative ways of providing for the taking of economic initiatives.

The previous paragraph points us to another crucial fact about the enterpriser. He or – whyever not? – she is essentially a risk taker. Notoriously, there are in our world, save death and taxes, no certainties. It is, therefore, utterly unrealistic and ridiculous to discuss the role and the appropriate rewards of the enterpriser while altogether ignoring the risk. Nor is that the sole absurdity of the devoutly socialist statements which follow:

> . . . consider the pure capitalist entrepreneur, who has no capital, but exploits the worker by virtue of his organizational skill. By bringing together workers whose abilities complement one

---

[15] Marx, *Capital*, Vol. I, Ch. XIV, p. 362.

> another, he is able to make them much more productive collectively than they could be in isolation. . . . the capitalist entrepreneur should at most be rewarded for the actual effort of bringing the workers together, not for the work done by those whom he assembles. (I say "at most" because he would not be entitled to anything if he is also instrumental in preventing the workers from setting up their own firm.)[16]

Since prudent people will not take big risks save in hopes of what may have to be perhaps disproportionately big rewards, governments which insist on taxing away what they like to denounce as "obscene profits" must thereby discourage the taking of those big risks which would eventually have turned out to have been richly wealth-creating.[17] Similarly, prudent people must strive to ensure that anyone who is on their behalf taking risks from which they hope to gain is himself subject to incentives and disincentives corresponding to those to which they themselves would be subject were they making the operative decisions directly and not by proxy.

So what are the alternatives to social arrangements by which enterpriser decisions are made by, or immediately on behalf of, the owners of the capital involved; and how is it proposed to ensure that the actual decision makers are subject to appropriate, and appropriately strong, incentives or disincentives? Our first, supposedly scientific, socialist answer was offered by Engels just before his collaboration with Marx began; and neither of them seems to have vouchsafed anything fuller in their later years. Engels starts with a favorite phrase, several times repeated in *Anti-Dühring* – itself the source of *Socialism: Utopian and Scientific*, which has been after the *Manifesto* the most widely read of all Marxist works:

> The present anarchy of production, which corresponds to the fact that economic relations are being developed without uniform regulation [planning], must give way to the organization of production. Production will not be directed by isolated *entrepreneurs* independent of each other and ignorant of the people's needs; this task will be entrusted to a specific social institution. A central committee of administration, being able to review a broad field of social economy from a higher vantage point, will regulate it in a manner useful to the whole of society, will transfer the means of

---

[16] Jon Elster, "Exploitation, Freedom, and Justice," J.R. Pennock and J.W. Chapman, eds., *Nomos XXVI: Marxism* (New York: New York University Press, 1983), pp. 293–294.

[17] The fury and the envy provoked by such extraordinarily large rates of profit may be to some extent assuaged by the reflection that – whatever the truth about the alleged tendency of the overall average rate of profit to fall – there most certainly must be a tendency for the rates of profit made by innovators to decline once, encouraged by the success of these innovators, competitors move in.

production into hands appropriate for this purpose, and will be specially concerned to maintain a constant harmony between production and demand.[18]

A second, marginally more specific answer came from a leading, much-loved Labor Party intellectual, R.H. Tawney, writing nearly a century later. Marxists would certainly describe him as a utopian rather than a scientific socialist. In this they would not be alone. Nevertheless, his stated appeal is to prudence. "A prudent community," he contends,

> will not rely, for securing that its essential industries are adequately supplied with capital, on the crude, extravagant and uncertain device of . . . trusting to chance. . . . It will follow the advice tendered to it by economists of unimpeachable propriety, and meet the danger that part of such supplies as are available may be wasted or misused by guiding the investments of capital into nationally desirable channels through the agency of a National Investment Board.[19]

When the third Labor administration to enjoy a working majority in Parliament proposed to establish (not a National Investment but) a National Enterprise Board there was (for reasons unfortunately not explained) no further mention of "economists of unimpeachable propriety." The two Ministers concerned, in a preparatory paper, announced that, "The task we face is nothing less than to reverse the relative decline of British industry, which has been continuous for many years."[20] To achieve this task the resulting 1975 Industry Act introduced two "powerful new instruments": planning agreements with major firms in key sectors of industry; and the National Enterprise Board (NEB), to provide the means

---

[18] Quoted at pp. 256–257 of Wolfe, *Marxism*; and compare F. Engels, *Herr Eugen Duhring's Revolution in Science*, trans. E. Burns and edited by C.P. Dutt (London: Lawrence and Wishart, 1934), pp. 23, 299, 301, and 311. The failure to grasp that there can be, and both in Nature and in human affairs is, order which is not imposed by directing intelligence should be seen as a failure to surmount even the *pons asinorum* of social science. Contrast A.G.N. Flew, *Thinking about Social Thinking* (Oxford: Blackwell, 1985), Ch. 3.

Anyone curious to discover how things really are done in the lands of "actually existing socialism" may be referred either to Romuld Spaskowski, *The Liberation of One* (New York: Harcourt Brace Jovanovich, 1986), or to any of the publications of the Centre for the Research into Communist Economies, recently established under the auspices of the Institute of Economic Affairs in London.

[19] R.H. Tawney, *Equality* [1931], with an Introduction by R.M. Titmuss (London: Allen and Unwin, fifth edition, 1964), p. 157.

[20] They were Denis Healey, then Chancellor of the Exchequer, and Eric Varley, then Secretary of State for Industry. The sentence quoted comes at p. 3 of *An Approach to Industrial Strategy* (London: HMSO, 1975 – Cmnd. No. G315). See also *The Regeneration of British Industry* (London: HMSO, 1974 – Cmnd. No. 5710).

for "direct public initiatives" (e.g., making investments or buying shareholdings) in key sectors.

No one was expected to raise, much less to press, the most obvious and crucial questions: "Why was it thought that there were in Britain then opportunities for wealth-creating investment which had been missed by all those looking for profitable places for 'investing their own capitals'?"; "How come that such definitionally greedy and grasping capitalists had, it seems, so feebly failed to serve their own sordid interests?"; "And what structure of incentives, disincentives and constraints was going, if not to ensure, at least to make it likely that National Enterprisers would do better than private enterprisers?"

Almost needless to say "the relative decline of British industry" has not in any event been reversed; while insofar as, under later and very different administrations, it has even been checked, this modest achievement cannot be attributed to the superior performances of National Enterprisers. The whole sad, distressing yet unsurprising tale is not to be told on this occasion.[21] What is relevant, and should here be sufficient, is simply to say that since World War II a great many investment decisions, especially some of those involving the largest sums, have been public rather than private. They have, that is to say, involved "public money" (money compulsorily extracted as taxes, or just printed) rather than "private money" (money freely, and hopefully, contributed by capitalists big and small).

But "public" investment decisions are actually made by (or somehow emerge from the interactions of) various individuals and groups whose common characteristic is that they are not merely not expected to have, but are often even expected and required not to have, any individual stake in the achieving of the maximum, or indeed any, return upon the capital employed. Being human – like even the cartoon capitalists of a socialist demonology, and of course like the rest of us as well – all such persons are inclined to strive to maximize their own utilities or, for those who prefer the jargon of Mr. Damon Runyon to that of the economists, to do the best they can for themselves and for their families. The trouble is that the utilities of such persons are very little connected with, if not more or less directly opposed to, the direction of tax monies into whatever investments will prove maximally wealth-creating.

---

[21] On the general record of the British nationalized industries see: G. and P. Polanyi, *Failing the Nation: The Record of the Nationalized Industries* (London: Fraser Ansbacher, 1976); J. Redwood, *Public Enterprise in Crisis* (Oxford: Blackwell, 1980); and R. Pryke, *The Nationalized Industries: Policies and Performance since 1968* (Oxford: Robertson, 1981). For more particular cases see F. Broadway, *Upper Clyde Shipbuilders*, C. Jones *The 200,000 Job*, J. Bruce-Gardyne, *Meriden: Odyssey of a Lame Duck*, and J. Burton, *The Job Support Machine* (London: Centre for Policy Studies, 1976, 1977, 1978, and 1979).

It appears, for instance, that the particular conceptions of the public interest pushed by public officials are, far too frequently for anyone else's good, closely coincident with the actual private interests of those hoping to flourish and to advance within their several bureaucracies.[22] Politicians too, especially elected politicians aspiring to subsequent re-election, often harbor their own excellent reasons for wanting to direct public investment to particular regions which have proved unattractive to private capital: unattractive perhaps because of their remoteness from markets and/or from raw materials, or perhaps sometimes because the available labor is such as would not be hired by anyone who had to meet the payroll from their own pockets. Again, the labor unions and other lobbying organizations possessing the most political clout are likely to be in heavily manned, sunset industries. (Their decline may well have been hastened by the rapacious and restrictive behavior of those very unions.)

There is now available much detailed documentation on the British experience. It extends over four or five decades and refers to decisions made not only by Labor but also by Conservative administrations. So let us conclude here by just mentioning three or four especially flagrant examples. First in time came the Solomonic judgment of (Conservative) Prime Minister Macmillan, a judgment requiring the state steel monopoly British Steel to construct two uneconomically small plants, one in Wales and one in Scotland, rather than the single, large and – it was hoped – highly profitable plant proposed by the technocrats. (Since there were no Conservative votes to be won, and precious few to be retained, in either of the regions standing to gain from this judgment, it has to be put down either as remarkably foolish or – perhaps even more remarkably – as politically quite disinterested.)

Next, there was the building across the River Humber of one of the longest single-span bridges in the world, a project undertaken in order to purchase victory in an especially important bye-election. Both that bye-election and the subsequent General Election were in fact duly won by the party which made the decision to build. So the bridge remains as a not very heavily used monument both to the never to be recovered costs sunk in its construction and to the political skills of (Labor) Prime Minister Wilson.

Third, there was the continuation of the Concorde program, when the particular Labor Minister most directly responsible just happened to

---

[22] See almost any contribution to the recent, rapidly growing literature on the economics of public choice. There are, for instance, three introductory collections, all from the Institute of Economic Affairs and all, presumably, edited by A. Seldon: *The Economics of Politics* (1978); *The Taming of Government* (1979); and *The Emerging Consensus* (1981). Compare D. Runyon, *Runyon on Broadway* (London: Constable, 1950).

represent the constituency[23] of those employed, at unusually high wages, to produce that beautiful piece of wildly extravagant economic nonsense.[24]

Finally, we come to what has been and remains by far the largest of these extravagances. This is the perennially increasing public investment in the massively subsidized, state-owned coal industry. It constitutes the best example with which to enforce the point that none of the various civil servants, labor union officials, and professional politicians who were involved in any of these decisions would have been prepared to subscribe to the equity from their own private pockets, or even from any trust funds for which they were individually accountable, though those labor unions and the particular political party which is almost completely funded and controlled by them have in recent years become eager to raid (other people's) pension funds in order to find (public) finance for pet projects which the (private) market refuses to support.

The example of the nationalized coal industry is especially suitable for enforcing this point: both because the (Conservative) Minister who during the recent strike repeatedly dared to boast of the huge sums which successive administrations of both political colors have continued to pour down these bottomless pits, had, as a merchant banker, before entering politics, made a fortune for himself by picking winners, not losers; and because among the originally offered reasons for socializing the industry in the first place was that no one was willing to make new investments of their own money.

Philosophy, Social Philosophy and Policy Center

[23] The term "constituency" in the UK is roughly equivalent to "district" in the U.S. and to "riding" in Canada.

[24] U.S. citizens are fully entitled to take a measure of national pride in comparing the behavior in this matter of their Senate with that of the British Parliament. For the U.S. Senate, despite the impassioned advocacy of the late Senator Jackson ("the Senator for Boeing"), defeated a proposal to vote a vast subsidy for the production of a supposedly commercial SST (Super Sonic Transport), even though Senator Jackson was certainly both much better liked and more widely respected than Mr. Anthony Wedgwood Benn.

CAPITALISM AND SOCIALISM: HOW CAN THEY BE COMPARED?

By Peter Rutland

INTRODUCTION

How is one to set about the task of comparing capitalism and socialism in a systematic fashion? The contest between capitalism and socialism has many facets. It is both an intellectual debate about the relative merits of models of hypothetical social systems and a real and substantive historical struggle between two groups of states seen as representing capitalism and socialism. Perhaps the intellectual challenge to capitalism thrown down by Marxist thinkers and the "cold war" contest between the U.S.A. and U.S.S.R. are such diverse phenomena that it is pointless and even misleading to try to treat them as part of a single problem. However, I believe that the theoretical and historical aspects of the capitalism/socialism issue are directly related. I would argue that a full understanding of, say, the cold war is not possible without understanding the socialist critique of capitalism – and that a purely abstract comparison of capitalist and socialist models would fail to do justice to the historical and empirical essence of these two grand conceptual schemas.[1]

In Section I, I expand upon these arguments, seeking to convince utopian socialists that they should not continue to rely upon invocations of a hypothetical future, but must come up with some empirical examples of what socialism is and how it works. After all, it is more than a hundred years since Marx and Engels railed against utopian socialists in favor of socialist arguments based on empirical reality. This is not to say that Marx and Engels were crude empiricists, accepting "facts" at face value. They laid great emphasis on the need to abstract from observable social phenomena. However, their intellectual exercise began with the observation of concrete phenomena and returned to observations, predictions and prescriptions of concrete phenomena.

* I would like to thank my former colleagues at the University of Texas at Austin, the participants in the Key Biscayne, Florida conference on "Capitalism and Socialism," November 1987, and in particular Ellen Frankel Paul, for useful comments on an earlier draft of this paper.
[1] A recent interesting collection on the debate broadly understood is T.R. Machan, ed., *The Main Debate: Communism versus Capitalism* (New York: Random House, 1986).

The second general methodological problem I tackle is the selection of the countries of the Soviet bloc as the relevant empirical test case for socialism. Some socialists would violently object to such a selection (although this would not be true, for example, of many socialists in Third World countries). My reasoning is simple: there are no other examples available of social formations with any degree of stability or magnitude (i.e., excluding short-lived, isolated communes) which would merit the title socialist. Beyond this simple take-it-or-leave-it argument, the objections to the selection of the socialist bloc as a test case seem to fall into the pattern of the well-known methodological divergence between historical and structural explanation. The argument is that the Soviet bloc countries are all unique historical phenomena, products of a particular chain of circumstances and events which cannot be captured by a structural model. In the third section I try to refute these arguments. My methodology is in fact very similar to Marx's own method of social analysis, which is appropriate in view of the fact that Marxism decisively shaped the terms of the debate between capitalism and socialism. Marxism is a clear example of genetic structuralism – rejecting a false dichotomy between historical and structural explanation, and arguing that structures themselves are the products of history rather than being ahistorical mental constructs. Thus, to argue that socialist country "A" or capitalist country "B" is a "special case" because of unique historical circumstances strikes me as a violation of Marxist methodology. Every social formation is "special": there is only one planetary history, and social systems rise and fall upon it. Non-Marxists, of course, have far fewer objections to the idea of taking the Soviet bloc nations as exemplars of socialism.

Thus, in our Section II, I try to defend the selection of the advanced countries of the Soviet bloc as examples of the socialist social structure in action. The next step is to carry out the empirical exercise of comparing the performance characteristics of the capitalist and socialist social formations. This takes the form of compiling a primitive scorecard where I try to illustrate in which areas socialism outperforms capitalism and vice versa. The problems involved in such a comparative exercise are immense, and in Section IV I discuss the cautious conclusions which can be drawn from the scorecard. Section V explains why, despite the deficiencies of this empirical approach, I am still more dissatisfied with philosophical approaches which try to make a narrow set of issues (such as rights) the litmus test of the virtues of alternative social systems.

The conventional approach to the issue of capitalism versus socialism is indeed to argue that the two ideologies are founded on two irreconcilably divergent sets of moral principles: equality versus efficiency; liberty versus solidarity; compassion versus self-interest. However, I will argue in

Section V that the debate between capitalism and socialism is not solely or even primarily a debate over conflicting moral principles. On the contrary, in many respects the antagonists share a common set of moral principles. The sides remain locked in dispute because of a disagreement as to what is empirically feasible just as much as over what is morally desirable.

The performance scorecard seems to show the capitalist nations performing better than the socialist countries across a broad range of variables, and only throws up a few examples where the advantage seems to lie with socialism. This crude empirical approach may be philosophically unsatisfactory, but in practical terms it can be argued that socialists are more likely to be persuaded as to the error of their ways if they are drawn into a debate about actual performance rather than being confronted with a set of conflicting moral absolutes where each side can retreat into its own abstractions.

However, in practice a real debate between the virtues of capitalism and socialism almost never takes place. Even if social thinkers are forced to confront this issue, the obvious response is to reject the dichotomy as false. The "reasonable" position would be to argue that both capitalism and socialism are flawed in theory and in execution, and that what is needed is some "middle way" happily combining the good points of both systems while avoiding their pitfalls. (Reference to Sweden usually follows at this point.) This type of escape comes easy to intellectuals, many of whom see their role as consisting precisely of a *critical* approach to the status quo (east or west). Justifying one social system in comparison with another is, for them, mere "apologism": an activity which is thought to be intrinsically less intellectual than criticism.

A critical intelligentsia is a useful, arguably necessary, social phenomenon, but at some point such an intelligentsia must give consideration to the consequences of their prescriptions, and assess whether their criticisms are likely to produce a state of affairs better than that already existing. (The critics must become self-critical.) In a nutshell: intellectual critics of capitalism (or socialism) must at some point step back and assess the relative performance of the system they are criticizing.

Intellectuals are reluctant to embark on such an exercise, which is indeed fraught with methodological and ideological controversy. Their conventional response to the accusation that they are enjoying the leisure of criticizing society without bearing any responsibility for social outcomes has been to propose concrete reforms – institutional changes which will embody their critical arguments. "Countervailing power" is a concept which captures this response: if the intellectual can identify a social group with excessive power, other groups or institutions must be mobilized to counter their power. Thus, in capitalism one should advocate more welfare support for the poor; in socialism one should encourage the liberalization of private enterprise laws. Critical intellectuals who adopt such a relativistic, pragmatic approach probably consider that they are immune to charges of social irresponsibility, and would decline to embark upon the sort of comparative evaluation of social systems which this paper attempts. Their skepticism as to the feasibility of overarching comparisons of alternative social systems should be borne in mind as we proceed with our own macro-sociological exercise in this article.

I. SOCIALISM: REAL AND UTOPIAN

My working definition of socialism in this paper will be the proportion of a nation's economy under state ownership. Any nation with more than, say, 70 percent of employment in state-owned organizations will be regarded as socialist: those with more than 30 percent in the private sector will be regarded as capitalist. This simplistic measure actually causes surprisingly few arguments over which country belongs in which box (although, as I will discuss below, there are strong disagreements over what the "socialist" bloc represents).

(Third World countries do not fit so easily into these categories. Limitations of space and a lack of familiarity with empirical studies prevent me from extending my discussion beyond the core blocs of the First World and Second World.)

Western socialists will, of course, object that the Soviet bloc does not represent "true" socialism, since there has been no full socialization of the means of production, no abolition of wage labor, no withering away of the state, and so forth. (The most extreme – and yet perhaps the most logically consistent – position is to regard the Soviet bloc as just another variety of "state capitalism."[2]) This position rests, essentially, upon a utopian leap of faith as to the mutability of human nature, and to the extent that this is the case its adherents cannot be shaken by rational argument. Nevertheless, it is worth spending a little time trying to expunge utopian elements from the argument between capitalism and socialism.

Utopian socialists reject the U.S.S.R. as a model of socialism, preferring to invoke a hypothetical future socialist society.[3] They insist upon the possibility and inevitability of change. Civilization, they argue, is not

[2] One of the few works coming out of the Left over the past 15 years which directly addresses the question of Soviet socialism adopts such an approach, treating the U.S.S.R. as indistinguishable from "other" capitalist nations is; A. Buick and J. Crump, *State Capitalism: The Wages System Under New Management* (London: St. Martins, 1986).

[3] Thus, for example, even a self-confessed "revisionist" socialist such as A. Przeworski has as his "worst case" that socialism be only *as* efficient as capitalism! A. Przeworski, *Capitalism and Social Democracy* (Cambridge: Cambridge University Press, 1985), p. 236.

confined to the set of social arrangements currently available. After all, modern capitalism is itself the product of change, and it acts as the motor of accelerating change. Capitalism would have seemed inconceivably utopian (or dystopian) to a medieval theologian. (It is still under attack by theologians from Managua to Teheran.)

These arguments are not convincing, however. The analogy between the replacement of feudalism by capitalism and the vision of a shift from capitalism to socialism does not hold water. The arrival of capitalism did not represent the triumph of a formerly utopian vision. The social analysts who foresaw the arrival of capitalism were not utopians, predicting some radical shift in human nature: they were practical men observing the fragmentation of feudal society. The early advocates of capitalism used practical, empirical arguments in defense of their new creed.

In trying to use the analogy of the arrival of capitalism, utopian socialists are blurring the distinction between utopianism and a general belief in the possibility of social change. Opponents of utopianism do *not* have to reject the possibility of change. Their position is simply that the course of change cannot be predicted with any degree of certainty or accuracy. Thus, they are objecting not so much to the specific *content* of a given alternative future suggested by the utopians, as to its inescapably hypothetical and speculative nature.

Of course, some defenders of capitalism do indeed oppose social change, but I personally see little merit in using arguments in favor of tradition and the status quo *per se* as a counter to utopian socialism. On the contrary, I would prefer to argue that capitalism itself is a powerful motor of social change – of the real rather than utopian variety – and stands in sharp contrast to less dynamic social formations such as feudalism and socialism. Within capitalism there are, of course, powerful interests at work seeking to defend the status quo (favoring monopoly over free entry, protectionism over free trade, and so forth) but these forces have not yet prevailed to the extent of undermining capitalism's ability to promote social change.

A second line of argument in defense of capitalism which I would *not* subscribe to is the use of utopian arguments in its support. Marxists accused of utopianism will often retort that capitalist ideology is itself saturated with utopian elements. It is indeed valid to point out that the popular mythology of the "American Dream" has strong utopian elements: not all presidents come out of log cabins, hard work is not always rewarded with success. Even intellectual defenses of capitalism often incorporate utopian themes. The way neoclassical models are presented in "Economics 101" is often utopian in nature, while fundamentalist free marketeers and supply-siders are almost pure utopians (invoking a desirable state of affairs which no actual society past or present has ever come close to representing).

However, the fact that some capitalist utopians exist is irrelevant to the general point I am trying to make in this section: to wit, that it is pointless to engage utopian socialists in argument. I am trying to clear the ground for subsequent sections where I compare and contrast existing socialist and capitalist systems. I am equally prepared to concede that there is no point arguing against (or for) utopian defenders of capitalism.

If one rejects utopianism, one is left with the need to embark on an exercise which investigates the character of known societies, past and present. If one rejects *hypothetical* societies as a vehicle for assessing the virtues of capitalism and socialism, one must turn to existing manifestations, or abandon the comparative project entirely.

Notwithstanding the existence of utopian elements within capitalist ideology, there is also a strong tradition of judging capitalism in terms of current performance. Capitalism's appeal rests primarily on pragmatic grounds: that it is performing better than any alternative form of social organization; that *this* is the good society, and not some other society which will come into being at some point in the future. An example of this willingness to defend capitalism in terms of its actual rather than hypothetical performance would be P.L. Berger's recent book, *The Capitalist Revolution*.[4] Although I would criticize the book for failing to seriously address many socialist criticisms of capitalism, its empirical approach strikes me as fruitful and promising.

There are relatively few Western socialists who are prepared to enter empirical arguments as to the relative performance of capitalism and socialism. Perhaps the most well-known example would be A. Szymanski's *Is the Red Flag Still Flying?*[5] Most, however, take the utopian position, and deny that the U.S.S.R. in any sense represents a valid test of their ideas of socialism.

Soviet leaders themselves have, at least since 1953, been willing to invite direct comparisons between the performance of their socialist system and its capitalist rivals. This willingness has been cautious and limited: much of the Soviet ideological appeal continues to rely upon the promise of future achievements, rather than pointing to actual performance past and present. Thus, for example, there are restrictions on the scope for critical analysis of the socialist record by scholars and journalists within the U.S.S.R. (Economic problems at least are discussed fairly freely, but social problems remained largely taboo until *glasnost*.) One should also recall Khrushchev's enthusiasm for comparing Soviet performance to that of the U.S.A.

[4] P.L. Berger, *The Capitalist Revolution* (New York: Basic Books, 1986). Also, on the general question of system comparison, see R.D. Eastil, *Freedom in the World* (New York: Freedom House, 1988).
[5] A. Szymanski, *Is the Red Flag Still Flying?* (New York: Zed Press, 1978).

(although this probably had more to do with superpower machismo than a serious interest in the relative performance of socialism and capitalism). Soviet leaders no longer share Khrushchev's optimism as to their chances for overtaking the U.S.A., but they continue to accept the comparison as valid. For example, the annual economic statistical handbook still includes a lengthy section comparing the performance of the socialist bloc with capitalist nations, and the U.S.S.R. with the U.S.A.[6]

Soviet political thinkers seem to have concluded that the main argument in favor of their system is that it *exists*: the principal achievement of Lenin was to forge a new type of state, thereby creating the possibility of an alternative to capitalism. Thus, the main challenge that they throw down to their Western socialist critics is that they have built "real socialism," as opposed to the various utopian schemas which have failed to come to fruition. (What the Soviets call "real socialism" the East Germans term "actually existing socialism."[7]) "Real socialism" is an ambiguous category. To some extent it invites the sort of empirical comparison I am about to engage in here. However, it also has strong utopian overtones, since real socialism's full potential has not yet been realized: it is real but unfolding.

Western socialists mostly remain unconvinced by these dialectical niceties. For Third World Marxists, however, "real socialism" exerts a powerful appeal.[8] Third World revolutionaries often find themselves leading a precarious existence, in the midst of states and even whole societies on the brink of collapse. Against such a background, the promise of "actual existence" is something not to be lightly rejected.

Third World Marxists are not, however, the only potential audience for this sort of dialogue between capitalism and socialism. Western specialists on the U.S.S.R. are, of course, engaged in studying the U.S.S.R. as a concrete entity (rather than a utopian project), and the question of comparing it with capitalist societies occasionally comes onto their agenda. In the 1940s and 1950s, when the Totalitarian Model reigned unchallenged, this was not a very live issue, as there was general agreement as to the sins of socialism (which were legion) and its virtues (which were nil).

Since then assessments of the Soviet system have opened up somewhat, with Western academics much more willing to discuss the strengths and virtues of the Soviet system. To some extent, the old orthodoxy of the

[6] There was, however, a change in the 1985 handbook: the comparative section was moved from its traditional place at the front, to the back. *Narodnoe khozyaistvo SSSR v 1985 g.* (Moscow: Finansy i statistika, 1986), pp. 578–627.

[7] On this, see A. Evans, "The Decline of Developed Socialism?," *Soviet Studies*, vol. 38, no. 1 (January 1986), p. 1; and L. Sochor, *The Ideology of Real Socialism* (Munich: Research Project on the Crisis in Soviet-Type Systems, 1984).

[8] See D. Chellappa, *Soviet Economic Achievements: Their Significance For Developing Countries* (New Delhi: Kalamkar Prakashan, 1978), for a not particularly edifying example.

Totalitarian syndrome has been replaced by a new orthodoxy which implicitly recognizes the socialist model as a viable alternative development path. Two concepts stand out as exemplars of this orthodoxy. First, it is held that there are strong pluralistic elements in Soviet society (perhaps as strong as in any other developed society), and that the most fruitful research strategy for scholars is to explore in detail the variety of pluralistic policy inputs and/or outputs.[9] Second, it seems generally agreed that the Soviet state has attained a degree of "legitimacy" in the eyes of its population (witness the absence of mass terror and the marginality of social unrest).[10]

These approaches represent, in my view, an insufficiently critical approach to the Soviet political system. They arose out of a distaste for the cold war Manichaeanism of the Totalitarian Model. To some extent the new orthodoxy is a natural by-product of the academic calling. Given the popular acceptance of the "Red Menace," academics may feel obliged to correct the ignorance of politics freshmen by leaning in a direction opposite to their students' prejudices. We may also be encountering the empathy which builds up as a scholar seeks to understand the internal dynamics of a particular period of social system (the academic equivalent of the "Stockholm syndrome" in kidnap-victims). This empathy may be reinforced by personal impressions gleaned during personal visits to the U.S.S.R. – Russians are friendly, the trains run on time, and so forth. Strongly negative reactions in visitors to the U.S.S.R. are at least as frequent, of course – but these people tend not to devote themselves to becoming Soviet specialists. A process of "natural selection" may be at work in the Sovietological community, leavened only by the arrival of émigré scholars, who tend to be resolutely anti-Soviet in most respects.

II. HISTORICAL VERSUS STRUCTURAL EXPLANATION

My simple definition distinguishes between "socialism" and "capitalism" on the basis of the pattern of ownership of the means of production: a structural, synchronic distinction. Can one move forward on the basis of such a definition to a direct comparison of the current socialist and capitalist nations?

Such an approach is open to challenge by the historical school, which

---

[9] S.G. Solomon, ed., *Pluralism in the Soviet Union* (London: St. Martins, 1983).

[10] For example, G.W. Breslauer advanced a theory of "welfare state authoritarianism" – see his *Five Images of the Soviet Future* (Berkeley: Institute of International Studies, 1978). The concept of a "social contract" wherein the workers offer loyalty in return for job security and welfare benefits is widely accepted. See, for example, P. Hauslohner, "Gorbachev's Social Contract," *Soviet Economy*, vol. 3, no. 1 (Spring 1987), p. 54.

argues that the functioning of current socio-political structures cannot be understood in isolation from their historical genesis. Methodologically, this is an open question: it may or may not be the case that the structures "socialism" and "capitalism" generate fruitful insights into the nature of human society. From a pragmatic point of view, however, this issue is absolutely vital. By introducing historical argument, defenders of socialism seek to explain away the current advantages of capitalism by referring to its unique historical record – the U.S.A. was unique in having a rich and almost empty continent to colonize; the West European empires were uniquely fortunate in being major actors at the inception of the modern "world system." The imperialist powers were able to lock themselves in to a position of privilege within the system, as defined by the established economic structures and trade patterns, the relative power of nation-states, the network of international institutions, and so forth.

An extreme historicist would therefore argue that each social formation is historically unique, and deserves separate treatment. This argument is often made with regard to the U.S.S.R. (although its theoretical under-pinnings are rarely made explicit). The U.S.S.R. is a "special case" because of the relative backwardness of Tsarist society and economy; the absence of a democratic tradition; the country's geo-political exposure to foreign attack; the depredations of the Second World War; the continued threat posed by "capitalist encirclement"; and so forth.

The historicist argument is difficult to defeat, but the rationale for proceeding with a structural comparison of capitalist and socialist systems would run along the following lines.

First, one can argue that capitalism and socialism represent integrated, coherent social systems, whose components are related to each other in a necessary fashion. One can show how state control over the economy necessitates the suppression of market forces, a shift of resources away from consumption, and so on, while in the political arena the command economy both presupposes and reinforces a one party system with concomitant limits on political liberties. One can also show how these structural relationships have been reproduced in each of the countries which have adopted the Soviet model.

The historicist will reply that it is no use multiplying the number of examples, since the course of development of all the socialist nations has been uniquely tied to the U.S.S.R., meaning that the particular "deformations" of the mother country have spread elsewhere, directly or indirectly. (Thus, for example, the Soviet model was crudely imposed on East Europe at the point of a gun, while the poverty and militarism of Cuba can be explained away by its U.S.A.-engineered economic and political isolation, in turn a product of U.S.A. fear of the U.S.S.R.)

However detailed one's structural analysis of socialism, the historicist can always argue that these structural relationships are accidental. Thus, a second possible riposte in defense of structural explanation is to take the historicists on at their own game, to take each historically "unique" feature and show how it has been shaped by structural factors. After all, the socialist system in the U.S.S.R. itself has been in place for seventy years. This is surely long enough for society and economy to have reproduced themselves many times over. Any imbalances and deficiencies present in 1917 should surely have been overcome by now. These points are clearest with regard to the economy: the U.S.S.R. has vast natural resources (a "unique" feature its defenders often omit), a large labor force, and a high level of capital investment, yet only converts these resources into products in an inefficient fashion. A structuralist counter to the Second World War argument would point out that the lost national product was mostly made up by 1948; that other countries also suffered population and infrastructure losses during the war of similar scale; and that the magnitude of Soviet losses can largely be attributed to structural features of Soviet socialism – Stalin's refusal to allow Red Army units to retreat or to surrender; his short-sighted pact with Hitler in 1939; the imbalances of the economic structure which produced lots of well-designed tanks, but without the radios and trained crews to make them effective on the modern battlefield.

This line of argument soon loses itself in a morass of historical detail. The simplest response to historicist criticisms of a structural comparison is to insist on the validity of structural analysis, even at the macro-social level. Whatever the particulars of the historical path by which the U.S.S.R. came to be the way it is today, we are interested in it *as it is*, as an example of a socialist system. The same historical accidents which "deformed" its rate of development (e.g., the tradition of a strongly centralized state) are also responsible for its being socialist. There are no other examples around of a "non-deformed" socialist state. If one wants to discuss socialism and capitalism at all, one has to deal with historically specific entities.

Given their very different histories, maybe comparing the U.S.A. and U.S.S.R. is like comparing apples and oranges. But this is better than no comparison at all, or than comparing apples and door knobs. Apples and oranges *can* be compared in terms of color, taste, vitamin content, and so forth.

Let us take it, then, that some sort of empirical comparison of existing societies taken to represent the structural features of capitalism and socialism is possible and meaningful. The problem then becomes one of selecting the most suitable pair-wise comparisons. There would seem to be five different ways in which such a comparative exercise could be conducted:

(1) The Best Case Approach

One could select the most successful current examples of capitalism and socialism respectively, i.e., the advanced capitalist countries of West Europe and North America and the developed regions of the U.S.S.R. and East Europe. This is the most obvious approach, and will loom large in the exercise I carry out in Section III.

(2) The Worst Case Approach

One could compare the worst examples of the capitalist world with the worst examples of the socialist world. This may make sense in Rawlsian terms – as we shall see, perhaps the best case for socialism can be attempted along "maximin" lines.[11] This approach cannot be used as the basis for a comparative study, however, because at the bottom end of the scale of development it is unclear whether struggling nations such as Uganda or Mozambique can really be said to possess identifiable capitalist or socialist structures. Even the level of information available about the functioning of these societies is usually inadequate to making such an assessment. (In any case, in the introduction I warned that Third World issues were beyond the scope of this paper.)

(3) The Neighbors' Comparison

An alternative approach is to try to control for level of development and cultural traditions by choosing countries which were very similar before one became socialist. Thus, one could compare East and West Germany, North and South Korea, Czechoslovakia and Austria, Cuba and Costa Rica, and so forth. This is methodologically robust, overcoming historicist objections as to the "uniqueness" of a given society to the maximum extent possible. I will draw upon such neighbor comparisons as have been conducted (the two Germanies have been a favorite object of study). There remains the problem that the two giants on each side – the U.S.A. and U.S.S.R. – do not have any obvious partners with a similar heritage.

(4) The Developmental Approach[12]

The third approach lumps together cultural and developmental factors. Modernization theory would argue that the general level of socio-economic development (as measured, say, by the proportion of the workforce

[11] J. Rawls, *A Theory of Justice* (Cambridge: Harvard University Press, 1971).

[12] This point was made to the author by J. Higley, who presents his own version of the theory in G. Lowell Field and J. Higley, *Elitism* (London: Routledge and Kegan Paul, 1980). For a review of the economic literature, and an application to the socialist countries of South East Europe, see M.R. Jackson, "Economic Development in the Balkans Since 1945 Compared to Southern and East Central Europe," *Eastern European Politics and Societies*, vol. 1, no. 3 (Fall 1987), p. 393.

engaged in manual work in industry) is the decisive variable determining social and economic life. They would argue that the impact of the level of development may overwhelm any differences resulting from the alternative social arrangements of capitalism or socialism. Thus, in order to examine the differential impact of capitalism/socialism, the comparison would have to be made between countries at the same level of development, rather than (as in the third approach) between countries which started at the same level. Thus, the comparison between East and West Germany would be invalid, because the differences may be due to the fact that East Germany has stayed at a lower level of development than West Germany (e.g., it has not entered the service economy). Instead, they would suggest comparing the U.S.S.R. of the 1980s with, say, the U.S.A. of the 1950s or the South Korea of the 1980s.

This approach is interesting, but I do not see why (or how) development should be separated out from the socialism/capitalism issue and given causal priority. On the contrary, I would suggest that socialism itself may be responsible for "delaying" the development of the socialist nations (as in the German example). The modernization approach has also been widely criticized as a disguised form of utopianism, in that it encourages us to imagine that at some point in the future the socialist bloc – under the influence of the allegedly independent development variable – will break through into a different set of social arrangements.

(5) The Historical Comparison

One could adopt the historicist paradigm, treating each country as historically unique and therefore adopting a "before and after" approach. The crudest variant is that favored by Soviet commentators – a direct contrast between the achievements of the U.S.S.R. and the levels attained by Tsarist Russia c. 1913. This is a rather pointless exercise, since it invites counterfactual speculation as to whether Russia would have turned out like the U.S.A. or more like Argentina had it followed a capitalist course this century.

A fairer test would be to conduct a dynamic comparative analysis, looking at trends in performance over time, rather than looking at achieved levels (as in methods 1, 2 and 3 above). Thus, one would compare the U.S.A. in 1917 and 1980 with the Soviet Union in 1917 and 1980. This is an extremely complex operation, however, as one is comparing four country observations rather than two (as in method one), and one is trying to bridge different historical periods. Problems of data commensurability are likely to be more than twice as difficult as in a simple, static pair-wise comparison.

* * * * * * * *

Thus, the question of selecting the suitable objects of study for comparative analysis is a complex and contentious issue. To work through all the evidence pertaining to each of these comparative methods is obviously way beyond the scope of this paper. For the purposes of moving my argument forward I will try to draw up a scorecard of comparative performance primarily on the basis of the "best case" approach (1), making due allowance for the materials available from "neighbors" comparisons (3), and trying to compensate for differences in the historical starting point of countries under the respective systems (5).

I should reiterate, however, that I am interested in a *structural* rather than casually historical/empirical analysis. In other words, I am looking for features of the various societies selected which can be analytically tied to the dominance of the socialist or capitalist social formation. I try where possible to discount features which can be argued to be the product of historical accident (problems of climate and terrain, for example, or the ethnic diversity of the country inherited from premodern times).

III.   CAPITALISM AND SOCIALISM: A SCORECARD

Most commentators who discuss the characteristics of capitalism and socialism imply that these terms mean something in the real world – that is, that the presence of socialism or capitalism as the dominant system of social organization will make a difference to social, economic and political life in that community.[13] In principle, therefore, it should be possible to draw up some sort of scorecard (see Table 1) listing the dominant characteristics of these two social formations. In this case, I go one stage further, and try to assess their relative performance, on the basis of what I hope to be common-sense evaluations of what is desirable (efficiency is better than inefficiency; more is better than less, etc.).

This leaves us open to two types of argument – questioning whether or not the features we attribute to socialism or capitalism are actually caused by those social formations (maybe they are mere historical accident, maybe we have our facts wrong); and questioning what we mean by saying that performance in any given sphere is "superior" under one social system rather than another. There are insuperable problems with regard to the second type of objection. Issues such as whether equality is intrinsically more valuable than inequality or the innate virtues of private versus public

[13] Two examples of works which try to provide a systematic analysis of the structural features of socialism are K. von Beyme, *Economics and Politics Within Socialist Systems* (New York: Praeger, 1982); and B. Mieczkowski and O. Zinam, *Bureaucracy, Ideology and Technocracy: Quality of Life East and West* (Charleston: East Illinois University Press, 1984). The present author also essayed an overview of the structural features of Soviet socialism; P. Rutland, *The Myth of the Plan: Lessons of Soviet Planning Experience* (La Salle: Open Court, 1985).

transport (or vice versa) will obviously not be resolved here. The scorecard approach should be seen as a heuristic device, rather than the Last Judgment as to the relative merits of these two social systems.

I have attempted a value-neutral approach, rooted in a fairly extensive familiarity with the literature on socialism and visits to socialist bloc countries totaling over two years' residency. Even so, it was virtually impossible to find a single person who agreed with *all* the rankings in the table: too much subjectivity enters into measuring the variables, and there are too many gaps in the empirical data – particularly on the socialist side.

Nevertheless, the author does believe that the table does in some meaningful sense represent the pattern of structural differences between socialism and capitalism. However, it is worth spending some time explaining some of the more controversial rankings in the table.

The first point must be to recognize that in creating two blocs of "advanced socialist" and "advanced capitalist" I am ignoring many country-specific phenomena. Thus, for example, the blocs could be broken down as follows:

within the socialist bloc –
U.S.S.R. performance better:
political stability

East Europe performance better:
general living standard
freedom of movement
food, transport, shopping, housing

within the capitalist bloc –
U.S.A. performance better:
general living standard
social classes

West Europe performance better:
living standard of poor
housing and health care for poor
freedom from crime
education

I do not wish to deny the historical uniqueness of each country: I am merely trying to rise above it in order to draw some conclusions about the impact of socialism and capitalism.

Let us take some of the more controversial and ambiguous rankings in turn.

(1) Racial Equality
The socialist bloc is not, of course, free of racial tension. The treatment of Jews in the U.S.S.R., Turks in Bulgaria, or the deported nationalities under Stalin indicate that socialism is not immune to racism. Capitalist systems have the advantage of greater respect for human rights combined

Table One
Capitalism and Socialism: A Scorecard

capitalism superior to socialism		NO major difference	socialism superior to capitalism	
strongly	weakly		weakly	strongly
political liberties	political participation	racial equality		
freedom of movement		some personal liberties (e.g., marriage, abortion)		
fair judicial system			freedom from crime	
economic freedom		worker alienation		full employment
	environment protection	economic growth		
economic efficiency		technical efficiency		
general standard of living	living standard of poor	social class	wealth & income equality	
food		social mobility		
transport	chance of being poor	gender equality		
housing and health care for non-poor		regional economic equality		
		health care for poor	housing for poor	
shopping/ consumer goods		"consumerism"		
leisure	high culture	education		
technology		social unrest		
religious freedom		political stability		
	military service**	military power***		

* By "capitalism" I mean the advanced capitalist countries of North America and West Europe. By "socialism" I mean the advanced socialist countries of the U.S.S.R. and East Europe.
** Capitalism is considered superior in that military service is voluntary in some countries, and terms and conditions are less harsh than in socialism.
*** Both sides can mobilize sufficient military power to defend themselves.

with legal systems with the autonomy to serve as a vehicle for the realization of these rights. However, the way the labor market works under capitalism – sucking in additional cheap labor, and keeping wages down through *de facto* labor market segregation in some cases – leads to the creation and/or perpetuation of ethnic underclasses (from immigrant workers in West Europe to blacks in the U.S.A.). The economic incentives to promote such international labor migration seem to be lacking under socialism, while the absence of a free housing market has generally prevented the emergence of ghettoes in socialist cities. Overall, I feel unable to conclude that either socialism or capitalism has any clear and consistent advantage in the way ethnic relations are managed.

(2) Political Participation

I list this as only a "weak" advantage of capitalism in recognition of the ambiguities and contradictions of the democratic process – low turnout, limited choice of parties, practical difficulties in aggregating the preferences of millions of electors. Also, in terms of local politics many specialists on the Soviet bloc are prepared to argue that local involvement in pothole/garbage issues is roughly comparable east and west (we would disagree, but the evidence is not there for a definitive answer, since it is difficult to come up with measures for the effectivity of participation).[14] In general, the Schumpeter argument holds: Western electors do have a choice, albeit a constrained one.[15] They *can* remove an unpopular government. Perhaps this should make political participation a strong plus for capitalism after all.

Capitalism is, of course, compatible with the *absence* of political participation, but in the developed countries which are the object of my "best case" comparison, democracy has been the preponderant form of political organization.

(3) Social Class[16]

Social class is a highly subjective evaluation: social stratification is probably a feature of all societies, and how is one to measure whether the

[14] For a representative work, see D.E. Schulz and J.S. Adams, eds., *Political Participation in Communist Systems* (New York: Pergammon, 1981).

[15] J.S. Schumpeter, *Capitalism, Socialism and Democracy* (London: Allen and Unwin, 1976). Schumpeter's analysis of socialism does not, in the view of the present author, match the perspicacity of his analysis of capitalist democracy.

[16] On these questions, see W.D. Connor, *Socialism, Politics and Equality* (New York: Columbia University Press, 1979); and B. Kerblay, *Modern Soviet Society* (New York: Random House, 1983). On income inequality, see J.M. Echols III, "Does Socialism Mean Greater Equality?," S. White and D. Nelson, eds., *Communist Politics: A Reader* (London: Macmillan, 1986), p. 361; and S. Jain, *Size Distribution of Income: A Compilation of Data* (Washington: World Bank, 1975).

sense of "us and them" is stronger in one society than other? Such data as are available suggest that social mobility on an intergenerational basis is roughly compatible in capitalist and socialist countries (being largely a function of the rate at which economic growth creates new urban and white collar positions). The occupational prestige hierarchy is also roughly similar. However, income and particularly wealth is more unequally distributed in the capitalist countries (although the more egalitarian capitalist countries such as Australia or Sweden overlap with the socialist camp).

(4) Economic Freedom and Employment Security

This means not only freedom to trade and run a business, but also economic freedom for the workers, in the sense of the freedom from a monopsony employer which workers mostly enjoy under capitalism. The obligation to work for the state in socialism is not only a problem for a small group of dissidents (who may be denied work in their profession): it also affects many ordinary workers and employees who do not want to put in their forty hours each week for the state (e.g., persons just below retirement age, mothers with older children who would prefer to stay at home, or persons wishing to develop their education). This twentieth-century state corvée system is the other side of the coin to state-guaranteed full employment – which is the only factor I identify in the table as a clear, strong advantage of socialism.[17] (There are, of course, other probable costs to state-maintained full employment – a lower level of economic efficiency, and a correspondingly poorer standard of living.)

(5) Worker Alienation

Worker alienation (or the related concept of "job satisfaction") would seem to be roughly the same in both systems, being shaped primarily by the nature of modern technology. In this regard a variety of "convergence theory" seems to hold true. Worker alienation under socialism may be partially eased by the absence of fear of unemployment. The tight labor market also leads to more relaxed industrial relations, with managers keen to placate and retain their scarce workers.[18] The resolution of individual labor disputes also seems fairly favorable towards the worker.[19] On the other hand, the absence of independent trade union activity is clearly a strongly negative factor from the workers' point of view, since under capitalism it seems to have brought higher living standards and at least a

[17] See the collection edited by David Lane, *Labour and Employment in the USSR* (Brighton, Sussex: Harvester, 1986).
[18] V. Andrle, *Managerial Power in the Soviet Union* (New York: Saxon House, 1976).
[19] N. Lampert, "Job security and the Law in the USSR," Lane, ed., *Labour*, p. 256.

partial sense of self-protection. The Solidarity phenomenon shows that such benefits of independent organization are also sought in the socialist bloc. Even in Poland, however, surveys also show strong support for the state's policy of full employment and state ownership of major industries.[20] In practice, however, there may be a trade-off between employment security and higher income, and we cannot say that the advantage is universally perceived to lie with the former rather than the latter. Thus we must leave worker alienation as neutral between capitalism and socialism. This in itself is a powerful indictment of socialism (if it is true), since protection of the workers' interests is supposed to be the rationale for the existence of socialism.

(6)   The Poor

"The poor ye will always have with you" remains unfortunately true for the socialist bloc. Socialist treatment of the poor is often cited as one of the system's main virtues, alongside full employment.[21] However, such a position is more a reflection of wishful thinking than a result of a careful empirical analysis of the plight of the poor in the socialist bloc (an analysis which, of course, is very difficult to conduct). We are interested primarily in absolute levels of poverty, and the comparison between East and West in absolute terms. What is the level of service (housing, food, health care) provided to the poorest groups in society, and what is the number of people falling into this category? Only a sketchy answer can be provided, as data is hard to come by. (No society, socialist included, likes to collect information about its poor.)

I would prefer not to get into arguments over the issue of "relative deprivation." (Are the socialist poor *less* poor because there are fewer Rockefellers to envy – or are they *more* poor because the range of wealth is narrower, meaning that the social perception of differences is more acute?) As to the causes of poverty, it is my overall impression that they are remarkably similar in the two societies – ill health, disability, old age, family separation, the arrival of children, chronically low wages, and so forth.

The best argument on the socialist side would seem to be that socialist societies have managed to avoid the tragedy of homelessness. However, some vagrants and beggars *can* be seen in the streets of socialist bloc cities,

---

[20] D.S. Mason, *Public Opinion and Political Change in Poland, 1980–82* (Cambridge: Cambridge University Press, 1985). For similar data from former Soviet citizens, see B.D. Silver, "Political Beliefs of the Soviet Citizen: Sources of Support for Regime Norms," J.R. Millar, ed., *Politics, Work and Daily Life in the USSR* (Cambridge: Cambridge University Press, 1987), p. 100.
[21] As in, for example, V. George and N. Manning, *Socialism, Social Welfare and the Soviet Union* (London: Routledge and Kegan Paul, 1980).

and the absence of more visible large-scale homelessness may be due to a policy of incarcerating vagrants and sending the children of the homeless to orphanages.[22] While redundancy and mortgage default are not present as causes of homelessness, family break up is a problem common to both systems (indeed, it is more serious in the socialist countries, where the tight housing market makes it extremely difficult for separated families to find alternative accomodation).

The living standard of the poor is low in socialism because income maintenance programs for those without a full work record are very weak.[23] Roughly 30 percent of the population may be living below the officially set minimum subsistence level in the U.S.S.R. (50 rubles per capita per month). Housing and utilities are cheap (4–5 rubles per month), but only a bare diet (bread, potatoes, milk, cabbage) can be sustained on these low incomes. In contrast, the U.S.A. has some 15 percent of its population subsisting on less than c. $250 per month. If these people are in receipt of food stamps or food bank aid, their diets will be better than those of the Soviet poor (and better, in fact, than the diet of the average Soviet worker).

Let us move on to health care.[24] The provision of health care to all on the basis of need, irrespective of ability to pay, is often cited as one of the decisive advantages of socialism – even by émigrés from the socialist bloc who otherwise have little good to say about their former homeland. However, in practice I doubt whether health care for the disadvantaged is any better under socialism than under capitalism – on the contrary, the advantage is likely to lie in the other direction. First, it should be noted that even in the U.S.A. private charities and state and federal agencies do provide a safety net of health care to the poor (notwithstanding the fact that the coverage may be patchy). (Most other capitalist countries do, of course, have universal state health provision.) Second, one should recognize that socialist countries tend to spend a lower proportion of their national income on health – of the order of 2–3 percent, as against 11 percent for the U.S.A. This is partly a product of their level of economic development,

[22] Glasnost has partially opened the door to public discussion of homelessness – in Czechoslovakia, at least. For example, one news magazine carried a story on a couple with two children who were living in a van in a Prague parking lot; D. Vondracek, "Ale maji se radi," *Mlady svet*, no. 2, 1988, p. 15.

[23] See A. MacAuley, *Economic Welfare in the Soviet Union* (Madison: University of Wisconsin Press, 1979); and M. Matthews, *Poverty in the Soviet Union* (Cambridge: Cambridge University Press, 1986). For recent data, see A. Trehub, "Social and Economic Rights in the Soviet Union," *Radio Liberty Supplement*, no. 3 (1988); K. Bush, "Retail Prices in Moscow and Four Western Cities," *Radio Liberty Supplement*, no. 1 (1987); A. Vinokur and G. Ofer, "Inequality of Earnings, Household Income and Wealth in the Soviet Union in the 1970s," in J.R. Millar, ed., *Politics*, p. 171. On the US side, see J.T. Patterson, *America's Struggle Against Poverty, 1900–80* (Cambridge: Harvard University Press, 1981).

[24] See Rutland, *The Myth*, ch. 8, for a review of the Soviet health care system.

but can also be attributed to the centralization of allocative decisions in a planned economy and the state's consistent desire to steer resources into defense and productive investment, rather than health care. The low level of health care provision must in part be responsible for the fact that Soviet aggregate life expectancy and infant mortality figures are among the worst in Europe, on the level of Portugal and Turkey. Third, it is important to bear in mind that goods and services which in theory are provided by the state on the basis of need in practice may well be skewed to the benefit of advantaged groups in society. It is generally recognized that health care provision in the Soviet countryside is very poor, while even in the major cities access to care is often rationed by bribes of "connections." This phenomenon of collective provision being manipulated to the benefit of socially advantaged groups has been carefully documented by I. Szelenyi with regard to the allocation of state sector housing in Hungary.[25]

(7) Economic Performance

The Soviet bloc economies have displayed fairly impressive nominal growth rates – although nothing out of the ordinary in comparison with Japan, or Korea.[26] There is also considerable doubt as to the ability of these economies to grow over the long run, once the initial phase of heavy industry expansion has been completed.

By "technical production efficiency" I mean both the efficiency of the machinery and of the work organization within the factory. It is commonly thought that socialist work organization is necessarily inferior to that of a capitalist firm, mainly due to poor incentive systems, but I agree with M. Burawoy that this is not necessarily the case.[27] Modern industrial processes can be installed in both systems, and this technology exerts a strong influence over surrounding work methods. Detailed studies of specific products or production lines show that some Soviet factories can meet Western performance levels. Some socialist firms are more successful than others, just as performance will vary widely across capitalist firms.

The key deficiency of socialism is not its ability to organize individual production processes, but its inability to do so across the whole economy on a systematic basis. Lack of market forces means that there is little pressure to retire outmoded technology or close inefficient plants. Even within this topic of economic efficiency at the level of social production,

[25] I. Szelenyi and R. Manchin, "Social Inequalities in Eastern Europe," M. Rein, ed., *Stagnation and Renewal in Social Policy* (New York: M.E. Sharpe, 1987), p. 110.

[26] F.L. Pryor, "Growth and Fluctuations of Production in OECD and East European Countries," *World Politics*, vol. 37, no. 2 (Summer 1985), p. 204.

[27] M. Burawoy and J. Lukacs, "Capitalist and Socialist Work," *American Sociological Review*, vol. 50, no. 6 (December 1985), p. 723.

there are considerable differences with, for example, capital productivity being much poorer than labor productivity (compared to capitalist economies) and their relative performance in agriculture being much poorer than in industry.

(8) Daily Life Issues

When we enter the area of daily life (crime, consumerism, education, culture, and so forth) it becomes very difficult to separate out the impact of the social formation (socialism or capitalism) from the general historical and cultural environment. It is with some trepidation that I include such variables in the scorecard. The motive for doing so was to confront those defenders of socialism who argue that the socialist societies systematically produce more desirable outcomes in these areas than do materialist, individualist capitalist societies. I do not see any such systematic structural advantage in the direction of socialism.

As far as crime is concerned, statistics from the socialist bloc are rather patchy, but it does seem that the extensive police network, punitive judicial system, and more restricted opportunities for crime (fewer private cars and houses, for example) do mean that major crime is less prevalent in the socialist bloc.[28] However, the difference between crime levels in Japan and West Europe on one side and the U.S.A. on the other swamps any difference in crime rates between socialism and capitalism.

"Consumerism" is given attention simply because an important theme in New Left critiques of capitalism is the idea of the moral and psychological void created by mass consumption in capitalist conditions. (This critique derives from Marx's aristocratic disdain for "commodity fetishism": better that one should hunt, fish, rear cattle, and read poetry, like the typical English country squire.) The present author is not convinced that "consumerism" means anything – as Peter Wiles once remarked, all that we know for certain is that people consume. Inasmuch as "consumerism" exists, however, then it is a flaw to be found in socialism as well as capitalism. Socialist consumers are admittedly free from the more intrusive forms of commercial advertising (although, as P. Hollander has argued, they are subject to political propaganda which constitutes a parallel form of value alteration[29]). However, socialist consumers show every sign of desiring the same sort of products as those in the West, and are subject to similar fads and fashions. They obstinately hold out for designer jeans or sports shoes; they will patiently queue for the "best" restaurants or for foreign

---

[28] For the bravest effort to compile data, see G.P. Van Den Berg, *The Soviet System of Justice: Figures and Policy* (Boston: M. Nijhoff, 1985), p. 15 for East European data.

[29] P. Hollander, *Soviet and American Society: A Comparison* (Chicago: University of Chicago Press, 1978), ch. 4.

goods; and they have gone to great lengths to circumvent the state's sustained efforts to limit private car ownership (bidding up the price of new cars and making superhuman efforts to keep old cars on the road).

The position of women in socialist society is one of the best studied aspects of their social system, and the verdict is clear.[30] While women have gained in terms of acceptance as full-time participants in the labor force, and in terms of access to education and the professions, they have made little progress in terms of average income compared to males, access to leadership positions, or gender equality in the home. There have been major advances in maternity leave and pay (although the motives of the state in introducing these have been driven more by a concern with a static birth rate than a desire to improve the position of women). Women under capitalism have done better in terms of their ability to organize themselves in defense of their own interests, and in terms of the provision of labor-saving devices which ease the burden of shopping and housework. Child care availability is better in East Europe, but not in the U.S.S.R. (where grandmothers still play a crucial role).

It is sometimes argued that the socialist states perform better in the educational arena, in terms of equality of social access, level of educational attainment, low proportion of dropouts, and so forth. There may be some truth in such arguments, although they do not appear to have been systematically studied in a comparative context. My general point with regard to education is the same as that made for crime, however: to wit, that East Europe is closer to West Europe in this regard than is West Europe to the U.S.A. Thus, what we are tapping into is national traditions rather than the influence of socialism or capitalism per se.

IV. ASSESSING THE SCORECARD APPROACH

What does one learn from the scorecard exercise? Objection about individual variables' positions in the ranking is not the main worry. Reasonable observers will differ about how to assess the evidence for the extent of poverty or whatever. More crucial problems arise as to the normative implications of the table.

Some commentators may even deny that agreement can be reached on how to rank the relative performance of socialist and capitalist nations as regards, say, worker alienation or racial equality. Perhaps these phenomena are so different in the two societies that they are incommensurable. This is on the surface a reasonable objection, but to accept it would place us well down the slippery slope of relativism. If there is no agreement on the

---

[30] See, for example, G.W. Lapidus, ed., *Women, Work and Family in the Soviet Union* (New York: M.E. Sharpe, 1981).

premises needed to study poverty or equality, then it becomes impossible to study these phenomena in any society, let alone in a comparative context.

Another objection would be to suggest that the variables discussed in the table are important and commensurable, but that they are not being determined by any differences between the socialist and capitalist forms of social organization. Rather, they would attribute causal power to some third factor – level of development, the logic of modern industry, or whatever. I am not congenitally opposed to these arguments – after all, many important social characteristics are listed in the table as exhibiting no major systemic differences. But it is my opinion that the differences discussed in the remaining four columns of the table are substantial, and can primarily be explained with reference to the political economy of capitalism and socialism respectively.

The greatest problem posed by such a table is the general question of the scope for meaningful comparisons between the capitalist and socialist formations. The danger in this scorecard approach is that it may encourage one to imagine that there is some divine observation point for assessing rival social systems, a throne of political economy from which judgments can be issued. Does there exist a set of universally agreed principles which can be applied to the enumerated variables, giving some overall meaning and significance to the scorecard exercise?

The table seems to show that socialism and capitalism have a differential impact across a wide range of social, economic, and political variables. It is doubtful whether their differences can be reduced to a simple question of equity versus efficiency, still less to collective versus individual welfare.

Some "public good" type issues seem to be handled better by capitalist states (environmental protection) and others (crime) by socialism. Socialism perhaps performs at a similar level in education, but lags with regard to science, technology, and high culture.

Take, for example, the situation of the poor, whose treatment is pivotal for moral thinkers east and west. Socialists traditionally argue that the undeniable economic gains of capitalism come at the expense of the poor, and images of the poor constitute the bulk of the Soviet propaganda assault on capitalism. Rawlsian liberals also recognize that how a society treats its poorest members constitutes a valid test of the relative moral worth of two alternative social arrangements. (The socialist bloc would, of course, fail the first half of the Rawlsian test, because of their failure to guarantee basic liberties.[31]) The evidence suggests that the socialist side cannot claim moral

---

[31] To my knowledge, no Soviet writers have directly addressed the question of how their society would measure up against the Rawlsian criteria of social justice. A Soviet philosopher, G.V. Mal'tsev, gave an accurate summary of Rawls's ideas in the book *Problemy gosudarstva i prava v sovremennoi ideologicheskoi bor'be* (Moscow: Yuridicheskaya literatura, 1983), p. 145. He

superiority on this score. In some respects their poor are treated better than under capitalism (with regard to housing, freedom from crime, and racial equality). However, in other respects (food, consumer goods, and the likelihood of being poor) capitalism seems to have the edge, while in the area of health care it is difficult to discern any systemic advantage. Thus, any evaluation of whether the poor are better off under capitalism or socialism would involve trade-offs between health care, diet, and housing which would be difficult to explain and justify.

Thus, the conclusion I would draw from this exercise would be to stress the need for an eclectic approach. It is not merely the case that different groups or classes enjoy different benefits under the two systems (the Marxist or pluralist answer to the question of system comparison), so much as the fact that a given group will experience a different mixture of costs and benefits. A group-by-group approach would make the commensurability problem a *little* easier, but would not overcome it completely.

The eclectic approach is probably compatible with the major competing schools of moral philosophy in the West, given that they recognize (and even value) the inevitability of ambiguity and inconsistency. Socialist moral philosophy of the Soviet variety, such as it is, is unlikely to be able to cope with such a fluid interpretation.[32] There is a hint of recognition of such a position in a joke reportedly told by Gustav Husak, President of Czechoslovakia, to the effect that the ideal situation would be to work under socialism and shop under capitalism.[33]

V. THE LIMITATIONS OF MORAL APPROACHES TO THE DEBATE BETWEEN CAPITALISM AND SOCIALISM

Conventional debates about the relative merits of capitalism and socialism have tended to concentrate on questions of moral and political philosophy. These usually take some hypothetical socialist system as a counterpoint to actual capitalism, although the conclusions of such debates are often applied to the comparison between existing capitalism and socialism.

Much of the debate proceeds at a fairly abstract level, raising issues which will remain "essentially contested" for the foreseeable future. They rest upon competing views of human nature: optimistic or pessimistic as to

---

is surprisingly uncritical of the content of Rawls's ideas (surprising because the book's title refers to the "ideological struggle" with the West), and merely reproaches Rawls for a lack of realism and a naive faith in the independence of the law.

[32] For a summary view of the state of Soviet philosophy, see J.P. Scanlan, *Marxism in the USSR* (Ithaca: Cornell University Press, 1986).

[33] Joke reported in *New York Times*, 6 July 1969, p. E6, recounted in O. Ulc, *Politics in Czechoslovakia* (San Francisco: W.H. Freeman, 1974), p. 45.

the possibility of change; stressing individuality or solidarity as a worthy end of human action; and so on.

Interesting though these controversies may be, it is not easy to see how they can be mapped onto the differing social formations of capital and socialism.

* * * * * * *

Take, for example, the subject of *individualism versus collectivism*. It is widely thought that Western society is essentially "individualistic" while socialist society emphasizes social control. It is indeed true that public behavior in the U.S.S.R. is highly conformist, that Soviet pedagogy lays great stress on collective effort and peer discipline, and that many of these traits can also be found in socialist societies from Bulgaria to Cuba. The dichotomy is given added currency by the fact that Soviet thinkers themselves enthusiastically embrace the division, heartily condemning the "individualism" of American society.

However, a moment's reflection will confirm that neither a theory of rugged individualism nor a theory of monolithic collectivism can stand alone. A theory of the individual needs a social framework within which the individual can exist and flourish: a theory of the collective needs some model of the individuals which make it up. Thus, for example, on the Western side, commentators on America from Tocqueville to Weber have emphasized that American individualists are also compulsive joiners, constructing a dense network of churches, fraternities, and other social groupings which seem to counterbalance their individualistic tendencies.

On the Soviet side, it is quite easy to get Soviet philosophers to agree that they are not trying to raise a nation of clones: they do expect individuals to be different. For example, they are keen to condemn Chinese society for being too collectivist (i.e., China prior to the latest liberalization). Soviet political texts often include Marx's condemnation (from *The Communist Manifesto*) of "barrack room communism"; and the sin of excessive collectivism is associated with Trotsky (because of his advocacy of labor armies in 1919). Soviet novels and plays do in fact explore individuality with great subtlety, and this question was even addressed in the hoary old classics of 1930s socialist realism. The fact that social control in the U.S.S.R. (and still more so in East Europe) is less than absolute can be buttressed by "sidewalk sociology." For every anecdote of old ladies telling foreign students in Moscow to stop whistling in the street, one can cite cases of the public (including the police) being tolerant and helpful to drunks.

Equating capitalism with individualism and socialism with collectivism becomes even more problematic if we widen our focus and recognize that capitalism seems to be able to flourish in highly "collective" societies such as those of Japan and South Korea. Also, one has historians such as Macfarlane arguing that, in the case of England, individualistic behavior can be traced back long before the arrival of the system of property relations characteristic of capitalism.[34]

This is not to say that there are no differences in the degree and nature of individualism in the U.S.A. and U.S.S.R. This could even be established through objective measures such as the rate of geographic mobility or the proportion of newlyweds living with their parents.[35] (Other measures, however, such as labor turnover or divorce rates would show little difference.) My main point is to question whether there is a clear moral dichotomy to be drawn between individualism and collectivism – and if there is, whether it is congruent with the division between capitalist and socialist social formations. I doubt whether any convincing moral account of the virtues of individualism can be constructed without also providing some justification for the particular form of collective entity they inhabit.[36] Similarly, any collectivist theory must account for individual differences, and the sources of virtue in individuals.

* * * * * * *

A second popular framework for the moral discourse between socialism and capitalism is that of *rights*. The socialist states are regarded as lacking in respect for the rule of law, never having developed an independent judicial system for applying the law in an equitable manner. The lack of respect for the law under socialism is traced back to Marx's refusal to recognize moral absolutes such as natural rights.

Much legal-philosophical brainpower has been expended on the question of conflicting theories of rights under capitalism and socialism. The arguments usually boil down to I. Berlin's difficult distinction between negative and positive liberty.[37] Socialism at best is held to promote the

---

[34] A. Macfarlane, *The Origins of English Individualism* (Oxford: Blackwell, 1978).

[35] Of course, phenomena such as geographic mobility or living with parents do not reflect the free choices of individuals within the U.S.S.R.: they are largely a product of state policies, the housing shortage, and other forces beyond the power of the individual citizen. However, they nevertheless *produce* a more collectivist culture, even if they are not *caused* by such a culture.

[36] This is the thrust of the widely discussed work by R. Bellah *et al.*, *Habits of the Heart* (New York: Harper and Row, 1986).

[37] I. Berlin, *Four Essays on Liberty* (New York: Oxford University Press, 1969). See also R.E. Howard and J. Donnelly, "Human Dignity, Human Rights and Political Regimes," *American Political Science Review*, vol. 80, no. 3 (September 1986), p. 801; and D. Lane, "Human Rights Under State Socialism," *Political Studies*, vol. 32, no. 3 (September 1984), p. 349; also A. Kadarsky, *Human Rights in American and Russian Political Thought* (New York: University Press of America, 1982).

"positive" socio-economic liberties of food, shelter, basic education and employment – while downgrading the "negative" liberties so well-protected by the liberal order (freedom of speech, movement, etc.).

Some would argue that this formulation of the issue is too generous to socialism. Surely, it could be said, the socio-economic rights found in the Soviet Constitution are mere window dressing, for without the core political rights the economic "rights" cannot really be protected as rights, and are in fact little more than policy declarations. (For example, how can one hope to correct governmental transgressions of economic rights without freedom of speech to bring them to the attention of the public?)

This is a sound point. However, one should not be completely dismissive of socialist rights. The Soviet legal system does seem to have been operating according to its own version of "due process" since 1953. Arbitrary arrest is no longer widespread. Arrested dissidents have always *done something* which they knew the authorities would not approve of – even if these actions were not clearly defined in the law. (And even if the actions would not be considered criminal in most Western societies.) The economic rights listed in the Soviet Constitution do seem reasonably protected through the legal system – reinstating workers unfairly dismissed, preventing eviction from housing, and so forth. Take, for example, the case of the right to housing, guaranteed in Article 44 of the Soviet Constitution. Despite extensive press discussion advocating a change, the new 1977 Constitution did not specifically grant the right to a separate apartment. The reason was that the persistent housing shortage means that at least for the next twenty years some households (currently one in five) will have to share kitchen and bathroom facilities. Thus, there is some attempt to take these economic rights seriously, and not treat them simply as propaganda, or a statement of policy goals. This impression is reinforced by the findings of the recently completed Soviet *émigré* interview project, one of whose main conclusions was that Soviet citizens (even those who have chosen to emigrate) value and respect the U.S.S.R.'s stance on economic rights (housing, health care, job security).[38]

In fact, I would argue that the socialist position on rights has grown increasingly closer to the Western position. Their record with regard to the core civil liberties is of course abysmal, notwithstanding pathetic attempts to equate Angela Davis with Andrei Sakharov, or whatever. Even though their motivation for defending their system in terms of civil and economic rights is probably rooted in a cynical desire to head off Western criticism,[39]

---

[38] B. Silver, "Political Beliefs."

[39] It is clearly a standard Soviet tactic to respond to Western criticism by turning the Western arguments around against the West itself. For example, one Soviet author keen to disprove the Totalitarian model did so by, among other arguments, accusing bourgeois society itself of developing a "totalitarian character"; Yu.M. Shikin, *Sotsial'noe edinstvo i totalitarnoe obshchestvo* (Leningrad: Lenizdat, 1982), p. 33.

it is instructive to note the energy and enthusiasm they display in utilizing the rights framework as a vehicle to challenge the capitalist nations in moral terms. (Rather than trying to bury the issue, they have made it one of the central planks of their internal and external propaganda.) The present author finds it difficult to resolve this ideological struggle between positive and negative liberties at the philosophical level. Certainly, in practical terms both sides find it easy to generate popular support for their respective interpretations within their own countries. (Not that this has anything to do with the rightness of their arguments.)

The argument that some of the positive liberties (food, shelter, etc.) are prerequisites for the enjoyment of "higher" liberties strikes me as a powerful one. I also find it difficult to grasp the meaning of the argument that the "higher" negative liberties are inherent in all human beings irrespective of their material position when the fate of millions of refugees this century has repeatedly shown that human beings who have the misfortune to fall outside a state system have no *inherent* rights – or at least no inherent means of realizing these rights.[40] Clearly, a recognized existence within some state system is necessary in order to realize one's "inherent" rights. The same point could be made with regard to aliens within the U.S.A. today – not in the sense that they are suffering in the way that refugees have suffered, but in the sense that they are not held to have any inherent rights, but only rights granted to them by Congress.

* * * * * * * *

Finally, let us turn to the issue of *migration*. Here I wish to play something of a devil's advocate role, since I am disturbed by the moral complacency of many defenders of capitalism who assume that the moral worth of the two respective systems has been settled once and for all by the erection of the Berlin Wall, and the fact that there is a flood of migrants into the West from the East. Of course it is morally outrageous that most of the socialist countries deny freedom of movement to their citizens, and of course it is tempting to select freedom to migrate as a clear, simple test of a social system's relative merits. Individuals can "vote with their feet" on the relative performance of different systems, and states which deny them the right of exit are tacitly admitting that their system is inferior to the system to which people want to migrate.[41]

However, I believe that this search for a simple moral litmus test of the

[40] M.R. Marrus, *The Unwanted: European Refugees in the Twentieth Century* (New York: Oxford University Press, 1985).

[41] See A. Dowty, *Closed Borders* (New Haven: Yale University Press, 1987), for a survey of the migration issue.

merits of a social system (i.e., migration) is ill-conceived. Migration is an individual decision shaped by a wide range of economic and cultural factors, and does not amount to the equivalent of a moral judgment on the virtues of an entire social system. The fact, for example, that several thousand Americans migrated to the U.S.S.R. in the 1930s may tell us something about the social problems that the U.S.A. was facing, but does it really help us to judge the relative moral worth of Soviet and American society at the time?

Consider for a moment some of the extraneous factors which enter into the decision to migrate, or to stay put. Cultural factors are usually loaded against the decision to migrate. It is not surprising that Hungary has been the most liberal state with regard to migration (along with Poland in various periods). Unlike the East German situation, there is no ready-made Hungarian-speaking community to welcome migrants. Also, questions of national identity play a role. The Hungarians are deeply conscious of being a small nation which has shrunk still further in the course of this century. Thus, national existence is at stake for Hungarians in a way that is not the case for Germans or Poles. A decision to stay in Hungary is just as much a "vote" for Hungarian national identity as a "vote" for socialism. Hungary does not in fact need a wall to keep its citizens in (they have one anyway, in order to prevent other East Europeans from taking advantage of their laxity by fleeing through Hungary). The relative liberalism of the regime does presumably encourage some citizens to stay who might otherwise have left.

Cultural factors also affect migration decisions at the capitalist end of the process. The pull of the native culture may cause migrants to, say, the U.S.A. to return home after a period of years. Roughly one-third of migrants in the decades leading up to the First World War subsequently left the U.S.A. to return to their country of origin, and this would seem to be the predominant pattern among Mexican nationals who have entered over the last two decades.

A more indirect way in which culture retards migration is that citizens are socialized into the political culture of their home nation and may find it difficult to alter their political attitudes later in life. Thus, surveys of Soviet émigrés to the U.S.A. suggest a fair degree of cultural conservatism – they continue to think that state provision of health care and control of major industries is a good idea, while deploring the uncertainty and "excess" of freedom they perceive in American society. This value inertia may deter migration.

On top of cultural factors, migration is also deterred by the significant transaction costs involved – the need to part from family and friends, to gain new credentials and employment, and so forth.

The thrust of my argument is that the cultural and pragmatic considerations which enter into the migration decision make it a shaky foundation upon which to erect a theory of the moral worth of the social system prevailing in a particular country. It is perfectly possible to imagine that an end to the migration restrictions currently in force in the U.S.S.R. might *not* lead to a mass exodus of the population. Such a situation would not alter the present author's opinions as to the relative merits of socialism and capitalism, which are based upon the sort of empirical evaluation of their respective performance which I carried out in Section III.

CONCLUSION

My purpose in this paper has been to try to shift the terms of the debate between socialism and capitalism away from the high plain of clashing moral absolutes down to the grubby reality of alternative social systems. At the very least, my hope was to remind participants in the debate – from utopian Marxists on one side to liberal moral philosophers on the other – that the issues raised by the clash between capitalism and socialism go beyond the traditional debates over the mutability of human character, the plausibility of natural rights, and so forth.

I argue that capitalism and socialism are distinct social structures which produce a distinctive set of features in social, economic and political life – features which cannot simply be dismissed as historical accidents, unique to the countries in question. I attempt in a crude fashion to summarize these respective characterics in the scorecard (Table One). This exercise suggests that the leading countries of capitalism are outperforming the leading countries of socialism across a whole range of indicators, and that the "innate" advantages of socialism alleged by Marxists have yet to reveal themselves in an actual society. For example, the exercise casts doubt on the fairly popular argument that "at least" the socialist bloc looks after its poor, thereby compensating in part for the absence of civil liberties and the generally low living standards.

However, the empirical exercise also suggests the need for caution in evaluating the claims made on behalf of socialism and capitalism. We are dealing with a wide and diverse range of social phenomena where the collection and interpretation of data is fraught with difficulty. On the one hand, the exercise does seem to show capitalism in fairly good shape when compared to socialism. On the other hand, the general thrust of my argument has been to suggest that it is mistaken to portray the rivalry between the two social systems as a simple black and white moral choice. Although I argue that capitalism and socialism are discrete social systems, each producing a distinctive pattern of social outcomes, I do not see that these separate structures translate through into a moral battle between right and wrong. On the contrary, moral issues such as rights, equity, individualism, and freedom of movement all include areas of ambiguity which bridge the distinction between capitalist and socialist social formations, and which furnish ammunition to both sides in their continuing debate.

Only the sort of abstraction from reality which utopian socialists indulge in can produce the appearance of a neat moral dichotomy. When faced with such arguments, defenders of capitalism would do better to stick with the empirical record rather than take off into the realms of moral philosophy.

Political Science, Wesleyan University